Money Makers!

Money Makers!

The Secrets of Canada's Most Successful Entrepreneurs

Kenneth Barnes

·

Everett Banning

McClelland and Stewart

McClelland and Stewart Limited
The Canadian Publishers
25 Hollinger Road
Toronto, Ontario
M4B 3G2

Canadian Cataloguing in Publication Data

Barnes, Kenneth.

Money makers

ISBN 0-7710-1047-8

1. Businessmen – Canada – Biography. 2. New
business enterprises – Canada. I. Banning, Everett.
II. Title.

HD62.5.B37 1985   338′.04′0922   C85-099655-4

Printed and bound in Canada by
T. H. Best Printing Company Limited

Contents

To Mari Banning and Marianna Barnes.

Introduction:
The Money Makers

Mellanie Stephens sold cabbages from the back of a pickup truck to earn the few dollars she needed to get by.

Frank Stronach landed on a friend's doorstep in need of a job and a place to stay. He had hardly a penny in his pocket.

Heather and Ken Dafoe admitted to the bank that they just didn't have the money to make the payments on their Brantford, Ontario, home.

Paul Abildgaard found himself travelling a lonely, dusty Alberta road in an attempt to escape the frustrations of retirement.

Ron McLelland worked ten hours a day for the $100 a week he earned in a Nova Scotia bank.

Chris Duffy mopped up the milk her children had spilled on the kitchen floor again, and vented the frustrations of a mother of six.

Troubling predicaments in the lives of Canada's disadvantaged people? Certainly something must be done to help these people, we are told. Politicians call for new government job programs and ambitious social initiatives to support the unfortunate. Media pundits offer scathing analyses to underline the injustices of a system that permits the few to build empires while many more suffer. Unions demand more power and higher wages from the fat cats in the business community. Social critics call for stricter rent controls, more comprehensive medical care, and a guaranteed annual income. Economists ponder the relationships between business, labour, and government. Everyone analyses, demands, and argues and few agree on the meaning of statistics on unemployment, inflation, deficits, prices, interest rates, and trade.

The government passes new laws and dispenses new billions of dollars to cure our economic maladies because it is seen as the conduit and control mechanism that can set everything right. It borrows more and taxes more to cover the costs of this bureaucratic beneficence. And after all has been said and done, there are greater numbers of unemployed, larger government debts, less affordable housing, more people in need of food and clothing, higher costs for services and consumer goods, and threats to trim public support programs to make them affordable. The system, it seems, never works the way people expect it should.

Mellanie Stephens abandoned her cabbage truck to sew canvas kit bags for the yachtsmen who called at Port Stanley, a small town on the north shore of Lake Erie. She rapidly expanded her product lines to include a vast selection of fashionable cotton clothing. By 1985, her coast-to-coast chain of Kettle Creek Canvas Company stores was expected to gross over $7 million.

Frank Stronach stayed with his friend in Kitchener, Ontario, for just two weeks until he found a job in the kitchen of a local hospital. However, he was a tool and die maker by trade, and he soon found work in a succession of machine shops. Before long he'd saved enough to rent his own shop and win metal-working contracts. Frank Stronach's 1985 gross revenues were projected to top $700 million dollars. His firm, Magna International, has become Canada's largest manufacturer of car parts. It employs nearly 7,000 people in seventy factories.

Heather and Ken Dafoe had difficulty paying their house mortgage because they hadn't yet found any customers for the personal hygiene products they were manufacturing with the help of one employee. They'd used the mortgage money to buy a sanitary-napkin-making machine and to rent space in an industrial mall. Less than ten years later, the Dafoes were operating six factories in four countries, with gross sales approaching $100 million.

Paul Abildgaard drove through Nanton, Alberta, and noticed the town's sign advertising "Canada's finest drinking water." In no time he'd set up a water bottling plant and five years later – at age fifty-five – is grossing millions in the beverage and meat business.

Ron McLelland used the knowledge he acquired while working for a Nova Scotia bank to establish a small mobile home sales lot in Truro. Within three years it rated among the top five mobile home sales companies in Canada. He sold it when McDonald's restaurants chose him to be the owner of their franchise in Bathurst, New Brunswick. McLelland is now a millionaire a couple of times over. He's invested his spare cash in his weekend hobby – running one of the nation's most successful stables of harness-racing horses. All of this he accomplished before he was thirty-seven years old.

Chris Duffy might have felt the frustrations of motherhood more than most, with six children in the house. But she was more frustrated with the open-top jugs they sold in supermarkets to hold plastic bags of milk. Mrs. Duffy designed a new milk jug that doesn't spill easily, and in partnership with her husband Earl she manufactures and sells them through their company, Totson Products Ltd.

There are at least a million of these money makers in Canada. Not all are rich, as the term "money maker" implies. But they are all makers of goods and services, the real money in our society.

Money makers give money its value. They provide the true "gold standard" for our currency. Paper money – worthless in itself – represents the value of the nation's total output of goods and services, all of which were invented, developed, put into production, and marketed by our money makers. Paper money is only a convenient medium of exchange. Its value comes from the ability of money makers to trade what they have produced with their hands and their brains.

Money makers are the entrepreneurs who make everything possible. Not only do they pursue opportunities, they actually make the opportunities. Not only do they respond to market demand, they actually make the market. They use resources, but they also create resources. They exploit technology and also develop technology. They are originators of wealth, yet most of them started with the most ephemeral of assets – their ideas, ambitions, time, and energy.

Money makers are the foundation of our economy. They provide our society with the wealth that can be taxed and shared to fund everything else, to fund everything government does, to support our schools, our medical system, our social welfare services, our research institutions. And they are the only true creators of jobs.

Our quality of life and our standard of living depend on the creative abilities and productive achievements of money makers. When they add new goods and services to the national marketplace, there is more for everyone – workers, bureaucrats, academics, artists, scientists, and those who require social welfare.

There are no eligibility requirements for money makers. You don't need money, or an education, or family connections, or the right friends, or government support, or a patented product to join their club. There are certain maxims, however, that define in a very general way the attitudes, approaches, and conduct of most of those who have become successful money makers. Here are some of the golden rules that lie behind the success stories in this book.

1. There are no golden rules. Everybody does it his or her own way.
2. Challenge the status quo. Do so with your best instincts because the "experts" are usually wrong.
3. Escape the comfort of the crowd until you're ready to sell them something.
4. Embrace risk and defy the odds. You'll be forced to believe in yourself and encourage others to support you.
5. Exploit your most valuable assets – your time and energy, your experience, and your ideas.
6. Make the market and create the opportunities, because supply attracts demand.
7. Attract people better than yourself. Trust them to do the job. Reward them for achievement.
8. Fear not failure.
9. Anybody can do it (except the government).

These rules might suggest that money makers are renegades, unsatisfied with the way things are, wild but not irresponsibly so, self-confident if not over-confident, daredevils who are prepared to lose everything on a gamble. Some certainly fit the swashbuckling stereotype, but most are as diverse as the human species. Here, in more detail, are the maxims we have derived from observing Canada's money makers.

1. *There are no golden rules. Everybody does it his or her own way.* Canada is one massive suggestion box. Our 25 million peo-

ple unknowingly make contributions every day merely through the serendipitous processes of their minds. Tens of millions of ideas swirl about. There is no order and no discipline to this maelstrom. But there is a selection process, which is a function of individual initiative. Those who are spurred to action by a pink slip, boredom, greed, disdain for an employer, the thrill of a challenge, poverty, power, excitement over an invention, the pressure of responsibility, the need to be boss, the desire for achievement, pride of workmanship, creative energy, and plain human necessity dip into this pool of suggestions and do something with them.

Money makers turn these suggestions to their advantage, creating new businesses, goods, and services. They do it by themselves, with a spouse, with a partner, with a group of partners, with their family, with their former co-workers, with a large number of investors, or with no support at all. Most start with no money, or very little money. Often they use all their personal savings, or get loans from family and friends.

Many conceive their prospective enterprises while working for somebody else. Some launch into an entirely new field of business with absolutely no knowledge of it at all. Others turn skills acquired at school or on the job into money-making ventures. Still others learn as they go.

Some do their own marketing. Others engage professional marketing people to do it for them. Many do their own manufacturing. Others contract it out. Many invent their own product or develop their own service. Others turn the inventions and ideas of other people into profitable enterprises. There is no golden path to money-making success.

2. *Challenge the status quo. Do so with your best instincts, because the "experts" are usually wrong.* Just because people say it is so doesn't necessarily mean they're right. Experts only measure what they understand. There is no effective way of measuring tenacity, blind faith, irrepressible optimism, ingenuity, and creativity. Economists can only work with history and general theory. Business schools have difficulty grappling with the diversity of the entrepreneurial mind. If you really believe you're right, why not give it a try?

That's what Suzy Okun and Elizabeth Volgyesi did when they founded a chain of sixty stores across Canada. Conventional wisdom suggested that palm-sized chocolate chip cookies and bran muffins were what people would buy. But the two women didn't have the money for experts, and they probably wouldn't have listened to them anyway. They gambled with their food inventions, trusted their own best instincts, and proved they were right.

Maureen Baufeldt believes the experts would have told her that a backwoods hamlet in Ontario called Violet Hill would be a foolish place to establish an enterprise. Today, she grosses several million dollars a year. And Eugen Hutka had always heard that Canadians don't build computers. Now he has a factory in Etobicoke that can barely meet the demand.

3. *Escape the comfort of the crowd until you're ready to sell them something.* John Masters, founder of Canadian Hunter Ltd., wrote of his astounding discoveries of oil and gas in western Canada in *The Hunters*. In his book he says, "every out-front maneuver you make is going to be lonely. But if you feel entirely comfortable, then you're not far enough ahead to do any good. That warm sense of everything going well is usually the body temperature at the centre of the herd."

Others criticized John Masters for being different. He broke with the conventional energy industry wisdom and worked on geological surveys by himself until he found one of the richest veins of hydrocarbon energy in modern Canadian oil and gas history. When he struck liquid gold, he sold it to the very industry that had doubted him.

Dare to be different. Be the trend setter. Lead with your own fashions, rather than imitating others. Who would have thought that people would buy bottled Alberta water? Or bun warmers in Violet Hill, Ontario? Or solid state transmitters in Nova Scotia?

You might be wrong if you break with the crowd, but you'll seldom be successfully right if you stay with it.

4. *Embrace risk and defy the odds. You'll be forced to believe in yourself and encourage others to support you.* We'd be nowhere as a civilization if nobody took risks. Progress only comes when risks are taken. When people take risks, all of us become more secure.

There is no other way to create wealth than to risk something. If all of us saved our money, it would soon become worthless because there wouldn't be the activity needed to build the economy. The less risk we're prepared to accept, the less will be our net gain.

Risks are required if we want new and better products and services, a better way of life, and more to share with others. Money makers take risks when they test and taste the market and hustle and bustle to produce new goods, widgits, and whatnots. They put their money, their time, and their futures on the line, and as the eighteenth-century classical economist Adam Smith reminds us, when money makers beat the odds and succeed, they end up dragging everybody else up the ladder of success with them.

The confidence a successful risk-taker exudes attracts others, because people like to be with winners. That's how the best money makers attract employees, investors, and customers.

It was risky establishing a Canadian hot-air balloon factory, a production line for plastic milk jugs, a line of cotton canvas clothing and fashions, and a design for a world-class communications satellite. But the risks paid off, and you'll meet the money makers who took them in this book.

5. *Exploit your most valuable assets – your time and energy, your experience, and your ideas.* You don't need money to be a money maker. You need you. The most outstanding characteristic of almost all of the money makers profiled in this book is their capacity for work. Ten-, twelve-, sixteen-hour days and seven-day weeks are common to almost all of them. They are sprinters, not just because they are people in a hurry, but because the rest of the world is sprinting, too. Competition makes them work. Competition makes them win. The capacity for work, the enthusiasm for work, and the need for work overshadow everything else required to become a money maker. The best ideas are useless unless they are backed with an enormous investment of time and energy. Time and energy are really money.

The recent business bestseller *In Search of Excellence* advises business leaders to "stick to the knitting." That means stick to what you know. It doesn't necessarily mean that your only hope of money-making success is fabricating waffle irons because you spent ten years in a waffle-iron factory. It does mean that you have experience with production techniques, inventory control, purchasing, employee training, and assembly-line design involving a home appliance. You might be able to exploit this experience in establishing an enterprise that makes electrical cords for appliances because you spotted a niche for a better, less expensive design. You might be able to use your waffle-iron experience in designing a better packing and shipping system or a better plastic material for small appliance housings. You might even establish an employment agency for small appliance workers, because your experience taught you that factories need temporary workers to gear up for production before the Christmas sales period.

Your ideas define your enterprise and give it the best chance of continued success, and you've got to have an eye for ideas, an intuitive sense. It's a state of mind. Sometimes, it requires a lot of careful thought to develop an idea for a product or service, and sometimes it's as if somebody simply pulled the cord on that proverbial light bulb people have in their heads. There are always things that have never been done before and new ways of doing old things. There's no particular formula for finding what will work in the marketplace other than learning to tune your mind into your environment in a constructively critical way.

The notion that the marketplace is controlled by large corporations and the wealthy elite is perpetuated by some commentators and social observers. But that's like suggesting that only people with strong forearms can plant cabbages and only people with Harvard MBAs can run businesses. There's no need to be concerned about others who have money – they can never hold a monopoly over your ideas, your capacity for work, and your experience.

6. *Make the market and create opportunities, because supply attracts demand.* Many widely accepted economic theories presume that a society's need for goods and services is finite. This leads to another presumption, that economies can be commanded and controlled to meet people's needs and desires. Capitalist or socialist governments, democratically chosen or otherwise, frequently err by accepting such theories and using them as the basis for government programs and regulations. The fact is that the people themselves don't even know what they need or want, so how could their leaders who plan their economies pretend to know?

Outside of the basic necessities, people don't develop needs or wants until a money maker happens by with a new good or service. There was no need for families to consider more frequent meals out in restaurants until Ray Kroc perfected Dick and Mac McDonald's fast-food concept, which created a market for inexpensive and convenient meals outside the home. There was no market for reasonably priced automobiles until Henry Ford developed the assembly line and used volume production to bring down the cost of what was previously an undreamed of luxury item.

Such pioneering entrepreneurs developed new products and services at reasonable prices that previously were not wanted by anybody in the marketplace. Their example is followed by many of the money makers in this book who have made their own opportunities, created the market, arranged for ample supplies, and watched the demand follow.

7. *Attract people better than yourself. Trust them to do the job. Reward them for achievement.* Money maker Robert Isserstedt, one of the co-founders of GEAC Computer, told us that a hallmark of a successful entrepreneur is the ability to let go of the reins when the company he or she created has grown to the point where new skills are needed. He reminded us that nobody can possibly know everything, that even the strongest, most successful pioneer must recognize the strengths others can bring to a company. Frank Stronach, who pilots the largest money-making enterprise profiled in the pages that follow, believes his company – Magna International – was able to grow so rapidly and profitably because he made his key employees his partners.

Ambitious people with creative minds will thrive and the company they serve will prosper if they can contribute, and if they benefit from their contributions. A company where product development and marketing strategy always come from the mind of only one person will become too narrowly focused and susceptible to mistakes.

8. *Fear not failure.* It's been said many times that nothing will ever be accomplished if all possible objections must be overcome first. This does not mean, however, that one should stumble blindly into new ventures. Learn everything possible; know the facts and risks; then act.

One of the great privileges of the free enterprise system is the freedom to fail. People profit from failure. The mistakes made the first time become valuable lessons for trying something else.

Many people fail in business. But many succeed, and there wouldn't be successes if everybody was paralysed by the fear of failure. More than one of the money makers profiled in this book failed but succeeded the second time round.

Investors who risk their money in new enterprises – venture capitalists – measure the risks this way: two-six-two. The ratio means that out of every ten new companies, two will fail, six will stumble along, and two will succeed spectacularly. Those aren't bad odds – a one-in-five chance of failure, a one-in-five chance of winning spectacularly. The odds of staying in business are four out of five, even though the payoff won't be much to speak of in three out of five cases.

Businesses must fail in a progressive economy. That sounds like a lesson from the jungle, and it implies pain and suffering, but victory isn't very sweet if you've never tasted adversity. Business must be competitive to benefit society at large, and competitions mean there will be winners and losers. In an economic sense, the losers are the producers of obsolete goods and services. If society, through government grants or other means, supports businesses that produce needless goods, then society begins to bear burdens that ultimately drag it down. Failure is part of the cleansing process that opens up new opportunities for progressive enterprises. Money makers avoid failure by being better than their competitors, managing wisely, and producing superior-quality products at lower prices. Overall, Canada produces more winners than losers. The Canadian Federation of Independent Business offers these statistics: in 1981, the year before the recent recession, 93,000 new businesses were born and 56,000 died. The next year, as the recession and punishingly high interest rates took hold, a still-respectable 87,000 new businesses were born, but nearly as many, 84,000, died. In 1983, things were booming again, with 96,000 births and just 64,000 deaths. For 1985, new businesses were expected to top 100,000 with just 50,000 failures. Overall, Canada has continued to gain, even in the worst year since the 1930s depression. And considering our total pool of businesses in Canada is close to 750,000 companies, the fear of failure need not be paralytic. Think positive.

9. *Anybody can do it (except the government).* Money makers are not an exclusive club. The people you are about to meet are young and old, women and men, some highly educated, others

not. None had access to extraordinary wealth. None was privileged or belonged to a small elite. But all had qualifications available to everybody if they choose to take advantage of them – a capacity for hard work, a willingness to invest their time and make sacrifices, the courage to take risks, and the determination to succeed.

We refer to the government's inability to engage in this vital economic process simply because so many expect that the government has the power and the capacity to set things right. We mean no malice toward the hundreds of thousands who exercise their public responsibilities with great dedication and skill. However, governments by their very nature are immune from the rules and realities of the marketplace. The insular nature of government makes the institution separate from the maelstrom of ideas and inventions that spew from the population at large. The natural sifting process of the marketplace, which rejects bad ideas and products and allows bright innovations to succeed, has no impact on government enterprise. The government won't go broke, and it is not driven by the relentless ambition and dreams of dedicated money makers. There is always, with government, the comfortable cushion of tax money to underwrite the losses of public enterprise. The nature of government bureaucracy, with management by committee and the political pressure always to please the voter, cannot deliver goods and services as profitably or efficiently as the private marketplace.

Government fulfils a necessary and important role in our economic life – to redistribute a portion of our wealth to the disadvantaged, to represent us on the international scene, to enforce rules and regulations for the humane conduct of national affairs, and to support programs that benefit society. Later in these pages, we will suggest policies and measures our governments should consider to help the money-making process thrive for the benefit of all.

The following success stories will underline our money makers' maxims. Every family, partner, loner, whiz, and visionary you will read about has experienced the challenges, frustrations, and rewards of entrepreneurial life in Canada, and we hope these chronicles will rally others to join them, or at least support them in their vital economic role.

Our money makers come from many regions across Canada, and they have excelled in many types of businesses. We had a million Canadian money makers to choose from, and we chose them randomly rather than scientifically. We met many of them while producing *Everybody's Business*, the Global Television Network's syndicated business and financial affairs program, which is broadcast in most major Canadian cities. Others profiled in this book have never been on our program and were selected from suggestions forwarded by friends and professional and business contacts. Our approach is personal and anecdotal, its aim being to present these people and the stories of their money-making enterprises as they represent themselves and their companies.

Money Makers is a snapshot, an informal progress report on the state of entrepreneurialism in Canada, rather than a definitive economic analysis or comprehensive critique. It represents the experiences of successful Canadians as they tell them. We believe their stories will inspire others to seek the extraordinary opportunities Canada offers.

Part 1: All in the Family

Most Canadian money makers are married for the simple reason that most adult Canadians are married. A married money maker who goes it alone in business invariably depends on the support of his or her spouse, perhaps to bring in an income while the business is in the incubation stage, certainly to give encouragement through the frustrations and difficulties of establishing a business, and often to take on additional family responsibilities while the other partner is investing countless hours in making the business successful.

With that kind of spousal involvement, direct participation in the enterprise is only a logical extension. In many instances, the children become partners as well. Family business ventures are as old as history. The pioneering accomplishments of our first settlers were usually due to family involvement, and that tradition has been perpetuated in the families Duffy, Baufeldt, Cook, Harley, Henke, Saksun, McLelland, and Dafoe. Their successful family money-making ventures were possible because of the support or participation of husbands, wives, brothers, sisters, and sons and daughters.

In these families, two or more minds and bodies were truly better than one. If the original money-making idea came from one family member, the business plan often came from another, and the time and effort invested to make it work from yet another. Families have more time available for a business, simply because there are more people who are willing to make sacrifices in the beginning for a hoped for payoff down the road.

The expertise that launched the Dafoe family multinational business came from Ken, but his wife Heather was able to start the business while he kept his old job during the first few difficult weeks. Young David Harley had an idea for a line of clothing, but it was his father's years of expertise in the fabric business that helped their fledgling company succeed. Maureen Baufeldt developed the family company's products, while husband Jim designed and built the store they are sold in. Earl and Chris Duffy relied on each other to take the risks required, including selling their home, to back a product she had invented and he marketed.

The roles and involvements of family members are different in each of the stories that follow, but these people are money makers in part because their businesses are family affairs.

HEATHER AND KEN DAFOE
Dafoe & Dafoe

Many of the faces in the Delta Secondary School yearbook of 1951 were destined to travel no more than a dozen stops on the Hamilton Street Railway that runs past the school to the steel mills on the south side of Hamilton Bay. One of those in the yearbook, Heather Dafoe, remembers her mother talking about the good jobs the men had there, and that the women who married them had no need to stay in school past the age of sixteen. Life would be comfortable and secure, as long as the steel mills' order books were full and there were no layoffs.

In 1975, twenty-four years later, Heather and her husband, Ken Dafoe, were leading a comfortable and secure life. They had a large house with a circular drive overlooking the Brantford Golf and Country Club. The mortgage was almost paid off. Their dreams had been realized. But there was a nagging undercurrent of dissatisfaction to their day-to-day existence, a feeling that they were capable of new challenges and greater accomplishments. "I was forty, Ken was forty-one, young enough to start all over again if we had to," Heather recalls. "The idea of starting our own company never scared us. We had already overachieved our life's goals. If we were going to fail, we would fail in the first five years. That meant we were young enough to recover. We knew we could work to get everything back."

They had never taken great risks before, but they had worked hard all of their lives. Ken and Heather married four years after they met at Delta Secondary School. He was twenty-one and a sophomore at the University of Michigan. She was twenty. Ken could afford college because he'd won an athletic scholarship. Even so, money was tight for the newlyweds. While Ken completed his studies, Heather got a job just off the campus with a small industrial supply house. That's where she learned the book-keeping and secretarial skills that would help the couple twenty years later when they would launch a multinational giant named – appropriately enough – Dafoe & Dafoe Inc.

After graduation they moved back to Canada so Ken could avoid the military draft. He worked as an insurance salesman in Hamilton for a few months and then became a travelling sales-man for Procter and Gamble, the American-based soap conglomerate. P & G operated twenty-two sales territories out of the company's London, Ontario, office at the time. Ken recalls that he took his territory up from twenty-first to second place in sales volume. He left the company when they wouldn't give him the promotion he asked for.

When he left P & G, he worked for a succession of companies in various parts of the world, but he stayed in one industry – personal hygiene products. In 1960, when Ken was twenty-six years old, he was hired by Johnson & Johnson for its subsidiary in Trinidad. Johnson & Johnson, headquartered in New York, is a vast worldwide empire of companies that develop and distribute hundreds of health-care products, including birth control pills, operating room equipment, feminine hygiene products, and items for the care of babies, such as disposable diapers, talcum powder, and cotton swabs. Ken and Heather spent five years in Trinidad, another four years in Jamaica, and another year in Mexico City, all for Johnson & Johnson.

The Dafoes' sons, Derek and Blair, were born abroad, and al-though Ken's North American salary permitted a luxurious life-style in the Caribbean and Mexico, the family wanted to return home to Canada. Ken joined Texpack in Brantford, a company that made products that competed with some of the personal hygiene products he'd sold for Johnson & Johnson. He stayed in the same business, when he switched jobs again, with a move to Stearns and Foster in Brantford.

By 1975, Ken Dafoe had spent most of his working life, fifteen years, in one industry. He knew the manufacturing processes, the products, the customers, the competitors, and he'd developed a network of contacts around the world. He'd also become adept at spotting market opportunities. That led to more business for his employers, perhaps some bonuses and promotions for himself, but he was still working for someone else. At this point he and Heather decided they should go into business for themselves.

Although the market for personal hygiene products was already well supplied by a number of large multinationals, including Johnson & Johnson, Kimberly-Clark, and Scott Paper, Ken and Heather decided their best opportunities lay with what they knew best. Conventional wisdom said the market was saturated. Ken's work experiences told him otherwise. His close contact over the years with supermarkets, drug stores, and department store chains led to the observation that a growing number of products were being sold in generic rather than brand-name packages. The stores were offering food and housewares, and even paper towels and toilet tissue – products close to his area of expertise – in packages bearing the names of their stores. However, Ken noticed that few outlets were selling their own brands of personal hygiene products.

The couple drew up a detailed business plan. The idea was to manufacture sanitary napkins; as the business grew they'd branch out into other lines.

Now they were ready to line up financing. Ken and Heather had hardly a penny in the bank. Their only major asset was the house they'd bought in 1970 at a price Heather describes as "a bargain." They set out to borrow against it to start their business and, approaching three of the major commercial banks with their plan, were flatly told it was hopeless: the market they wanted to break into was too competitive. Undaunted, they approached the Federal Business Development Bank, the lender of last resort for many business people. Ken met with FBDB officials in Hamilton, filled out all the appropriate forms, and waited. He never heard back from them. Perhaps the application got lost or was simply ignored. They never found out. Then an old family friend who knew someone in the bank's Kitchener office volunteered to make a personal approach on their behalf. Three days later, the Dafoes were presented with a cheque for $150,000 secured against their home; the FBDB demanded a 20 per cent share in the ownership of the business as additional security. Its investment impressed the Royal Bank, which advanced a further $50,000.

The Dafoes immediately placed an order for a sanitary-napkin-making machine from West Germany. They rented a 10,000-square foot space in Brantford's Braneida Industrial Park. Heather still remembers the rent, exactly $1,783 per month. They needed a person with unusual mechanical skills and a knowledge of the personal hygiene business to help them set up their factory. Don Brennan, who had worked with Ken at Tex-pack in Brantford, left his job and became the Dafoes' first employee. He also became a co-owner of the small company, with 1,000 shares in his name. In September, 1975, they were ready for business.

Brennan installed the machine and operated it. At first, they only had enough business to manufacture napkins one day a week. Heather learned to drive the forklift and did all the shipping and receiving. She packed whatever Brennan made. Ken handled sales while keeping his full-time job at Stearns and Foster – they needed the income.

The company's growth was painfully slow at first, something Ken can be philosophical about now. "You have to prove yourself to retailers before they'll take a big order from you. Some, like Shoppers Drug Mart and Bi-Way, will back you to the hilt. But there are too few retailers controlling the market in Canada, and it makes it very difficult to break in. There is only a handful of supermarket chains – Loblaw's, Steinberg's, A & P, Safeway, Provigo – that's about it with Dominion gone. We're fortunate because we export so much of what we make in Canada. I wouldn't want to be only selling in Canada. It would be very difficult to do business that way."

Their first customer was Wyant and Company of Montreal, which bought individually wrapped sanitary napkins to put in their washroom vending machines. They were able to get the machine operating two and three days a week when they signed a contract with G.H. Wood Ltd., also in the vending business. Then Stearns and Foster found out Ken was moonlighting and fired him. By January, 1976, they were almost broke. They phoned their banks and told them they couldn't make payments on the loans.

Often, delinquent companies are forced into bankruptcy by creditors who see no hope of recovering their loans in the normal course of business. They appoint bankruptcy trustees to wind down the business and auction off the assets. The creditors then recover what they can. That did not happen to the Dafoes.

Heather thinks their survival was due to two things. First, this was before the recession and the banks weren't as strict then. Second, they'd been meticulous about keeping the banks informed about everything they were doing. "We gave them complete year-by-year business plans and projections. We'd filed financial statements with them every month. We shared everything with them from the very beginning. I'm convinced to this day that the banks appreciated our forthright approach. It helped them to understand what we were trying to do. I really believe if you're open and honest with the banks, if you keep them informed all the time, if you give them more information than they need, that they'll stay on your side. That approach pulled us through then. And to this day, we believe in full and honest disclosure in our financial dealings."

Meanwhile, Ken was still busy on the phone and travelling to potential customers. Early in 1976, they won a contract with the Shoppers Drug Mart chain to produce Life brand sanitary napkins. "That's when we crossed the line between loss and profit," says Heather. "We still supply the Shoppers chain today, and we're both very proud of it. We maintain a close relationship, because we both know that their contract was responsible for pushing us over the top."

Other Canadian companies were difficult to win over, so they exploited some of Ken's old contacts in the U.S. Their sales of generic store-brand hygiene products in the U.S. quickly surpassed their Canadian volume.

The Dafoe husband-and-wife team didn't sit around to savour their fledgling success. They wanted to broaden their manufacturing base with a wider selection of products. In 1977, they started hunting for venture capital to launch a line of generic disposable diapers. The giant INCO company of Sudbury was turning handsome profits at the time, and INCO management wanted to use some of the money to fund promising young businesses. INCO had appointed a Boston firm, Venture Founders, to screen applicants for funding. It meant Ken and Heather had to go to

Boston to apply. Although the business was breaking even, there wasn't much spare cash around, so they drove from Brantford, staying with friends along the way. It was worth the effort. The meeting won them a chance to appear with twenty-four other finalists at a question-and-answer session held for INCO executives at the Harbour Castle Hotel in Toronto. Only three companies were chosen. Dafoe & Dafoe was one of them.

INCO put up $350,000 to put Ken and Heather into the diaper-making business. In return, the mining conglomerate got a 24 per cent share in the company. It has become INCO's most profitable venture capital investment, because Dafoe & Dafoe achieved as much success with generic diapers in major retail chains in North America and Europe as they had with sanitary napkins.

The INCO investment was the last time the Dafoes sold shares in the company. Some shares have been set aside for employees, but the rest of the company will remain in family hands. "We don't give up shares any more," says Heather. "We've learned now that you don't have to give up ownership, if you have a track record and you're profitable. People will lend you the money if you need it and run a good business."

The Dafoes have now recovered the shares they sold when they started. The FBDB paid only $2,000 for its 20 per cent in 1975. Three years later, in 1978, the Dafoes paid the bank $40,000 to buy the shares back. That year, they also paid off the original FBDB loan with interest.

In the ensuing years Dafoe & Dafoe has periodically borrowed money to expand into new facilities and develop new product lines. A million-dollar loan from the Ontario Development Corporation helped put the company into what Heather calls the most beautiful factory building in Brantford. It's a buff brick complex, with 87,000 square feet of factory space, set on twelve acres of landscaped property.

The Dafoe & Dafoe name does not appear on any of the products they make or in the stores they are sold in. Their sanitary napkins, disposable diapers, cotton swabs, and cotton pads are sold in Shoppers Drug Marts, Sears, Bay stores, Woolco, K-Mart, Steinberg's, Miracle Marts, Loblaw's, and A & P. In the U.S., they serve the 1,300-store Revcor Drugstore chain, K-Mart's 1,400 stores, and more than 100 other chains most Canadians have never heard of, including King's, Weis, Topco, and Price. There is a similarly impressive list of customers in Europe. All are supplied from six factories – the main one in Brantford, Ontario, and smaller units in France; Britain; Atlanta, Georgia; Malvern, Pennsylvania; and San Diego, California. The company now has 500 employees, more than half of them in Canada.

The rapid expansion to six factories in less than ten years has been fueled by their growing market share. The factory in France fell into their empire by some unusual circumstances, however. Ken and Heather were contacted by the French owners, who said they had lost so much money on the operation, and would face such substantial severance costs for the staff if they shut down, that they were prepared to hand over the operation for only one French franc! The Dafoes accepted, and now make money in France.

The factories produce a wide variety of hygiene products – various sizes and designs in the feminine hygiene line, an assortment of cotton swabs and cotton pads, and four sizes of generic disposable diapers. Revenue from these products has now reached $100 million a year, but the Dafoes will not disclose how much of that is profit to be shared among themselves, employee shareholders, and INCO.

Some of their earnings were used to start a second company in 1982, Blarek Inc. (a contraction of their sons' names, Blair and Derek), which produces plastics. Some of the plastic products are used in the Dafoe & Dafoe Inc. business – diaper liners and packaging. But prudent business people use their machinery and the skills of their staff to full advantage, so Blarek Inc. now bids on plastic moulding contracts elsewhere. As a sideline the firm supplies trim for the major Detroit automakers.

Heather Dafoe says they are a winning business because they have always kept their costs low and their quality high. "We don't furnish our offices lavishly, and our people are capable of doing a number of different jobs. If we get big orders for diapers, and fewer for cotton products, our staff is flexible enough to take on other duties and fill the orders. We work closely with our customers on product development, so we don't have major R & D expenditures. And our products carry only the names of the retail chains selling them, so we don't have to engage in national advertising the way our competitors do."

Ken and Heather Dafoe are unapologetic about their success. Says Ken, "I see nothing wrong with wealth. I love to be wealthy. I'm willing to work for it." And Heather adds, "We're just tipping the iceberg." Their ambitions for their enterprise are virtually unlimited. Says Ken, "I see no reason why we can't be a billion-dollar company. We've got the people, we've got the product, and God knows, we've got the desire." Heather concurs. "You have to grow. If you're in business, you can't stay steady. You have to grow every year by more than 10 per cent in order to keep your head above water. You're not just doing it for yourself. You're doing it for your employees, because they don't want to stay stagnant either. They don't want to start as a packer at the end of a machine, and be a packer all of their lives. They want that chance for advancement. They want opportunities."

The Dafoes savour the lifestyle they've achieved for themselves and their sons, whom they hope will join them in the company. They still live in the 4,500-square-foot home overlooking the Brantford Golf Club that they had before they started the company. There have been some noticeable improvements, however. There's a pool in the back garden, and Ken and Heather drive to work in a Rolls-Royce. The company owns a ten-passenger Cessna Citation twin-jet, which they keep at the Brantford airport for management trips to their American factories.

This unusually successful family partnership excels, in part, because husband and wife work so well together. Ken and Heather share the same goals and the same working philosophy. They don't always agree on who is the real boss: "We have our problems," Ken says. "I've made decisions, and she's changed them. She's made decisions and I've changed them. We work together, and our people know who to get, who to go to for whatever they want. Some of them will come to me for certain things, and some will go to Heather for things." Heather adds, "Some of them run it by me first, and what they're really asking is what I think Ken will think of it. It usually works out. If I say absolutely not, no way, they just drop it. It's finished." And Ken concludes with this comment on their management relationship, "Heather is the tough one really. I'm the easy guy. If you want something, come to me."

This comfortably shared authority is a reflection of the shared approach to life that enabled the Dafoe family to risk forfeiting comfort and security to become successful Canadian money makers.

CHRIS AND EARL DUFFY
Totson Products

Irreplaceable milk. In the fall of 1982 that memorable advertising slogan took on new meaning at the Duffy house in Thornhill, Ontario. Six children all had their turn dumping the contents of slippery milk pouches over the kitchen table. Their mother, Chris Duffy, cursed the dairies and the makers of those open-topped milk pitchers that were supposed to hold the milk bags firmly in place. Yet the bags always slipped out and spilled.

Her complaints about spilled milk did not go unheeded. Her husband, Earl, had some responsibility for the problem. He was president of Silverwood Dairy, and Silverwood was one of the companies that sold milk in plastic bags. The problem wasn't the bags, though. It was the way they were used.

The Duffy family seemed to have reached that idyllic pinnacle of upper-middle-class Canadian life: a mortgage-free home in an upscale Thornhill neighbourhood; the comforts and perks that go with an executive's salary; children in their late teens and early twenties beginning to leave the nest. Life was good, except for the small day-to-day annoyances, such as spilled milk.

"Why doesn't somebody invent a better pitcher?" Chris Duffy asked.

"Why don't we invent one?" Earl replied.

So Chris Duffy sat down with a sketch pad and drew her own design. Her pitcher was taller than the ones they sold at supermarkets, so it could hold the entire bag. It had a slide-on lid to cover the top of the milkbag, with just a small spout at one end, where the corner of the plastic could be cut off so the milk could be poured. Simple.

But converting this artistic vision from paper to reality would prove to be a formidable task. Friends and relatives thought the product design was brilliant, but such support hardly constituted adequate marketing. Chris and Earl turned to the phone book and found a number of firms listed in the Yellow Pages that specialized in product engineering. They chose Delmo Engineering of Toronto to produce blueprints and perfect the design, to be sure the jug would work. An engineer from the company made blueprints and took them to a prototype maker who made three pitchers.

Then the Duffys took the prototypes to a professional marketing firm, Creative Research on Eglinton Avenue in Toronto, to sample customer reaction in major cities across Canada. The research firm took photographs of the jugs, and with the prototypes at hand, they polled shoppers in stores. About 400 people were interviewed. By April of 1983, the Duffys were presented with a comprehensive survey on the milk pitchers. The survey, which provided the reactions of shoppers in various age groups and income categories, was overwhelmingly positive. Now the Duffys had proof their product would sell!

At this point they had spent $16,000 – $5,000 for the product engineering, $2,500 for the three handmade prototypes, and $8,500 for the market research. It had taken half a year, and it had consumed most of the family savings.

But they still had to have moulds made for manufacturing. They had to sign a contract with a plastic products company. And they had to sell the pitchers to major supermarket chains, department stores, and other distributors. For that, they had no money. And they were soon to lose Earl's income. During the engineering and research stages, Earl resigned from Silverwood to join a supermarket chain. There was a disagreement and Earl was out of a job. (He says he'd rather not discuss the details because the matter is before the courts.) The family had to make a choice: scrap the milk pitcher project, write off the $16,000 they'd already invested, and seek employment; or redouble their efforts and risk everything to make the pitcher project viable. They chose the latter. Their pitchers became a full-time project.

Chris and Earl were both fifty-one years old, a time in life when most people are planning retirement, not setting up a new business. But they felt their relationship could withstand another challenge. After all, they'd been together since high school, helped each other through nursing college and chartered accountancy training, and managed to raise six children. They sold their Thornhill home and moved into a rented house. This freed up $100,000 cash – the proceeds from their lives' work – to get the milk pitchers into production and onto store shelves.

"At any point along the way, the feedback might be bad or the circumstances might be difficult," Earl says, "but you've got to get your bathing suit wet. You've got to make the jump and commit yourself." And Chris adds: "We wanted to get it onto the market ourselves. We didn't want to give up control of it to somebody else. I had decided that this could be job creation. With a large family, and unemployment the way it is, we really thought we'd like to provide a means for those children of ours to do something themselves. If they had any entrepreneurial spirit, they could come to the company, and they might have an opportunity to do many things out of the company."

They called their company Totson Products. The *Tot* comes from Tottenham, Ontario, where Chris grew up. The *son* is from Nelson, British Columbia, where Earl was born and raised. (His parents sent him to Toronto to attend St. Michael's College for his high school education, and she attended St. Joseph's College for girls in Toronto. They met at a "tea dance" held at St. Joseph's.)

In May, 1983, Chris and Earl went knocking on doors. They spoke with a number of mould-making companies. "It's important to shop around, learn as much as you can, and get several estimates," advises Earl. Tradesco Moulds of Weston, Ontario, quoted them $78,000 to make two finely polished pieces of engineered metal that would serve as cookie cutters for an endless stream of plastic to make hundreds of thousands of plastic jugs. One mould would be for the body of the jug, the other for the handle and lid.

The Duffys signed a contract with Tradesco in August and made a 40 per cent deposit – $32,000 – up front. The mould-making process would take several months; they were promised the moulds for the following spring.

While they were waiting, Chris and Earl sent brochures and

sales information to the purchasing managers of every major store chain in the country. "First we just sat down with the Yellow Pages and phoned everybody. We'd ask their switchboards who was in charge of purchasing, get the name, and phone back. The purchasing people didn't want to see us, but they did ask for pictures and product descriptions, so we mailed it to all of them," Earl recalls.

The brochure cost $5,000 to produce, but it was a worthwhile investment. Purchasing managers from major chains – such as Kresge's, Towers, Canadian Tire, and Woolworth's – began calling the Totson Products company office, set up in the basement of the Duffys' rented home. "I told them that the moulds would be ready in the spring, and we expected we could start shipping product soon after that," Earl says. What they didn't count on was the change that was taking place in the Canadian economy. As the Canadian economy emerged from the recession, Tradesco was flooded with orders for moulds from their regular customers. "It created a big backlog, and we didn't get our moulds until July, 1984. We had to phone all the purchasing managers at the stores and ask them to wait."

Unfortunately, the delay meant that some chains couldn't get the Duffy milk jugs into Christmas catalogues and Christmas sales programs. A number of prospective orders were put on the back burner for half a year.

When Chris and Earl finally received their moulds, they sought quotes from manufacturers, among them "a couple of people, who just like us, were starting out on their own with a small plastics plant in Concord, Ontario." The company seemed a natural fit. "People had faith in us, and we were small, so we figured we should have faith in others that were starting out." Mysan Plastics won the Totson contract. They offered to make and package the pitchers for $1.90 each.

Chris and Earl were satisfied with this manufacturing cost, "but that didn't matter to the big chain stores," Earl discovered. "We sent them our first production pitchers, and they could immediately identify with them – almost everybody has spilled milk and they could see the usefulness of our product. They were enthusiastic and took the samples to their purchasing committee meetings. That's where they decide what the product can be sold for. Canadian Tire was the biggest customer, with 350 stores, and they told us the pitcher would have to sell at $3.49. With their mark-up for their stores, it meant they'd pay us only $1.90 a pitcher. That was our production cost! We wouldn't get anything back to cover our development costs, and there wouldn't be anything there for us."

It was back to the drawing board for the Duffys. They had expected that the pitchers would retail at around $4.50 and that they would get about $2.25 a jug. If they sold to Canadian Tire at $1.90, they'd have to sell for the same price to other stores. "Mysan Plastics said they couldn't make them for less than $1.90. We suggested they eliminate the shrink-wrap packaging. They said that would save maybe ten cents a pitcher. We phoned Canadian Tire, and they said the shrink-wrapping didn't matter, so we cut that. Our cost was down to $1.80. Then we suggested we cut the stick-on labels. Everybody said okay, and we saved another nickel. We decided to cut out the small instruction leaflet we were going to put in the package, and we saved more. After we'd cut five cents here and ten cents there, Canadian Tire still had the product at the price they wanted, and there was enough money in it for us.

"We had to remember that stores like Canadian Tire sell about 30,000 items, and whether they have our product isn't going to make much difference to their business. It meant everything to our business. If you don't have the big chains carrying your product, you haven't got anything."

The Duffys hired a trucking company to pick up their first shipment of plastic milk pitchers at Mysan Plastics on September 1, 1984. Ten months later, they had sold 150,000 pitchers. Earl expects the business will average 200,000 jugs a year. "Our marketing research done before we launched into this showed about 5 million Canadians had purchased the old style of jugs. We calculated that the potential market share for our product was about 20 per cent – about a million pitchers."

The Duffys regret one oversight. They filed for patent protection in Canada and the United States, but they weren't fast enough in Europe. They took a number of their pitchers to a trade fair in Frankfurt, West Germany, and European businessmen snapped them up. They think a European company might copy their product before they can license somebody to

34

make the pitchers in Europe. However, the opportunities in the American market look good. Earl says the plastic milk bag is about to be reintroduced in the U.S. "Plastic bagged milk was introduced in both Canada and the U.S. around 1968 or 1969. The design wasn't very good then, and the product was withdrawn from the U.S. market. The dairies stuck with it in Canada and developed better bags, which didn't leak so easily. Now, Dupont is relaunching bagged milk down there. Dupont used our pitchers in their market tests, and the results were very encouraging."

None of the Duffys has become wealthy as yet from the family's kitchen-table creation. Earl takes no income from the company, although he has the title of president. He puts in as much time as he can; the rest is spent on another project he prefers not to discuss. Chris, who is executive vice-president, earns $25,000 a year, while their son, Ken, who is responsible for marketing, earns $24,000. The company has not yet turned a profit, although it is covering expenses. Their stated cost to launch the milk pitchers was $99,000, with several more dollars spent on travel, telephone, stationery, and sales. The project also cost both Earl and Chris two years of unpaid time, as well as their life savings.

Was it worth it? "We sure think so," says Earl. "We have a very valuable company here. The purchasing managers at the chain stores are obviously impressed with us. They've already been phoning us and asking what other products we have to offer. We don't have any at the moment, but we're working on some ideas. We've got our foot in the door. Our name is in their computers, and that obviously matters."

A good product idea, a creative design, a willingness to risk life savings, and a home are the assets that have made the Duffys a family of money makers.

HORST AND RICK HENKE
Children's Playgrounds

In 1972, Horst Henke emigrated to Canada from Germany. His younger brother Rick stayed in their homeland and eventually got a job in Sweden selling power transmission equipment, not an unusual course for a mechanical engineer. Horst was an economist by training, but in Europe he had worked on the design and marketing of children's playgrounds made from wooden and plastic materials.

In North America, he soon discovered, "Playground equipment was still made of metal and it was easily twenty years behind that sold in Europe." So he decided to sell similar new designs in Canada. "I was really marketing a new way of perceiving the basic function of a playground. Traditional playground equipment separates children and forces them into individual and specific single activities. A metal slide standing alone, for instance, dictates to the child that he must go up and down by himself, and do only that. On a swing, he swings alone, a prescribed back and forth, back and forth. The new playground equipment combines activities, leaves children free to experiment with uses and combinations and to interact with others. That's creative and sociable play." Unlike traditional metal equipment, Henke's free-flowing wooden playgrounds would be individually built to match each location, with a variety of innovative attachments, such as tree houses, plastic and metal slides, nylon climbing nets, chinning bars, suspended tires, and even plastic tunnels.

His original idea was to find a Canadian company to manufacture his designs; he would simply sell the product. But he lacked capital. "I only had $10,000 cash so I saved my money by moving into a rooming house where I served as building superintendent." He quickly realized as well that no one was going to take a chance and build the equipment for him without a proven market and solid financial backing. Besides, Henke had come to the conclusion that it would be difficult to get the quality of craftmanship he wanted from a company whose people didn't work directly for him. And so, with a still-limited knowledge of English and only his personal savings – but with a lot of faith in his concept – he set out to build his own wooden playgrounds.

Workers were his first priority. "I needed to find a pool of readily available labour in an area where the cost of living was relatively low so that I could make what little money I had stretch as far as possible." He went to DREE (the federal Department of Regional Economic Expansion) and consulted their maps showing depressed areas. The Ontario Ministry of Industry and

Tourism put him in touch with a councillor in Apsley, a small town north of Peterborough. On his first visit there, the politician invited local builders interested in the project to meet with him. Only one person showed up, but this was all Henke needed. "I told him that I had no orders, but that I expected to get them and would pay him whenever I got paid. He agreed to do the work and we started building the new designs on his front lawn." It was now spring 1973. Henke had been in Canada less than a year.

Soon there were a number of local people working with Henke and the Apsley builder. Each person supplied his own hammer and nails and worked on spec. After several weeks his unpaid staff said they could wait no longer. But Henke had nothing to pay them with. He'd spent his remaining money on a promotional catalogue illustrated with his own hand-drawn designs. This he had sent with letters to possible buyers – schools, hospitals, and municipal recreation departments. Just as it looked as though his workers were going to lay themselves off, the mailing began to yield results. As the orders started to come in, morale improved. Soon he was able to pay the men.

During that first year Children's Playgrounds sold enough to get the word out. The biggest order was from Toronto's Hospital for Sick Children for a playground donated by Queen Elizabeth on behalf of the province. It received full media coverage in the newspapers and on television. Children's Playgrounds was off and running.

When it got too cold to build, Henke closed down the manufacturing operation for the winter. He was still holding onto his job as rooming-house superintendent and spent the winter in Toronto, marketing his product. "I got pretty good at doing mailings and found I could stuff 400 envelopes in one night." His targets now included summer camps and landscape architects. The following spring he was back in Apsley. With a saw set up outdoors, he and his small contract crew worked through the next summer. In February, 1975, he moved into a barn rented for the princely sum of $35 a month and they worked for the rest of the winter.

Henke's free-form wooden designs, solidly built for institutional use, were slowly springing up in playgrounds across Ontario. "We were turning out $350,000 annually in sales over the next few years, but when you subtracted the labour, lumber, and other costs, the company was not very profitable." Eventually, Horst Henke set up a small office in the basement of a building near fashionable Yorkville, in Toronto. His only other expense was the answering service he'd had from the beginning. That was the extent of Children's Playgrounds' office facilities and it was all that he needed. Municipalities began ordering more and more of his durable, innovative wooden playground designs.

Still the company wasn't generating enough cash flow while selling to this narrow market. "Our prices were not cheap, compared to metal equipment," says Henke, "and although some wealthy Torontonians had purchased large units I realized that we would have to have lighter, less expensive designs for general use in people's yards." So he made a deal with an American wooden playground manufacturer who gave him the rights to produce its designs in Canada. The Americans had also picked up some European ideas and the new line complemented Henke's originals. "It was the best thing to do at the time. They agreed to stay out of Canada and we were able to use their designs and promotional material."

By 1977, overseeing the construction as well as selling the designs had grown into a formidable task. The first place he turned for help was his brother Rick, who had by now moved to Sweden. Rick's engineering background made him ideally suited to help in the equipment designs and in overseeing the manufacturing side of the business. Rick was willing and Children's Playgrounds Inc. became a family partnership.

Sales grew at a rate of about 25 per cent a year and the company set up a second shop, this one for home playground equipment, in a converted garage in north Toronto. Then the brothers made one almost fatal mistake. They decided to get into the parquet flooring business. "It looked simple," recalls Horst, "but we quickly found out we did not know the market." With quality-control problems due to faulty installation without adequate supervision, the flooring business floundered, and it almost brought Children's Playgrounds down with it. "We called a meeting at our factories and I had to announce that this was Chrysler day," says Horst. "We fired our parquet installers and consolidated the work at our Toronto plant. Our Apsley employees were fantastic. They said, 'We'll come and work in Toronto, but when the financial picture improves we want your word that you will move the institutional division back to the Apsley area.' "

Now the pressure was on. Like many small enterprises faced with adversity, Children's Playgrounds became more efficient than ever. Horst and Rick ran flat out and the following year sales approached $1 million for the first time. Some of the employees were switched from hourly wages and put on contract. With the help of the Ontario government, in 1982 the company was also able to form a small business development corporation that invested in Children's Playgrounds. This is an Ontario financial instrument permitting investors to obtain a 30 per cent tax-free credit in Ontario-based manufacturing companies.

With brothers Horst and Rick sharing the responsibilities (Horst in charge of marketing, Rick in charge of manufacturing), sales went from $1 million to $3.5 million in three years. And, true to its word, in 1982 the company returned its institutional manufacturing to Peterborough (near Apsley) and moved its employees back near their homes.

Children's Playgrounds is now entering a third phase by expanding into the United States. A small office has been set up in Cambridge, Massachusetts, and the quality of its work has already won it some major contracts and produced word-of-mouth sales. Its first job was for a $100,000 installation at St. Mary's Hospital in New York City, and it is currently putting in a playground for the United Nations school. The facility is being built on a concrete abutment extending out over the East River.

Horst Henke is aware of the challenge of mounting a profitable marketing campaign in the U.S. "Although the public sector in the U.S. is poor relative to Canada's, there are an infinite number of privately owned amusement parks, commercial spaces such as shopping centres, and restaurant areas such as Burger King and McDonald's." In Canada and the U.S. Children's Playgrounds now offers a sophisticated line of equipment geared to specific age groups and has developed special facilities for the handicapped child.

The brothers Henke admit today that their biggest problem remains lack of capital for advertising and promotion. It takes a six-figure amount to put together a respectable campaign in the

U.S. and the firm simply doesn't have that kind of cash on hand. "The unique feature of our business is that it does not provide us with collateral for the working capital we need to finance our growth," says Horst. "We have some lumber, materials, a pool of labour and design know-how, but it's impossible to convince lenders that this is adequate." As a result, the firm has resigned itself to growing slowly but surely.

Both brothers work six-day weeks, though Horst admits to taking one month off a year to travel. Still a bachelor, he has seen a lot of the world and plans on seeing more. Apart from travel he takes pleasure in collecting old maps and original paintings. Rick is married and has a family. Other than an annual trip to a warm climate, his main form of relaxation is playing his flute.

Children's Playgrounds Inc. is an evolving success story of which the final chapter is not yet written. Money maker Horst Henke started with an undeveloped market for a new product and set out to supply it. He entered that market with innovative designs and high-tech quality construction. He kept his competitive edge by catering to its special characteristics: "Each project is uniquely unpredictable. We're hard to copy and we have the special appeal of individuality in an age when 'mass production' has an unpleasant ring to it. We are holding our course. We believe in it." And finally, his own total commitment, dating from the pioneering days of the company, has been matched by that of his brother.

There has been a quiet revolution in children's playgrounds over the past decade. In Canada at least, Children's Playgrounds Inc. has helped to make it happen. In 1985, in order to meet the challenge of the American market a new partner was brought into the company. Horst is now in charge of U.S. sales, Rick is Canadian sales manager, and the new man oversees manufacturing. The company is changing from a family-owned and -managed enterprise into a firm with specialized responsibilities. How well the transition is made will determine its future success.

RON MCLELLAND AND FAMILY
McDonald's, Bathurst, N.B.

Ron McLelland looks back on the twenty years between the time he left school and the life he now leads in Bathurst, New

Brunswick – where the unemployment rate tops 15 per cent – and figures all of his life's experiences have made him a millionaire a couple of times over. Ron McLelland owns and operates the McDonald's franchise in Bathurst.

McLelland began making money selling mobile homes with his brother; today, despite the tempting offers to sell his McDonald's franchise, he continues in the hamburger business with an eye to the future when his children can become involved in yet another family enterprise.

He and his wife Gail have enough extra cash to maintain a growing stable of harness-racing horses, all named after McDonald's and the town of Bathurst. One of the older horses is called Nobody, as in "Nobody can do it like McDonald's can." A more recent acquisition is We Do It All For You. Another is named Drive Through, because Ron was one of the first to ask for a drive-through serving window at their McDonald's store. He tried to name a horse Quarter-pounder, but harness-racing officials wouldn't let him register it. Bay of Chaleur is a fast trotter named after the picturesque inlet on which Bathurst was built, and North Shore Tremor was named the year the north shore of New Brunswick was shaken by a small earthquake. Turmeric is not an ingredient of McDonald's hamburgers, but the horse doesn't fit the pattern either. He was the number-one money winner on the harness-racing circuit in 1982, with total purses of $205,000. But Turmeric took sick the next year, and the McLellands' dreams of earning several million in stud fees evaporated. Turmeric's winnings helped to cover the costs of trainers and managers for what is essentially their weekend hobby. The day-to-day business is McDonald's.

The story of McDonald's restaurants around the world has been told frequently: restaurant equipment salesman Ray Kroc established the first franchise in Des Plaines, Illinois, on April 15, 1955, based on a concept developed by Dick and Mac McDonald in San Bernardino, California. George Tidball, currently head of the Keg and Cleaver restaurant system, opened the first Canadian McDonald's, in British Columbia in 1967. The current president of McDonald's of Canada, George Cohon, brought McDonald's to eastern Canada with a store in London, Ontario, in 1968. Tidball sold his interest in McDonald's six years later.

By 1985, George Cohon had built McDonald's Canada into a chain of over 500 outlets, employing more than 50,000 people.

Annual sales hit $1 billion. For that, Canadians who passed under the golden arches consumed 50 million pounds of beef patties, 70 million pounds of French fries, 22 million pounds of chicken, 26 million dozen buns, 12 million litres of milkshakes, and 4 million litres of juice! McDonaldese has now become part of the Canadian language; the golden "M" part of the Canadian landscape; Ronald a character that fascinates small children; and meals at McDonald's at least a weekly routine for many Canadians. There isn't a business success story like it, and countless thousands of business people keenly line up to get in on it.

But McDonald's sets rigorous standards for prospective franchisees. Only a small number of applicants qualify. There is no simple check list of qualifications. The best way to describe what's needed to become a McDonald's franchisee is to describe money maker Ron McLelland.

He was born on his dad's dairy farm, sixty miles outside of Halifax, on May 25, 1948. At an early age he learned to get to work early and work hard. His days started at five in the morning: the cattle had to be milked, fed, and watered and the barn cleaned out before school, and it had to be done again when he got home. He was an adequate student until high school, then he started to lose interest. "I wanted to get out and work at something." He knew when he wrote the grade twelve Nova Scotia provincial exams that he hadn't done well (he barely passed with a 55 per cent average). But the results wouldn't be mailed until summer. "So I rushed out after school to get a job before my marks came in. I went to the Canadian Imperial Bank of Commerce branch in town, and they took me on as a teller trainee. I don't think they ever found out about my school marks!"

Ron was a fast study, and a hard worker. He rose quickly through various junior banking positions – teller, clerk, accountant's assistant. The bank transferred him to various branches to gain new experience. He spent time in Anne Murray's home town, Springhill, and in Montegue, P.E.I. Then they moved him to the Halifax regional office, where he became an audit assistant. For four years, he travelled throughout the Atlantic Provinces, auditing Bank of Commerce branches. The audit team he belonged to was also responsible for the bank's branches throughout the Caribbean, so Ron spent several months in Antigua, St. Lucia, Grenada, and St. Vincent. That won him an assistant manager's job in Dartmouth, and then a promotion to the regional office corporate credit department in Halifax.

"All my other bank jobs required long, long hours. Now, I was basically in a nine-to-five job. I was earning $8,000 a year, and I was getting bored. I was young and aggressive, and I was frustrated with working in a bureaucracy." His wife Gail – whom he'd married in 1970 – was working in the psychology department at Halifax General Hospital at the time. They decided to make a move.

McLelland noticed from all the loan applications he was processing that the mobile home business in the Maritimes was growing. His brother, Gerry, was actually living in a mobile home at the time, and liked it. So the two of them researched the manufacturers and the market. "We really did our homework. I remember it took us from September, 1971, to the next March."

They decided Glendale Mobile Homes were the best in the business. "There was no point doing anything unless we could offer our customers the very best." They applied for and received a Glendale franchise for their home town of Truro. The franchise cost nothing; all they needed was a sales lot, a sign, and one or two display models.

The next problem was capital. "Gail and I had saved up $3,000. We borrowed another $7,000 from one of the bank managers I used to work for, with our life insurance as collateral. Then, I took all of our money – $10,000 – to the local credit union in Truro." Ron's years with the Bank of Commerce must have helped. He needed $20,000 to buy two mobile homes from Glendale and lease a display lot. As security, he offered the credit union the $10,000 he'd already scraped together and the mobile homes. He got the loan.

In April of 1972, Ron and his brother set up the two display models on a lot they rented for just $50 a month. They put up a sign and started selling. Things went slowly at first, but Gail had found a job at the Colchester County Hospital nearby and supported the family while the business grew. They saved money by living in a rented cottage without any running water. Ron now says, "Gail is the most important person in my life, and she has been very supportive. She really made it all possible."

Both brothers worked hard – from nine a.m. to ten p.m., six

days a week, and often on Sundays. When they weren't selling, they assembled the homes, which came in kit form. The sales began to mount. "That first year, we sold forty-five mobile homes, almost one a week. That brought in $400,000 in gross sales. The net profit was $16,000 – twice what I'd been making at the bank. It was like somebody had given me a million!"

The next year they hired a service man who helped assemble the homes and dealt with any problems covered by warranty. In the 1973-74 year sales were over $2 million and net profit was close to $200,000. The McLelland brothers now ran the largest mobile home distributorship in eastern Canada – and were one of the top five in Canada. They were also beating out the local competition. When they opened there were ten other mobile home distributors in the area. Soon only one competitor was left.

Ron attributes the company's success to the combination of low prices and top quality bolstered by excellent service. If a customer had a problem, it was fixed. On one occasion they replaced an entire unit, no questions asked. "I worried about dealing with the manufacturer later." He always passed on rebates and manufacturers' discounts to his customers. "I believed in giving people a deal. I never took more than our usual profit margin. I believed in spoiling the customer, because that's what builds your reputation and brings people back." Ron McLelland also proved to be an astute investor. A mobile home dealer in New Glasgow, Nova Scotia, became ill. McLelland purchased his inventory, land, and good will, for $300,000. He ran the second lot for two years, then sold it for an immediate profit of $75,000 plus a further $50,000 profit from mobile home sales. The McLellands had become wealthy in a comparatively short time. Within two years, they'd earned enough to buy a farm and modern home on Truro's town limits, for cash.

Four years after starting this first business venture, Ron began looking for new challenges. The business was declining: prices were going up and so were interest rates. And mobile home insurance was getting more expensive. Then he heard that McDonald's had purchased a property right across the road from the Truro lot. So, he applied to McDonald's head office in Toronto for the Truro franchise.

"I don't believe in fooling around, once I've made up my mind to do something. I phoned Peter Bigalki, McDonald's licensing director, and he sent me an application right away." The application was processed and Ron was invited to Toronto for interviews. "They were very detailed meetings, and I spent a lot of time speaking with McDonald's president, George Cohon. They went over my entire background, what I did, my full financial background, my philosophies on business." He was too late, though, to get the Truro franchise, but he was put on the list for future franchises. McLelland qualified for the franchise that was to be established in Bathurst, New Brunswick. It was scheduled to open in October, 1977. At the time, McDonald's required each franchisee to have $125,000 in unencumbered cash, which made him eligible for bank financing of another $325,000. The total cost of establishing a franchise then was $450,000.

When you join McDonald's, they expect you to make the restaurant your main business interest. Ron consulted with brother Gerry and they agreed to sell the mobile home business in May, 1977. Gerry took his share and returned to family farming near Truro. The buyer was their best salesman. Since he'd put a lot into the business they handed it over to him for the value of the inventory. Ron quickly reorganized his financial affairs and disposed of his other business interests. Altogether he and his wife had saved up approximately $300,000. They kept the house and farm in Truro.

Then, like every new franchise owner, Ron McLelland joined McDonald's at the bottom. "I put on a crew uniform and worked at every job there is to do in a McDonald's store. I cleaned up the parking lot, cleaned the washrooms, washed the floors and tables, made the French fries, made the Big Macs, the fish fillets, worked the counter and served customers. I enjoyed it. I'm a real people person. I believe in serving the customer."

After you've worked in a McDonald's outlet for 300 hours, you take the Basic Operations Course. McDonald's calls its training centres the Canadian Institutes of Hamburgerology. There are three of them – in Vancouver, Montreal, and Toronto, and more than 12,000 people are now graduates. In 1985, 2,400 management and franchise people were scheduled to take the course. According to Peter Beresford, McDonald's director of marketing, the curriculum "includes the study of operations, financial analysis and forecasting, marketing, consulting, employee relations, and equipment operations and maintenance. Students participate in class discussion and role-playing management techniques." A computer system developed by McDonald's is used to present the students with all possible management challenges, and it simulates the results of management decisions and how those decisions can affect business.

Ron took the course in Toronto with about twenty others, not all of them franchisees. Every manager hired for a McDonald's store must take the same course. Students are constantly reminded of founder Ray Kroc's philosophy: "None of us is as good as all of us." And they learn George Cohon's credo: "We talk the quality of our product. We talk the cleanliness of our restaurant. We talk the nature of the service that we give. We call that QSC, quality, service, cleanliness."

When Ron McLelland completed his training at the Institute for Hamburgerology, he was sent back to work in another McDonald's store for three months, this time as assistant manager. Because the store in Bathurst was delayed due to some permit problems, he ended up staying six months.

The restaurant finally opened in April, 1978. By then McLelland's $450,000 start-up capital was practically gone. He'd spent extra money up front to make his franchise state-of-the-art, including drive-in windows, which were just being introduced. He also put an office in the store basement so he could be close to the staff. And he had to hire managers and have them trained.

On opening day he had 150 employees, twenty-five of them full time. "Business was good right from the start. We paid off the $325,000 bank loan in two and a half years. We're completely debt-free now." McLelland reports that his annual sales of $2.4 million are about 20 per cent above the average McDonald's in Canada. But he keeps his profit lower than many because he believes in reinvesting in the business and in the community. In the first three years his profit was less than 6 per cent of sales. The average for McDonald's is between 10 and 15 per cent.

Since Bathurst is a small place, and money can be tight, he invests a lot of money in community activities – sports teams, the handicapped, senior citizens, fund-raising programs organized by local service clubs. He offers a complimentary breakfast to all the graduating students at the two high schools, one French, the other English.

In spite of McDonald's intricate formula for all aspects of restaurant operations, the licensees have nearly complete freedom in matters concerning money and supplies. McLelland sets his own menu prices and wage scales. He is conscious of the state of the Maritimes economy and tries to keep his food prices at a reasonable level. His wage rates are higher than the industry average, and most of the full-time employees have been with him since opening day. "I love this business. I think McDonald's is fantastic. You're involved with a lot of people, especially young people, and that keeps me young. I know all of the staff on a first-name basis, and I try to help them out if they have a personal problem. I like to take care of them. I believe in treating people fairly." He also believes in buying as much of his restaurant's supplies as possible from local businesses. All of his buns are baked locally, and the drinks come from a local bottler.

Ron McLelland has expansion plans for the community he serves. "Bathurst wouldn't support a second McDonald's, but there are opportunities for what we call mini-Macs – smaller operations in shopping malls, that sort of thing. That's what I'm considering in Bathurst."

The McDonald's in Bathurst, New Brunswick, will likely remain in the McLelland family for some time. Ron says he and Gail have no intention of selling and would like to get their three children involved in the business when they're old enough. "I'm a workaholic. I'm here six days a week. I know I'd get a lot for the business if I wanted to sell, somewhere between 45 to 60 per cent of our sales volume, and I know I'm a millionaire a couple of times over. But I'll always want to do this. I enjoy work. I'm aggressive. I'm not happy unless I'm working.

"I believe anybody can be successful, as long as they have the best possible product, and they give customers value. You spoil your customers, and you'll appreciate the way they say thanks.

"In business," he says, "you've got to take chances. You've got to be different. I'm not a genius. I know the Maritime economy is bad. There are very few people who are prepared to take a chance today. When they have a job, they want to hang onto it.

They worry that if they try something new, that they might not make it, that they'll lose everything. But that's the only way. You've got to be prepared to risk everything."

JOHN SAKSUN AND SON
Accuform Golf

John Saksun watched the opening ceremonies of the 1976 Summer Olympics in Montreal on his home television set, but few who were in the stadium could have done so with as much intensity. He held his breath as the runner mounted the long steps to the Olympic bowl, torch held high, then touched it to the rim of the huge dish, setting afire the Olympic flame that would burn steadily for the next two weeks. Blinking back tears, Saksun savoured the moment with a sense of joy and accomplishment. It was his torch that had lit the flame and launched the Olympics that year.

Eighteen-year-old John Saksun arrived in Canada from Czechoslovakia in 1938 to join his mother and stepfather. When he landed in Halifax he had thirty-five cents in his pocket. "I remember when I arrived in Toronto for my first meal with my parents. There was a basket of apples on the table. After a long conversation I realized I had eaten every one of the apples. My stepfather told me then that in Canada you can have everything you want. You never have to be hungry. It was quite a revelation."

Looking for a profession in his new country, Saksun quickly settled on tool and die making. "They earned more money than teachers," says Saksun, whose education in Europe had prepared him to enter either the academic world or the priesthood. He apprenticed himself to a small Toronto company called Viking Engine and Tool and began to pay his dues. He worked an eighty-hour week and took home a $5 paycheque. After work each evening, he'd ride his bike to Western Tech where he was studying drafting and design. In 1939, when the war broke out, Saksun was made foreman of a group of boys from the technical school who came to work at Viking. This was his introduction to aircraft work, a field in which he would become expert. He and his team worked with Mosquito bombers and Lancasters.

In 1943 Saksun got married and went briefly into business for himself manufacturing ornamental iron work and magnetometers (used in prospecting for metal ore). After two years and with marginal success he decided to close down and continue his training as a tool and die maker. But he soon became restless again. "They were union shops. There were a lot of rules and guidelines. I wanted to make my own decisions and set my own standards. I knew the time would come when I would need to try it on my own again if I were going to be really happy."

In 1951, at thirty-one, Saksun set up on his own for good. He named his company Queensway Machine and entered the very competitive machining business by going after the difficult jobs, the ones other companies couldn't complete to specification. This approach demanded persistence. "I remember going to De Havilland Aircraft every Saturday for about six months," reveals Saksun. "I would ask if they needed any work done and the answer was always no. Finally one day they called me in and said they were having problems with the wing tips for the Beaver airplane. They couldn't get them to fit properly. By Monday I had them made, both left and right wing tips, and they fit perfectly. I've been working for De Havilland ever since." He now builds aircraft frames to the demanding specifications of aircraft manufacturers such as De Havilland and McDonnell Douglas.

Saksun's tenacity has today given him a small company, employing on average eighty people. He has built an enviable reputation for the finest precision work. "If a hole is off by five-hundredths of an inch," he says, "the whole job is no good. It has to be right." It was this reputation for unparallelled precision and craftsmanship in tool and die making that made the firm fit company for Olympians. The torch for the 1976 games had already been designed at McGill University when Saksun was approached to give his expert opinion. He considered the welded object unsightly and set out to machine torches from solid material. He produced 1,800 in all, including the gold-plated torch that was presented to the Queen.

"I remember when we supplied the first two torches to the

Olympic Committee for their approval. They couldn't believe that we had made the torch out of one solid piece of metal. So they took one apart to assure themselves it was genuine. They had never seen anything like it."

While Saksun was building a reputation that would take him to the Olympics he was also raising a family. In 1948 his wife gave birth to a daughter, followed in 1952 by a son. By the time John, Jr., was old enough to join his father's business, the old man was about to get into a different, though related, line of work – manufacturing golf clubs. "I took up golf about twelve years ago because people told me I should relax. My well-wishers never thought golf would become work. Anyway, simultaneously we began to do some contract work for another golf club manufacturer. They had some financial difficulties and, after consulting my accountant, I took over the business."

When he saw how the clubs were being made, he was horrified. "I saw the workers assembling the irons by eyeing them, and I realized that was the way most manufacturers still assemble their clubs." One of his mottoes is, "If you cannot measure it, you cannot make it. If you think you can, you're a damn fool." So he decided to design and build his own clubs. First he brought in Ben Kern, a former touring professional who is now the pro at the National Golf Club in Woodbridge, Ontario. "Ben looked after the aesthetics of the club and I worked on the material, balance, and feel," says Saksun. "One of the first things we did was to build a machine which precisely measures the loft and lie of every golf club. It is our assurance of accuracy and uniformity."

John, Jr., was in charge of the new company soon after it was incorporated on July 5, 1978, and dove head first into the competitive world of sports marketing. It left John, Sr., free to run Queensway.

The elder Saksun loves to tell a story, and a favourite of his is how one of Ontario's leading amateur golfers, Nick Weslock, discovered the newly named Accuform golf clubs. "Nick came in one day with his clubs and he was playing a Tommy Armour Silver Scot set. His five iron was head up in the bag, of course, and I found myself looking at it. It had a spot worn close to the handle, which was where Nick had discovered the sweet spot. I prefer to call sweet spots [where the ball should make contact for the best shot] sensor points. And sensor points should be in the middle of the club's face. If they aren't the club isn't properly balanced. And if every club has been only 'eyeballed' instead of precision manufactured, you have sweet spots here, there, and everywhere. The golfer has a favourite club because he's spent time learning its idiosyncracies. That's not the way things should be. The professionals may be okay because they monitor their clubs' manufacture, but the average golfer can't rely on consistency or balance. We'd like to change that."

Saksun, Sr., also likes to describe the day Lee Trevino came by his plant. "He told me that he could always get another wife, but not another good driver. I said, 'Mr. Trevino, you are absolutely wrong. I can duplicate your driver for you exactly.' He had never before seen the equipment we designed to measure our clubs, and was taken aback by the sophistication of our relatively small operation."

Nick Weslock, Dan Halldorson, Barb Bunkowski, and a growing number of golfers are discovering the quality of Accuform clubs. However, Accuform refuses to pay professionals to promote its equipment. "We let the quality of our equipment do the talking," says John, Jr., "and we now have a growing number of U.S. college kids playing our clubs, simply because they want to. I know the word is spreading."

Queensway Machine Products Limited and Accuform Golf do not disclose their earnings. Both companies remain privately owned. But Saksun admits to revenues of $2.5-$3 million a year. More revealing is the fact that he is installing $750,000 worth of equipment in 1985 and is self-financing and privately financing the purchase. "My financing is very simple. I never buy anything without having the money. My bankers visit me, see the new equipment, and ask if I need to borrow money. I have never gone to the banks for money." His wife is trained in accounting and does the firm's books.

Queensway Machine likes to hire young people with a grade twelve education and train them. Job candidates are asked one question. "Do you want to work, to learn, to make money?" If the answer is yes, and if the employee follows strict company discipline ("If he's late for work three times, he's let go"), then he has a future at Queensway.

Queensway's challenges today are fairly typical. "We're

always looking for orders, and finding the right people to work for us is not easy." The golf business, however, represents a different challenge. "American manufacturers keep coming up with gimmicks to sell their equipment. One year it's lightweight, the next it's hollow irons. I can't subscribe to introducing a new golf club unless it's thoroughly tested and properly made. If Accuform puts out something, it has to be right."

John Saksun, Jr., delights in taking the head of an iron off the rack and balancing it on the end of a pencil. The point where the pencil is placed under the iron is exactly in the middle of the club. But traditionally the golf business requires more than a well-made product. John Saksun and his son have decided to allow the quality of the product to speak for itself. This was a successful strategy for Queensway, but it remains to be seen whether or not it will work for Accuform Golf.

MAUREEN AND JIM BAUFELDT
Granny Taught Us How

The tiny hamlet of Violet Hill, Ontario, is barely on the map – a dozen houses, an old church, a one-time Orange Lodge, a former one-room schoolhouse, and a Shell gas station. By 1974, the wooden church was closed because there weren't enough parishioners; the schoolhouse was shuttered because students were being bussed to larger schools in the larger towns; and the Orange Lodge was empty. Only the gas station was in business, to serve motorists on Highway 89 that bypasses the village. The few residents commuted to the nearby towns of Alliston, Shelburne, or Orangeville.

Eleven years later, in 1985, Violet Hill is no larger and only subtly different to the eye, but much has changed. The evidence is in the bright curtains that adorn the windows of the church, the schoolhouse, and the Orange Lodge, in the neatly trimmed lawns bordered by flower beds and shaped hedges, and in the freshly raked gravel in the parking lots in front of the school and the Lodge. The school now bears a sign – "Mrs. Mitchell's." A woman by that name taught there for more than twenty years. On the Orange Lodge, another sign tells passersby that "Granny Taught Us How." And on a weekend afternoon, forty or fifty cars line the streets of the hamlet. This tiny speck of rural Canada is headquarters to a multimillion-dollar-a-year enterprise.

Inside Mrs. Mitchell's, visitors are greeted by a woman in nineteenth-century dress and a man with knee-high leather boots and a knee-length top coat. They are serving lunch, and they are Maureen and Jim Baufeldt, waitress and waiter, cook and maitre d', manageress and manager, owner and designer of this country dining spot. The Baufeldts are a husband-wife team of money makers who have put their complementary talents into a winning combination.

Mrs. Mitchell's restaurant occupies a large part of their time, but it is only a small part of the Baufeldts' Violet Hill conglomerate. Across the road, Granny Taught Us How is the retail outlet for a bustling craft, toy, and collectibles business that grosses several million dollars annually. A new subsidiary, Canadian Country Folkart, brings in another million dollars plus. The Baufeldts' product lines can be found on the shelves of major department stores throughout Canada and the United States. And this all started in 1972 when a cocktail waitress and her husband, an aspiring restoration contractor, were living in a small Toronto apartment.

At the time, Maureen was working in the Runway 23 bar at the Skyline Hotel on Toronto's airport strip, and was pregnant with their younger daughter, Heidi. Their daughter Heather was then seven. Maureen needed some gifts for people, so she "designed and made three little bun warmers – one for my mother, one for my husband's mother, and one for a very good friend of mine for a Mother's Day gift." Then one day, a friend asked how much she would charge for a bun warmer. "I didn't know. I told her, five dollars or so. She said she wanted to take one back to the office, to show some of the people she worked with. She came back about an hour and a half later and said she needed eighteen for that Friday. I thought I'd never get eighteen bun warmers made in four days, but I did it anyway. Then, I got a call a week later, from one of the recipients of one of the eighteen bun warmers. Her sister owned a store, she said, and she wanted to buy some for the store. That's how it started."

The apartment kitchen was very small, with a round kitchen table. "My sewing machine took up half the table, and the rest of the family sort of ate around the other half. I never had time to take away the sewing machine." Within a few months she was supplying six or seven stores and "just going crazy." Her husband Jim had just had an accident at the time, and he was propped up on the couch in a body cast, threading elastic through the bun warmers so she could get the Christmas order out – about $600 worth. "The apartment got so full of material and bun warmers, we couldn't move. We had to get out of there, the place was bulging. It was my materials or my family!"

But money was an obstacle. "We looked out in the country, because we thought we could find something cheap, and because Jim is a restoration designer, we thought we could find something old and fix it up. That's how we discovered Violet Hill. The church was for sale. We borrowed a bit of money from our family and got a mortgage from the bank to make up the $13,000 they wanted for the church."

They moved to Violet Hill in the fall of 1973. While Maureen pursued her rapidly growing bun-warmer business, Jim turned the church into a home. He refurbished the interior in natural pine, built a three-sided loft for the bedrooms in the peaked roof, put a living room, dining room, and kitchen under the loft overhang, and created a dramatic floor-to-peak entranceway. It became a comfortable home, but an inadequate production facility for Maureen, who regularly displayed her expanding product line at trade and gift shows in Toronto and other communities. At the shows, she met store owners and distributors, who began to place large orders for Maureen's crafts.

"The church was full. The busier I got, the more product I had to move, the more fabric I needed, the more boxes that were half packed. The orders were all over the house. The business just grew and grew. Then the old Orange Lodge, which was built in 1878, came up for sale. I decided we'd buy it for a craft shop."

In the spring of 1976, the Baufeldts had accumulated enough profit from the burgeoning crafts business to pay cash for the Orange Lodge. Jim cleaned up the original brick and stonework and fitted the lodge with shelves and sales counters. Maureen, meanwhile, contacted other crafts people she'd met at various trade shows and arranged to have them supply the store with pottery, wooden toys, kitchen decorations, hand-knitted clothing, carvings, and collectibles. Her own line of crafts had expanded from bun warmers to include several dozen designs of clothing accessories, carrying bags, and items for homemakers. She purchased a wide selection of fabrics to keep in the store, so customers could buy material to sew their own clothes, curtains, or whatever.

Since the shop had such a homespun atmosphere to it, and because many of Maureen's skills had been passed to her through her family, they named it Granny Taught Us How. The sign facing Highway 89 outside Violet Hill attracted the curious, and the shop rapidly became a regular stop for those enjoying drives in the country.

Over the next eight years Maureen kept attending craft shows and making contacts. She developed an array of product lines (they now number over 100), including stuffed animals, sewing bags, crib comforters, wall-hangings, placemats, and pot holders. When she felt she was ready she made arrangements to have her products distributed throughout Canada and in the U.S. David Youngson and Associates Ltd., a Toronto-based distributor, agreed to represent Maureen in Canada, and David Moriphy of Atlanta became her American sales representative. "These people approach all the stores and get the orders. They pass on the orders to me, and I ship directly to the stores, and I pay the sales reps on a commission basis. I still go to two gift shows at the Canadian National Exhibition every year, and two shows at the International Centre by Toronto airport. That's where all the exhibitors gather, so all the store buyers can see what's available. We also participated in trade shows in Dallas and Denver to get into the American market."

Maureen doesn't sew much anymore. Her bulging order book led her to recruit a small army of home sewers; there are now ninety. "It's become a large cottage industry. When somebody is interested in sewing for me, I give them a few items to do, to check the quality of their work. I do all the design work. I draw up the patterns. I supply the materials. When she comes in, I'll have everything cut up for her, with the patterns and even the thread. I ask her how much she can produce a week. If she says forty, and I need eighty done, I'll find somebody else to sew the eighty. They get paid by the piece. They have to supply their own sewing machines, their own work space. They're really in business for themselves. My sewers earn anywhere from $70 to

$400 a week. Most of them do it in their spare time, so that's not bad money."

The volume of sales grew so quickly that the Baufeldts set up a warehouse and distribution centre in nearby Shelburne. The warehouse and the store together employ nine people. Another nine are employed by Canadian Country Folkart, which developed from Jim's hobby, reproducing eighteenth- and nineteenth-century rocking horses, whirlygigs, and wall plaques. Yet another nine people have jobs at Mrs. Mitchell's restaurant, which specializes in country cuisine. A number of homemakers in the Violet Hill region supplement their income by supplying Mrs. Mitchell's with baked goods.

Like other entrepreneurs, she complains of the difficulty of finding and keeping good staff. "So many lack the work ethic. They know the social system. They want to keep getting government benefits, and want me to pay them under the table. I won't pay anybody under the table. I've reached the point where I can spot those people who just want a job for twenty-one weeks or whatever the minimum qualifying period is for unemployment insurance. I won't take them on. I judge people by a personal yardstick. I measure them against me. I used to be an employee. I waited on tables. I know that anybody can do anything as long as they work. You don't get up at nine in the morning and go to bed at nine at night. You have to work twelve hours a day, seven days a week, for ten years or however long it takes to accomplish whatever you want to accomplish. Nothing comes to you easily."

Maureen and Jim Baufeldt haven't had it easy. And they've certainly earned their success. As Maureen says, "You know, if a high-powered organization from the city had done a feasibility study on the potential of the old Orange Lodge in Violet Hill, beside the Shell gas station, in a hamlet of a dozen houses, they'd have said to forget it."

NORMAN AND DAVID HARLEY
Far West Mountain Wear

It was the summer of 1977 and twenty-three-year-old David Harley was washing dishes at the Banff School of Fine Arts. Having recently earned his degree in economics from Simon Fraser

University, in British Columbia, he was saving up money to finance a period of hiking and skiing in the Rockies. Harley was a keen outdoorsman, an adept skier and mountain climber. Back home in Vernon, B.C., David's father Norman was busy raising his other three sons and running the family business, Harley's Fabrics, a successful chain of fabric stores dotting British Columbia and Alberta. The senior Harley had earned an MBA from the University of Western Ontario and worked as a department store fabric buyer before setting up his own store, which grew into the chain. That summer Norman had no intention of leaving the business he'd built up for a new enterprise. And David had no plans to go into a new business with his father.

While working in Banff, David kept noticing that many of the jackets being used by American tourists visiting the Rockies were made from some special, new material. He soon found out that the good-looking, lightweight fabric carried the U.S. trade name, Gore-Tex, and he decided it was perfect for use in Canada. Gore-Tex is a fabric laminated with a thin skin of Teflon-like material. It was developed in the early seventies for medical uses, notably for artificial heart valves, veins, and arteries. It is entirely inert, meaning that it won't rust or dry out or cause any reaction at all when in contact with living tissue. American clothing manufacturers quickly recognized its potential as a revolutionary recreational fabric since Gore-Tex is water- and wind-repellant but allows moisture to escape so the body can breath. It is also rugged enough to stand up to repeated outdoor use. To David Harley it seemed ideal for the Canadian market.

David went for his hike and pondered the scheme that was forming in his mind: he would design a line of Gore-Tex jackets himself and use his first-hand knowledge of the conditions facing a wilderness athlete to put them through a series of demanding in-use tests. Then he would manufacture and market them himself.

That fall David was back in Vernon working for his father, plugging away at his jacket design in his spare time and saving capital toward his venture. Seeing his son's determination, Norman gave him some financial assistance. With the money, David hired a seamstress and started making prototype parkas for friends. It took several months of designing and redesigning the rugged jackets until they would stand up to his "torture tests," but eventually the new Gore-Tex outerwear was ready for showing at sports shows in western Canada. In a few short months he'd gone from being a dreamer to the brink of entering the rough and tumble of the clothing industry.

Up to this point Norman didn't take the whole thing seriously. "But when David came home with his first large order for 3,000 jackets, I had to sit up and take notice," he recalls. Many men in his comfortable position would have been reluctant to make a major change. But like his son, Norman Harley is a money maker. "We met that first order by scrambling like hell. But Gore-Tex's sales appeal had been proven by David. I decided to sell the fabric stores and work with David full time on Far West. They say that change is good for everyone."

Far West had discovered that it was able to produce the comfortable, stylish jackets that the consumer of the eighties was seeking, but at a price range that still placed it below the extraordinarily expensive prices of comparable imports. Father and son formed a formal partnership and set to work. Far West Mountain Wear Ltd. was officially incorporated.

David Harley threw himself into a routine of seven-day weeks, designing and overseeing the manufacture of the clothing line. The proceeds from the sale of the fabric chain were used to help build up the new manufacturing business and Norman was free to take over the responsibility for sales. "The key to our success," says the senior Harley, "was to decide where we wanted to go. We decided to target the higher range of the clothing market and not try to make clothes for everyone." Marketing was nonetheless a tough proposition because it entailed simultaneously educating buyers about the product and selling it to them. "It's still our number-one problem today. We're still out selling to major accounts. But the quality sports stores know we exist and the word is getting out."

David Harley discovered Gore-Tex eight years ago, so Far West Mountain Wear could hardly be described as an overnight success. With the recent emergence of a sports-minded, relatively affluent shopper who is prepared to pay for a quality garment, Far West is riding the crest of what promises to be an increasingly heavy wave of consumer demand. "We're just starting to hit the mainstream of demand for our product," says Norman. "Sales have increased by 25 per cent each year for the last few

58

years and I have no doubt this will continue." Revenue was $3 million last year and will go over $4 million in 1985 and he confidently predicts revenues of $10 or $12 million will be attained over the next five years. Right now, well-designed assembly-line methods allow for the production of 70,000 garments a year with plenty of flexibility to handle growth.

Today, Far West purchases its own material in Canada and ships it all the way to Maryland, where it is converted into Gore-Tex. The finished material is then shipped back to Canada. There are about thirty-five items in Far West's inventory; retail price for an average jacket is from $180 to $210. David now oversees a modern, airy 12,000-square-foot plant in Vernon that employs about fifty people.

The Harley family likes Vernon, B.C., and sees little reason to move to a more heavily populated area. "We don't wear a shirt and tie in the office," says Norman, "and home is just minutes away." In his spare time he likes to pilot his own Beech Bonanza aircraft, which he also uses for business.

Norman is away about thirteen weekends out of the year on sales trips. He's now backed up by full-time sales people in the Maritimes, Quebec, and Ontario (where another son is now sales manager) as well as in the West. But the company is not entirely a family affair. In January, 1981, they brought in a chartered accountant from the firm of Thorne Riddell to act as financial controller.

David is slowly returning to the outdoor sports he loves so much, after nearly exhausting himself emotionally and physically while Far West was getting off the ground. The mountains where he skis are only a twenty-five-minute drive and he recently bought a sailboat, which he keeps at nearby Kalaamalka Lake. He is enjoying remodelling his modest home and has no interest in living more lavishly, particularly if it means incurring debt.

"I'm very conservative when it comes to money matters. I don't even like mortgages. In fact, I don't like 'owing,' period," explains David. "I've lived very frugally, pouring virtually everything back into Far West. I wanted to give it every chance to succeed and I couldn't relax and spend until success was a safe prognosis. We also made sure that the company's growth didn't outdistance the funds available to support it. Going too far too fast has undone quite a few entrepreneurs. We planned carefully and moved forward with our eyes wide open. Looks like it's working and now I can take it a little easier and be, well, kind of young again."

Far West Mountain Wear is a textbook case of seizing an opportunity to introduce a product for which a ready market exists. But the company's burgeoning success can be partly attributed to its management team, consisting of designer, salesman, and financial officer. It has discovered how to mobilize and run an efficient manufacturing operation, and it is learning how to market its products effectively across Canada. As a result, it is quietly revolutionizing the way Canadians are dressing for sports and other outdoor activities.

JOHN COOK
Sundance Bars and Restaurants

Money maker John "Bull" Cook left Newfoundland in 1975, at the age of thirty, to make his fortune in Toronto. But it was not to be. He sold sporting goods for a while at Doug Laurie's store at the front of Maple Leaf Gardens and rented a place at Harbour Square for only $250 a month because it was new and not yet fashionably expensive. He had Tuesdays off but worked Saturdays to midnight selling to the hockey crowd. Meanwhile, he and a few friends worked up a scheme to open a new sporting goods store on Avenue Road. The great plans for the new store never amounted to much, and within a year, John Cook returned to St. John's with a lot of good stories but not much of a fortune.

Ten years later, at the age of forty, Bull Cook is called Atlantic Canada's bar tycoon, with a small empire of eight restaurants and bars expected to gross $5 million in 1985. Cook looks every inch the king of Newfoundland publicans. He's six feet tall and a solid 220 pounds, complete with a grizzled beard. (His father must have known something when he gave son John the nickname Bull when he was only two.)

In retrospect Cook's success seems a long shot. He dropped out of high school after grade nine and at age seventeen got a job with the Mitchell Agencies as a "traveller," which is food-business jargon for a travelling salesman who tries to convince supermarket and corner grocery store managers into stocking more of his brand X than somebody else's brand Y. The job paid

$50 a week, but the company gave him a classy car to drive around the province, to impress the customers.

For the next nine years, Cook sold products from the Mitchell Agencies, and his customers passed on to him countless scraps of business knowledge. Equally important in the education of this young salesman were the observations he made after work hours, while relaxing in the pub of whatever town he happened to find himself in. He became a bar critic, etching reviews in his mind: where he thought publicans were making bad business decisions in the quality of the food, the courteousness of staff, the attractiveness of the decor, and the cleanliness of the establishment.

In 1972, he broached the subject of a Cook family bar with his father, Lewis, and his brother, Doug. Lewis Cook, fifty-nine at the time, was taking early retirement after a career with Bain-Johnson and Company, a large Newfoundland conglomerate active in the insurance, furniture, and fishing industries. Doug had just completed a law degree at Dalhousie University in Halifax and was looking for a job in St. John's. Among them they were able to come up with $5,000. They were able to negotiate a $35,000 line of credit at the bank, based on John's income from the Mitchell Agencies and his father's retirement income and equity in the family home.

The three Cooks believed there was potential for a pub near Memorial University in St. John's. John had noticed that the one pub near the campus was usually empty, and that the staff didn't seem to care much about their customers. So, the family partnership signed a contract to rent a vacant store with 1,800 square feet of space in Churchill Square, a small shopping centre near the university. The location was between a bank and a drug store, and the rent was $800 a month. The three spent their evenings and weekends refurbishing and equipping the place they came to call Big Ben's. The name was not coincidental – the pub was given a distinct British flavour, with Highland pictures and wainscotting on the walls, ploughman's lunches and Scotch eggs on the menu, and a variety of ales on tap to oil Newfoundlanders' well-known love of a good yarn and a tall tale. The ambience appealed to the local university crowd, which made Big Ben's a habit after classes and sporting events. The Cook family gambled that their business venture would fill a void in the neighbourhood, and they were right on target.

"We opened the doors at three o'clock one afternoon, and for five years, you couldn't get into the place," John remembers. "We didn't expect to be that popular, even though at the time there wasn't much competition in St. John's. We'd opened it on a wing and a prayer and a hell of a lot of hard work. The money we put into it wasn't much for a pub or restaurant, as I found out later. But people liked the place. It did so well, that we paid off the loan we got to open it in six months!"

John stayed on at the Mitchell Agencies and Doug began practising law in St. John's while their father managed Big Ben's. In 1975, John left Mitchell's for his brief foray into the sporting goods business in Toronto. "I could have stayed in St. John's, but I might have spent too much time sitting around and drinking!" By the time he returned home, his third of the profits from Big Ben's had grown to $20,000. He pooled this amount with money from three friends, who became silent partners. Then he approached the manager at his local Toronto-Dominion Bank branch with a detailed plan for a waterfront bar and disco to be called Uncle Albert's. The bank happily advanced a further $80,000 since John and his family had already established a reputation for prudent management.

The Cook family instinct proved itself again. Uncle Albert's became another hit with St. John's young people, but it didn't become profitable until John toned down the music and let it become more of a social gathering spot. By 1979, nearly four years after he had developed the Uncle Albert's concept, the bar had generated the cash for a $240,000 investment in a larger, 300-seat restaurant and bar, the Sundance Saloon, complete with a bold brass and mahogany bar, stuffed animal heads on the wall, horseshoes and branding irons on the walls, and steak and roast beef on the menu. The Sundance Saloon was timely because St. John's was crowded with westerners, attracted by the scent of oil off Newfoundland's shores. "We had a large out-of-town business clientele. You could see it in the cash register every night. So many of them paid with oil company expense accounts." It, too, became a hit and made money.

By 1985, Sundance Bars and Restaurants Limited had expanded into a small conglomerate of five establishments in St. John's (not including Big Ben's, which remained under separate ownership, managed by the elder Cook) and two bar-restaurants in Halifax. Every one of the seven outlets has a distinctive style, menu, and atmosphere to appeal to a specific market segment.

On St. John's Water Street, across from the main courthouse, John opened Peppers, based on the light lunch, salad-and-quiche places he'd seen in some of the chic corners of Toronto. In Halifax, where seafood is a restaurant staple, he opted for beef and chicken.

John Cook confidently predicts the Sundance chain will gross close to $10 million by the end of the decade. He won't say how much profit current sales generate, but he earns enough to drive a BMW and keep a thirty-five-foot racing yacht near St. John's. But most of his money goes back into the company to fuel expansion.

Cook believes his company grew and prospered in large measure because of rigorous control of expenses. He tries to keep rental costs below 10 per cent of projected gross sales; staff costs below 20 per cent; food and bar supplies below 35 per cent; and other expenses, such as furnishings, utilities, and maintenance, to less than 25 per cent.

Doing business in the Atlantic Provinces is difficult because of geography and climate. "Everything costs us more here – fuel, electricity, beverages – and it is difficult to get top-quality food. It sometimes happens that a shipment of fruits and vegetables for our restaurants gets stuck in North Sydney for a week, because of weather. The sales tax in Newfoundland is 12 per cent, which discourages people from buying things. We think very carefully before we invest in something for the company, because of the taxes."

He also knows his market well, particularly in St. John's where he grew up. "There isn't that much for people to do here. If they lived in Montreal or Toronto, they might go out in the evening and drop $40. We just don't have the recreational facilities, the theatre. There's no pro hockey here, no pro football. So people go to a bar for the evening. It's someplace for them to go. They'll easily spend an evening in one of our places and spend $20."

John Cook's money-making story really began with a successful family partnership that gave him the credibility and the confidence to branch out on his own. He thinks his example proves there's a lot of opportunity in Newfoundland for those willing to look for it. "The key thing is people have to start things happening. Activity creates jobs. People are thinking of new businesses for St. John's, especially in the downtown core. We can't wait for people to come in from outside. We've got to do it ourselves."

Part 2: Partners

Good business partnerships can be unbeatable combinations. But they must be structured carefully to take full advantage of each partner's attributes and assets, while avoiding destructive conflict. One partner might bring an idea or an invention to a business relationship; another contributes the management and marketing expertise. Some partners might bring in money to start the business, while others invest their time and experience. The contributions and skills of the various partners are not always equal, and ideally the management and ownership structure reflects that fairly. The majority partner by virtue of his or her investments often recognizes that another is a better leader, best suited to run the company day by day. Successful partners recognize each other's strengths and weaknesses, and a prudent corporate structure that capitalizes on each partner's virtues can have the potential to steamroller the competition.

Ian Innes was the motivating force at Feathers, which became a winning business when his skills were exploited while his partners remained silent financial backers. The founders of GEAC each brought diverse talents into the enterprise, which enabled the company to thrive in the complicated, competitive world of high technology. A real estate salesman, a banker, a computer programmer, and an accountant blended the knowledge of their various professions to develop lucrative new products at Aftek. James Mackenzie found partners willing to back his first attempt to cater to the working woman. Though that venture failed, he'd learned enough to try again on his own. Other permutations and combinations of personalities, skills, and contributions turned the partnerships at Three Buoys, Treats, and International Verifact into money makers.

IAN INNES AND PARTNERS
Feathers

The greatest motivating factor in the life of a money maker can be a pink slip. Such was the case for Ian Innes, fired from his position as real estate sales manager at a Canada Trust branch in 1979. The dismissal coincided with his parents' first visit to Canada in the thirteen years since he had emigrated from Scotland. Innes recalls the event with a combination of mild bitterness and amusement. Apparently, his work performance didn't matter. "They gave me a psychological test, which said I wasn't a good manager. The boss canned me. It had a shattering effect. I vowed then that I would never, ever put myself in a position like that again. I'd been thinking of opening a pub of my own for years. Getting fired was the push that made me do it."

Innes's yearning for his own pub was more than a desire to be independent, to be his own boss, to have his own business. The man has Highland ale in his veins. He still has fond memories of the snug comforts and genial ambience of Edinburgh public houses, with games of darts, talk of football, and pint mugs of Younger's Tartan or Tennant's Lager. When he first arrived in Canada, drink was still being consumed in bureaucratic darkness. Though things had improved in Toronto by 1979, Ian Innes saw room for the kind of pub he remembered from home.

Innes's knowledge of pubs was acquired from the patron's side of the bar. Like many people in Britain, he was a regular at a particular local, which he visited most days after work in an Edinburgh computer company. In 1967, Toronto-Dominion Bank recruited him for the bank's Toronto computer centre. Two and a half years later he moved to the data-processing division at Lilly Cup in Toronto, and a year after that he switched careers by going into real estate sales.

With his untimely dismissal, Ian decided to learn more about pubs and earn an income by working in one. He waited on tables, washed dishes, cleaned the floors, and tended bar in a restaurant called the Crown and Mitre in midtown Toronto. He had his mornings free, so he spent them scouting locations for his own pub. "I wanted a mainly residential neighbourhood, with a strong sense of community. I felt the people in the area had to be mainly of British heritage, the type of people who would enjoy imported British ales on tap, who would adopt the place as their own local."

After a year's experience at the Crown and Mitre and months of visiting possible pub sites, Ian settled on a narrow, depression-era brick building a couple of blocks west of the Kingston Road streetcar loop in the Beaches district in east Toronto. The building could be bought for $110,000 and Innes calculated it would cost another $200,000 to renovate the former furniture store on the ground level and furnish it as a pub. This money he did not have.

Innes approached a number of friends and friends of friends until he assembled an investment group of eight people, including himself. Five of the partners each contributed $10,000; three others, including Innes, contributed $20,000. This yielded a total investment pool of $110,000. All were convinced that "The Beach," as long-time residents refer to their community, was ripe for Ian's pub. Most of the group were in their late thirties and early forties. They owned their own homes, and the money they invested in the pub idea was what they'd been able to sock away in savings accounts or borrow through personal loans from banks.

All of the money was spent on the building on Kingston Road, bought for cash. So far so good. But when they tried to borrow the $200,000 for turning it into a pub, they were flatly refused by a succession of eight banks and finance companies. "They see restaurants and bars as a hellishly high risk," Innes observes. "They have statistics to prove it – and at that time, the summer of 1980, interest rates were between 18 and 20 per cent. You'd need one hell of a successful business to generate the cash to make those high interest payments."

Those interest rates were the major factor in setting off the worst recession the Western world had experienced since the 1930s depression. While politicians and social commentators focused more on the massive unemployment that resulted, little was said about what high interest rates did to entrepreneurs. Innes and his investors were faced with debt payments triple the size their parents' generation would have faced twenty years earlier.

He and his partners simply couldn't find a lender until they approached the Federal Business Development Bank. The FBDB lent them the $200,000, taking a mortgage on the building and the future business as security. The interest rate on the loan was 18 3/4 per cent – meaning staggering interest rate payments of over $37,000 per year, which wouldn't even retire the debt.

There wasn't any point spending money on renovations, however, until they were certain the Liquor Licence Board of Ontario would grant them a licence to serve beer, wine, and liquor. The LLBO refused to do so. Inspectors felt that the planned pub put too much emphasis on drinking and not enough on eating. They insisted on a design change, so that more food could be served. And they suggested food prices be increased. Anybody hoping to establish a restaurant or pub must cope with an army of building, liquor board, health department, municipal, and labour office inspectors. Anyone going into business on his own must be prepared for similar bureaucratic hassles.

Innes and partners got their liquor licence approval a month later, after they had added more tables and a more expensive menu to their original plan. They named the prospective pub Feathers, after a popular establishment of that name in Ludlow, near the Welsh border in England's Shropshire County. They wanted the Toronto pub to be as authentic as possible, so they hired an Irish designer named Jim Naughton. Graham Savage, one of the partners, is British, and his contracting firm handled the construction. Restaurant consultants Floody and Associates were retained to ensure the business would be run as efficiently as possible.

Innes recalls that one small change involving the location of the glass-washing machine eventually saved so much staff time that it almost paid for the consultants' fee alone. "It meant that the bar staff's time wasn't being wasted filling the glass washer, and they concentrate on dispensing drinks, which is where the money is."

The renovators had about 2,400 square feet to work with: 1,800 square feet were set aside for the public area, the rest for washrooms and kitchen. The building was completely gutted. Walls, wiring, plumbing, heating and air-conditioning systems, three smoke removal systems, and a full bar, hand-built from mahogany, and cooking facility were installed. Rugged Axminster wool carpet was imported from England for the pub floor. Plaster cornice was installed where the ceiling meets the walls. A pillared mahogany front was put on the building, with a hand-cut Feathers sign. In the basement, they built a large walk-in cooler with pumping systems for six draft beers. One partner, television cameraman Terry Culbert, who'd won national news awards at both the CBC and Global Television, decorated the walls with a collection of his photographs and pen-drawn caricatures.

Innes chose to offer domestic versions of British Toby and Danish Carlsberg on tap. He imported Newcastle Brown, Younger's Tartan, Guinness, and Tennant's Lager in kegs from England, Ireland, and Scotland.

Ira Jones, who'd grown up in Wales, was hired to supervise the kitchen. She developed two menus. One is a light snack selection common to British pubs – Scotch eggs, steak and kidney pie, Welsh tart, and a ploughman's lunch. The other is a more sophisticated selection for the ten-table dining area – steaks, roast beef, Yorkshire pudding, and gourmet burgers. "You can't make your liquor licence food ratios in Canada serving bangers and mash," says Innes. "Besides, Canadians demand a lot when they go out for the night. They want service and quality. If this pub were in Britain, it could be run by a family, a staff of six people or so. In Canada, you have to offer so much more, on two shifts, and seven days a week, so we employ more than thirty people."

The pub was ready to open in March, 1981. At the time, Feathers' partner Janice Roberts and her husband Harry were working in England on a teaching exchange. On opening day, they travelled to Ludlow and asked the mayor and all the townsfolk to join them at the original Feathers, whereupon they placed a telephone call to Canada. Thus the British Feathers was linked to its Canadian cousin for the official Toronto opening. On Kingston Road, however, there wasn't anything more than soda pop on tap. The liquor licence would not receive final approval for another two weeks.

Being a dry pub for the first few days turned out to be an advantage. "It gave us a chance to work out all of the wrinkles, to get the kitchen operating smoothly, to get the staff trained." Once they finally got permission to begin pulling pints from the beer kegs in the cellar, Feathers became a resounding success. "It was gangbusters. People came because we had the right location, good atmosphere, good food, good drink, and good times. Some people have become such regulars that they're here every day for a pint. We bring in the British papers, so people can catch up on the news back home. We've set up a couple of dart boards at the front of the pub, and the customers choose their own captains and run tournaments. There are two soccer teams based here, and a baseball club. We stage feast nights when everybody joins in the fun. And we've got fish and chip nights, too. It's like a social club, really."

Innes is the only partner who takes an active role in the management of the pub. That's the way he wanted it from the beginning. The other seven trust him to run the place properly, and they share ideas and make major management decisions at regular board meetings. Only one of the original partners has left the group, which recouped its original investment after three years. They are still locked into the five-year loan agreement with the Federal Business Development Bank, but they've been able to pay the principal down to $130,000 in three years. Now all of the partners are earning what Innes calls "a handsome profit" from the pub – not enough to make any of them wealthy, but a pleasant complement to their other incomes. Innes derives his entire income from Feathers through his share of the profits and a salary earned as the pub's general manager.

The Feathers' partners have no ambitious expansion plans, no interest in opening more pubs or selling franchises. However, Ian is an active supporter of a lobby group called Campaign for Real Ale. CAMRA started in Britain, where ale afficionados demanded that regulators allow small, regional breweries to make cask-conditioned ale. The British beer market has been dominated by six major brewery corporations, and CAMRA members demanded beer without artificial carbonation or chemicals, and beer made without heat-treating and filtration. A Canadian chapter, CAMRA Canada, was formed, and it has had some success. Innes says he'll be one of the first to buy "real ale" from a new brewery being built by CAMRA supporters in Guelph, Ontario. He plans to carry two brews at Feathers from the new Wellington County Brewery. He thinks real cask-conditioned ale will add a new dimension to the pub business in Canada.

Ian Innes meets many people who would enjoy owning their

own pubs. He warns them it is much tougher than it looks. "This isn't Britain. You can't underestimate the difficulties of the business in Canada. It is very demanding, and you've got to be prepared for a lot of hard work, a lot of frustration, and many unexpected problems. We are doing well, but it hasn't been easy."

JAMES MACKENZIE
Molly Maid

"We're just tickled pink to have you as a customer" are the words on a card that welcomes every new client to Molly Maid, one of the first maid-service companies in the world to be organized into a proper franchise system, and certainly the foremost Canadian chain of its kind. There are now 120 franchises across the country, and these don't include a recent expansion into the U.S. and U.K. Forty-one-year-old money maker James MacKenzie is the president of Molly Maid and it was his drive and management skills that took the operation from $100,000 in sales in 1980, when he organized it, to sales of about $10 million annually in 1985.

MacKenzie graduated from Queen's University with a degree in commerce and economics, then worked as a plant accountant for Ralston Purina. Eventually, he made the switch to marketing, and, when he left the company in 1979, he was director of product management.

MacKenzie had always had an enterprising spirit and right from university days envisioned himself in an independent, entrepreneurial role. He liked the idea of bringing together a select group, launching a business, and making it big. His goal in entering accounting had been to learn all he could about financial management. The switch to marketing was also deliberate. He read everything he could about starting a business, listened to anything well-informed associates could teach him, and keenly researched the needs of a changing society.

He came to believe that the kind of business that would succeed would in some way cater to that burgeoning section of the population, working women. The method for making it big

70

would be franchising, one of the subjects that MacKenzie had spent years investigating. He was an armchair expert.

Just before leaving Ralston Purina he formed an investment company with three partners. Together they raised $100,000 in working capital. They borrowed, they drew on their savings, and then they put their assets on the line to arrange for financing. In all there would be about a quarter of a million dollars to draw on. Then after working with Price Waterhouse on the development of a business plan, they acquired the Canadian franchise rights to a U.S. chain of haircutting salons called Great Expectations.

The venture proved a disaster. "We hoped to appeal to working women by offering hairdressing without an appointment in convenient mall locations during extended mall hours. But we couldn't get into the shopping centres and so couldn't open and operate enough units to support the cost of strong marketing and management. We would have needed to amortise operating expenses over several locations to be efficient. It was no go."

Though the enterprise failed, he still clung to the idea of catering to the working woman, and in 1980 he discovered Molly Maid. It was a residential cleaning business located in the Toronto suburb of Mississauga owned by a former nurse. Although it was marginally profitable, MacKenzie was attracted by its concept, name, and logo – an eye-catching pink maid's cap on a navy blue background.

MacKenzie bought the existing business for $15,000 and converted it into a franchise, which he sold back to the previous owner for a dollar. Her trademark was purchased for $15,000. The original owner, now a franchisee, was made a major shareholder and member of the board of directors.

By the fall of 1980 a complete franchising system was put into place and a push to expand from the Mississauga home base began. "We had developed a franchise formula for the previous business, but this time we had the right product," says MacKenzie. "We identified the profile of a franchisee and put in place a system that would enable her (or him, since a few of our franchisees are men) to run her own business." This time MacKenzie had found an undeveloped market.

MacKenzie made full use of experts in setting up his company.

He used two well-known accounting firms, one to develop an internal accounting system and the second to construct a package for franchisees. A legal expert on franchising developed the franchise agreement, and a firm specializing in trademarks and patents set up the rules for use of the logo. Finally, a research firm conducted an in-depth study to ascertain customers' knowledge of maid services and the potential for their use.

Essentially, Molly Maid looked for women who had no previous management experience and who were frustrated at the lack of growth opportunities in their current employment. The women would be between the ages of twenty-five and forty-five and share two essential characteristics: a determination to succeed and a willingness to work.

The company offered a management system wherein each franchisee was trained at head office and backed up by mass purchasing of cleaning materials, business insurance, and bonding services as well as national marketing and promotion. Important support services such as uniforms, letterheads, and invoices were also supplied. The Molly Maid logo – unchanged from the founder's original – instantly conveyed the nature of its business. In 1980, the price for a franchise was $4,500, including several thousand dollars worth of materials. (It is now $9,000.)

MacKenzie stresses that "one of the absolutely key ingredients of our success is the standardization of procedures. This allows us to monitor every franchise with expedience through weekly reports and monthly analyses by our operational team. We provide guidelines to our franchisees that they can follow towards success; and, since we have the regular input, we can solve most of their problems before they snowball. In a word, everyone involved in Molly Maid has a sense of direction, the *same* sense of direction. We've been called the McDonald's of the maid-service industry and we're delighted with the comparison.

"The franchisees are the heart of our business and really are partners in Molly Maid," says MacKenzie. "People don't realize that our franchisees are not cleaners themselves. They hire an average of ten people each. Their job is to ensure customer satisfaction and to manage a profitable business." The average franchisee also makes about $30,000-$35,000 a year, which, in owner-managed enterprises, translates into more purchasing power than from a salary alone.

Molly Maid was careful to map out a plan of steady growth. "We could only grow at the rate which we could comfortably support the franchisees," says MacKenzie. "I mean by that there has always been an emphasis on budgeting (both time and money) for strong marketing and management support. And in-depth research is conducted on every new market. We have controlled growth from day one." In four years the chain has grown to 120 franchises ("We're about five ahead of our projections") and MacKenzie expects soon to reach 160, the maximum number Canada can support.

Competition in the maid-service industry, in part inspired by Molly Maid's success, has been a healthy influence. (In 1980 the Mississauga telephone directory listed just five maid services; in 1985 it lists twenty-five.) Molly Maid's management system has made the difference. "There are a lot of maid services starting up, and a lot are failing. When I first looked into the reasons for so many maid services having disconnected telephone lines, I discovered that their greatest weaknesses and what most likely forced them out of business had been a lack of strongly defined, regulated management procedures and real 'networking.' "

MacKenzie's main concern is improving the training of his franchisees and their maids. To underscore the point he lists the agenda for Molly Maid's annual convention. There will be lectures from experts on customer relations, workshops on cleaning, supervisory skills, and public relations, and a seminar on personal financial planning. Every manager is also expected to take a Dale Carnegie course as part of the ongoing training program.

One of the advantages of a large franchise operation is that it can afford to advertise and promote its service. MacKenzie has arranged joint promotions with companies such as Pepsi, McDonald's, CP Air, and Johnson's Wax. But he admits that "the main selling factor is performance. We are highly aware that when you allow a cleaning service into your home, it is a very personal act. And it's word-of-mouth recommendation that wins us most of our customers."

Molly Maid has a staff of ten people in the Oakville head office. In the beginning Mackenzie spent a lot of time in Oakville but now he travels two weeks out of every month. Part of Molly Maid's system involves field visits with every franchisee, which means a direct one-on-one meeting and a review of problems and performance. The firm has also developed a system of awards and incentive travel. Last winter fifteen franchisees and their spouses enjoyed an all-expenses-paid trip to Jamaica.

With the saturation point in maid services fast approaching in Canada, MacKenzie is looking to the future. He has already granted master franchises in the United States, United Kingdom, and Australia and Molly Maid is now carrying out research aimed at delivering other home-care services to householders.

The boardroom of Molly Maid's head office is lined with an impressive array of photos of its franchisees. They are there not just as a reminder of the firm's rapid growth, but because every time he calls a meeting they illustrate MacKenzie's central theme: developing the franchisee is the single most important activity. That's why a number of franchises are now owned by former maids, and the firm's vice-president, field operations, is a former franchisee. And it is why regional refresher seminars are held on topics such as equipment maintenance, provincial labour laws, and personnel management skills.

When James MacKenzie goes for a cruise on his yacht *Molly Maid*, with its Molly Maid logo emblazoned on the sail, he can take considerable satisfaction in having stuck with his original vision and found an undeveloped market where he could make it work. In the process he has tapped a relatively unused pool of management talent – women in dead-end jobs or housewives looking for a career. He's also helped to solve a real problem for the modern working couple. "Studies have shown that disputes over housework are now a major cause of marital friction in homes with two wage earners. They have the money to pay for a solution to the problem and the solution is Molly Maid."

NAZIR KARIGAR, MEHBOOB SHARRIFF, AND PARTNERS
Aftek

In the spring of 1979, Nazir Karigar was looking for a job. He was twenty-nine years old, newly arrived in Canada from Pakistan. He had a degree in chemistry but most of the jobs available required a knowledge of computers. So Nazir decided to try something new. He bought a Commodore PET computer and taught himself how to program it. His new skills got him a job as a programmer in the general accounting department of the Manufacturers Life Insurance Company in Toronto. He'd found a new profession in a new country. However, the task of buying a new home led to an unexpected series of developments that quickly made Nazir Karigar one of Canada's more successful high-tech money makers.

During negotiations for the purchase of a condominium apartment, Nazir met Mehboob Sharriff, the owner of the Century 21 real estate franchise in Don Mills, Ontario. Sharriff's casual interest in computers led to a discussion about the possible applications of computers in the real estate business. He believed that a number of apartment building owners he'd come to know through his real estate transactions could use a computer program to manage their buildings more effectively. He guessed that there might be a vast market for such a computer program in Canada.

Sharriff invited his brother, Hufain, and their brother-in-law, Amin Amlani, to a meeting with Nazir. Hufain is a chartered accountant. Amin has experience in banking. And with Nazir Karigar's knowledge of programming and Mehboob's experience in real estate, the four men set out to design a computer system for apartment building managers. Once they had what they wanted and had tested it thoroughly, the four pooled $25,000 in savings to market their product across Canada. The development of this kind of computer software is not capital-intensive, because software is really an organized collection of ideas and concepts that instruct a computer to behave in a specific way. Software is the result of an intellectual effort, and the major cost is brainpower. The software industry is growing astronomically, with some software development companies reporting sales gains of more than 400 per cent a year in the mid-1980s. While Sharriff and his partners focused on the Canadian market at first, advertisements they placed in industry publications quickly led to sales in the U.S.

That first year of operations, 1983, when they called their company Distributed On-line Systems, they sold $100,000 in programs. They reinvested their profits in the fledgling company and kept learning about the computer business.

Of course, they couldn't sell computer programs to clients until the clients had chosen computer equipment. Well-known IBM and Apple systems were selling at over $3,000, although a number of small companies were selling close copies of the brand-name products at much lower prices. The four partners decided – after less than a year in business – to become copycats, too. Since their new strategy was to offer a top-rate computer machine at a much lower price, they changed their company name to Aftek, for "affordable technology."

They faced some formidable problems, however, not the least of which was their near total lack of knowledge about how to build computers. And they didn't have the money to do it. But reputation can be worth cash. Their computer software for apartment managers had won the admiration of Toronto apartment building owner Ken Kassum. Initially, he lent the four original Aftek partners several hundred thousand dollars for a computer factory (in 1984 Kassum became a senior partner in Aftek, and took on executive responsibilities).

Traditional lending institutions had been distinctly unenthusiastic. "We approached the banks," says Karigar, "but they are very conservative and didn't really want to put their money into a venture they thought was extremely risky. That's one of the difficulties in starting companies in Canada. You've got to arrange your initial funding through friends, family, and business contacts, and then establish a strong balance sheet, before the banks show any interest."

Once they had the money in place from Kassum, the four partners went hunting for talent. They recruited a top Toronto computer designer, William Leary, to direct the creation of Aftek's IBM-compatible computer and a production line on which to make it. Of course, it was against the law to copy the IBM design exactly, but they were within their rights to design a computer composed of off-the-shelf parts that does exactly what the higher-priced brand name product does. The most sophisticated part of a computer is the microchip circuitry, which provides the computer's brain and memory. Such chips are available to anybody from large microchip manufacturers such as Intel and Texas Instruments, which supply most of the big computer makers in the market today.

The Aftek team found a small circuit-board maker in St. Catharines, Ontario, Proto-Circuits, which was contracted to mount the computer chips on circuit boards. They hired Fox Metal, a sheet-metal shop in Markham, Ontario, to build the computer housing. And they rented factory space in Willowdale, a Toronto suburb, for an assembly line.

Eighteen people were hired from various technical training schools, including the Devry Institute and George Brown College, to staff the assembly line. "We selected these people very carefully. We brought them in for a two-week probationary period, to watch them work. It is a difficult, time-consuming process, but in the end we had a team of people who are able to work by themselves, with little direction or supervision. They are highly motivated individuals," concludes Karigar.

By January, 1984, the basic Aftek computer was coming off the assembly line at the rate of about 200 a month. At the same time the company offered customers a line of off-the-shelf accessories – keyboards from Keytronics in Chicago, disc drives from Shugart of Japan, and a wide variety of video displays and printers. The price for a complete Aftek computer with accessories was $2,200, some $1,300 less than a competitive IBM machine would sell for.

All of this gave Aftek a unique product for apartment building managers around the world – a software program designed specifically for them, plus a very competitive computer hardware package that could be plugged into any IBM compatible equipment and could use almost any software program written to the IBM standard. The move to manufacturing also meant that Aftek could go after the entire desk-top computer market.

Aftek computers came onto the market in February, 1984. By September, they were selling computers to the Canadian government and a large number of institutions. Corporations were less daring, because they knew what they were getting when they bought from IBM, Honeywell, Control Data, and the other computer giants. Aftek, they had never heard of. "Too many small computer companies have failed in the past," observes Karigar, now Aftek's vice-president of operations. "Breaking into the larger companies is one of our biggest challenges. We must work hard to get over their initial reservations, because they don't want to buy from a firm that won't be around to back up its product."

Aftek intends to be around for a long time. Ken Kassum, who

is now Aftek's chairman, has increased the company's capital base to $500,000. Sales are mushrooming. By the end of 1984, gross revenues hit $1 million. In January, 1985, monthly sales topped $200,000. They zoomed to $350,000 in February, and $500,000 in March. Kassum estimates annual sales of $12-$15 million by 1986, and he thinks that is conservative.

These sales projections are not based solely on Aftek's computer clones. Company president Hufain Sharriff and his co-founders expect that their computer manufacturing will last only a few years in a field where new products supercede the old within months. Sharriff believes Aftek must innovate to survive. They capitalized on loopholes created when the computer giants rushed to market with new products and failed to cover their tracks with patents. Aftek and other clone makers were able to imitate without fear of legal reprisals. As these renegades become a larger force in the marketplace, the giants are less likely to repeat their oversights. That's why Aftek's strategy for the future is to find product niches that the big companies are unlikely to touch.

Aftek's first such product is Datasafe, a tape drive for micro-computers. "It is an external tape unit for data storage to be used primarily for back-up, to avoid the accidental loss of data," explains Nazir Karigar. "It is a comparatively slow system, but well worth the time spent loading it, because it could protect six months' worth of effort. We were the first in the world to capitalize on the need for such a system, which allows random access to any data stored in a tape back-up system."

Aftek recently accepted a government invitation to display its product at an international trade fair in West Germany. That exposure resulted in distributorships in West Germany, Holland, Spain, France, and Britain. The company expects Datasafe to be its biggest source of revenue in the near future.

Datasafe and other product ideas that Aftek's executives don't want to talk about just yet are being developed by some of Canada's top high-tech wizards, although they are not on Aftek's payroll. Aftek is still a relatively small company and does not have the resources to maintain a large research and development department, so they approach researchers and electronics specialists at universities and hunt for talent employed by larger companies who are willing to do product design on a spare-time contract basis. "It's up to us to decide what we want made. Then we go to the experts and say 'This is what we need, and this is what we want it to do. Can you design it for us?' Canada is loaded with the right kind of expertise. You just have to make an effort to find these people and encourage them to develop the products you need for the marketplace," says Karigar.

"Developing the product hasn't been the difficult part. It's the time and effort. We still work seven-day weeks. That's my wife's chief complaint. But you have to do that, initially. We're living fairly well now. We're a long way from being millionaires. Perhaps we won't ever be, because we don't intend to let the company grow past a $45-million-a-year operation. That's when you've got to go to the stock market." This is because high technology requires more research money than other industries. "As long as we keep it below $45 million, we can maintain control. It's been a fight, but we can see the light at the end of the tunnel."

Nazir Karigar, Mehboob Sharriff, and partners all started in different lines of work. None had anything to do with computers. Yet, they were alert enough to spot opportunities. They had saved enough from their other jobs to invest in their dreams. They combined their expertise and experience in other businesses with developing technologies in order to launch unique products, which in turn attracted other investors and gave them the capital base to launch a new Canadian enterprise. They are well on their way to becoming real money makers.

DOUGLAS ARCHIBALD AND IAN CUMMING
International Verifact

The only product of International Verifact Inc. is a credit-card- and cheque-clearing terminal that looks something like a medium-sized calculator. Called the Terminus I, it sits on the checkout counter of a store or restaurant or at a hotel front desk and permits the clerk to instantly clear any credit card transaction (it handles up to nineteen different cards). By punching the right code and running the credit card through the machine, which is connected to, say, VISA or Mastercard central terminals, a transaction can be cleared in seconds. Terminus I is even equipped with a device that notifies police if the card is stolen. It seems like an idea whose time has come.

"It took no formal market research to determine the need for our product," says Ian Cumming, vice-president of International Verifact and one of the two founding partners. "But we did do a market analysis. We checked with the banks to find out if they could use such a product, and they certainly could." Cumming's partner is Douglas Archibald, now the president of the company. When the two first met in 1972 Archibald had just been fired by the investment dealer he was working for and was looking for something to do. Cumming was "full of talk about a new product called a credit card verifier and I felt sure he was on to something with real potential."

Archibald's enthusiasm for the idea may have been helped by the fact that, like Cumming, he was born in Scotland of a Canadian mother who had likewise advised him to seek his fortune in this land of opportunity. Both had come to Canada as young men and had similarly diverse backgrounds with one major theme in common: data processing.

Archibald was trained in accounting and after arriving in Canada worked with a variety of companies, including Ford Motor Company, Canadian Imperial Bank of Commerce, and National Trust. He became a systems analyst, responsible for analysing and improving the efficiency of data-processing departments.

Ian Cumming began in Canada as a trainee loan officer with the T-D Bank and quickly transferred into its programming group. After working for an insurance company and then a trust company as a co-ordinator of systems and procedures, he switched to the field of executive search, where he set up his own firm that concentrated on data-processing. He was in the midst of settling a dispute with a partner when he came across the great marketing opportunity. Then he met Archibald.

They formed their partnership with virtually no capital. Archibald remembers "it was tough going. Initially we ran out of money to pay the rent and even began working out of hotel lobbies. It was tricky when the pianist started to play in the mid-afternoon, but I was able to intimate to the person at the other end of the phone line that it was just my wife's regular afternoon piano practice."

With their market research completed they were convinced they had the right product; now they had to build it. So they enlisted the considerable talents of Ronald Crowe, now vice-president of manufacturing. An engineer and circuit board designer, Crowe surveyed the competing machines in the field and came up with the design and software for the Terminus I. Archibald and Cummings immediately hopped a plane to VISA headquarters in California to show off their prototype. VISA was impressed and suggested modifications. Ten days later the changes were made and they had the official seal of approval.

"VISA was knocked out by our product and our enthusiasm," says Archibald, "and insisted we Canadians would teach the world a thing or two about product development. In a way, the people at VISA were right. At least we could tell the rest of the world that developing the product is the *easy* part."

The next step was to find the financing to keep the company afloat and to underwrite the expensive marketing push. They couldn't go to the banks for financing, because they were the ultimate customers, so the partners met with several venture capitalists. But they were dissatisfied with the percentage of the company they would have to give up to obtain the money they needed. "We would have been working for the venture capitalists, not ourselves," says Archibald.

Archibald and Cumming decided to raise money in the stock market. This meant going to the Vancouver Exchange, the only Canadian market that would list a fledgling enterprise with no track record. They went to an investment company in Vancouver with a fourteen-page draft proposal typed up by Archibald's wife the night before they left. "We had fourteen meetings in two days covering investment dealers and lawyers," says Cumming, "but we left Vancouver with a guaranteed agreement for the underwriting." It then took ten and a half months for the prospectus to be written. Finally, in January, 1984, shares were made available to investors and $600,000 was raised. International Verifact was off and running.

Now the product had to be sold to both the large financial institutions and retailers. Since everything depended on the big guys – and because they can take a long time to make a decision – they were approached first. It took fifteen months of work with some of the banks before an order was obtained.

This period of the company's development was particularly harrowing. The stock, issued at a dollar, plunged to fifty cents during the first year of operations. "We were under pressure to issue announcements about our plans, but I refused," Archibald states firmly. "I insisted we would only issue news releases of fact, announcing a confirmed sale." It was a policy that paid off in the long run.

In 1983 the company presented its product at the American Bankers Association annual convention. Their booth stood out, and so did Archibald and Cumming. They wore name tags adorned with a picture of a buffalo and accosted bankers in the aisles with their convention motto, "Don't be buffaloed by fraud." The result: "Sixty-five serious sales opportunities," and the company's first sale to a U.S. bank.

Every lead was followed up and slowly the results began to show. A few months later a California cheque authorization company gave International Verifact its first million-dollar order. Then came breakthroughs with American Express in Canada and the Toronto-Dominion Bank. Today virtually all of Canada's banks are testing Terminus I with their retailers in the field and its quality and performance are winning new orders.

With the major financial institutions starting to come around, the company was ready to take on retailers at a National Retail Merchants Association convention being held in Toronto. "We did not want to pressure the banks through the retailers," says Archibald, "but we felt they had a right to know about the existence of our product." Shoppers Drug Mart, Idomo, and Toys R Us now have the unit in their stores and the list is growing. "There is no question that every retailer in the country will eventually have a terminal at every cash register," says Cumming confidently.

These days International Verifact's office and warehouse in north Toronto are humming with activity. Newly hired computer experts assemble the dark grey units and put them through stringent tests while Cumming and Archibald spend their days on the telephone. Recently an Australian firm was given the marketing rights down under. And inquiries are now coming in from Europe.

The dark days of 1983 are definitely history. The stock has risen slowly from the low of fifty cents a share and as of this writing is close to the $5 mark. There were certainly times when the pressures took their toll and there was friction between the partners and between members of the key management group. "You have this image of starting your own company and being your own boss," says Cumming, "but in fact that's not how it is. We had to learn to work together. We were helped by our common desire to see our product become a success. But still, it was a little surprising to find you don't have as much autonomy as you thought you would. There's always compromise."

International Verifact has put together a board of directors carefully designed to meet the needs of its shareholders and demonstrate its management strength. Apart from Archibald and Cumming, it includes a well-known investor, the company lawyer, an ex-bank vice-president, and an ex-trust company president. The firm now has considerable management depth to guide it through the growing years ahead.

In the spring of 1985, VISA International based in San Francisco chose International Verifact to build a prototype machine incorporating a new technology. A new device, called a watermark, is now being built into credit cards to prevent their duplication. International Verifact's new terminal permits instant readership of the old card as well as the new. It gives the company a competitive edge in the new technology.

Archibald, Cumming, and Crowe today work an average of eighty to ninety hours per week at their company. In 1985, for the first time in three years, Archibald managed a two-week holiday in the sun. "The fact is," admits Cumming, "you work virtually all your waking hours on the company. People want to hear our story. When I went to a party with my wife recently she admonished me not to talk about my company. So I tried, I really did. When I was asked what I did for a living I said, 'marketing.' The next question was what do you market, 'hardware and software,' I replied, but then came the next question, what kind of hardware? Bang, I was off and running. When I next looked at my watch it was two a.m. and there were still people standing around me."

Money maker Douglas Archibald is only forty-two. His partner Ian Cumming is thirty-nine. Their story, though it's still being written, is a textbook case of how to start an enterprise despite severe handicaps. First come up with a product that fills a definable gap in the market. Then find the financing to develop the product and test it thoroughly. Finally, combine the right amount of moxie and energy to galvanize a marketing program into producing hard sales. Soon, few consumers will have to waste time waiting while a clerk dials up the credit card company to discuss their credit limit. They can thank the founders of International Verifact.

SUZY OKUN AND ELIZABETH VOLGYESI
Treats

Money makers Suzy Okun and Elizabeth Volgyesi sell treats. If you like muffins, you have your choice of banana, strawberry rhubarb, peaches and cream, and forty-seven other flavours. If you prefer cookies, you can buy Swiss chunks and pecan, peanut butter chocolate, white chocolate chunk, and seven others. And that's only the beginning. They've invented snacks they call munches and desserts they call crunches. These treats are available at any of the partners' sixty-three Treats stores across Canada.

What they don't sell you is food. "We sell a concept," says Suzy. "We take what the palate already knows, and we make it electric! We take what the customer has already seen, and we do it differently. We are making the fashion. We are constantly evolving our treats. We were one thing in 1978, and now we're something else in 1985."

In 1978, the two women ran only one Treats store. In 1985, their coast-to-coast franchise system is expected to gross well over $8 million, and they are making plans to bring Treats to the United States.

The two friends began modestly. Elizabeth had been on holiday in Europe and came back with the idea of importing Swiss chocolate. Suzy suggested they make their own chocolates. They both were raising families and this was something they could do at home. So they made truffles and sold them to Winston's, a posh Toronto restaurant, and Creeds, an upscale Toronto emporium.

This lasted for a year. They soon realized that the market was very limited, so they started looking for a new way of selling.

Suzy observed that almost everywhere food was sold and served, the chef or the baker was "the hidden wonder" in the back room somewhere. "I remember the old-style pizzerias that we used to pass on Yonge street in Toronto. The pizza maker was right in the front window, and we used to stand there watching him flip pizza dough into the air. That was a restaurant event. We thought that whatever we did, it should be a food retailing event."

The two stress that although they are both good cooks, that was incidental. "In business, we gravitated to food," explains Suzy. "We weren't food people. We're not cooks let loose. What we really believed we had was a marketing concept. We chose food, because it is the most irresistible."

Their idea was to put the baker and the candy maker up front where customers could see them and to make the customer a participant. "We'd make candy turtles, but we would let the consumer decide whether the turtle would have a chocolate fudge filling, or mocha walnut, or coffee walnut, pecan, caramel, or marshmallow. We'd let the consumer decide the shape of the cookies and the mixture of the cookie flavouring. We'd let them decide what kind of muffins they wanted," explains Suzy. "Our customers would be able to exercise their own choice, to present something to their families which was a personal statement."

This was wonderful brainstorming, but in 1977 the two partners had only the experience of making chocolate truffles in their home kitchens. They possessed little more than pocket money, and no store, no equipment, and no resources but their own ideas and their willingness to test them out. They would have to borrow some money.

They took their enthusiasm and their concept to the local branch of the Canadian Imperial Bank of Commerce and applied for a $12,000 loan. The bank manager tried to convince them the money would be badly spent on a cookie store, that they should consider some other form of retailing – the clothes business, perhaps. "But he must have been impressed with our personalities and energy," Elizabeth says. They got the loan.

There was no sophisticated marketing information available to these ambitious but neophyte businesswomen. They decided that the bustling Bloor-Yonge-Yorkville Avenue district of Toronto would be a plum location for their Treats. It was an area where they could be sure customers would notice them. As Suzy says, "Bloor Street is Toronto's Fifth Avenue. We just felt we had to be there."

They rented 280 square feet of retail space at 82 Bloor Street, an area no larger than the average living room-dining room of a home, but it was promising and affordable, considering their borrowed nest egg of just $12,000. The annual rent was $30 a square foot, payable monthly, with the first and last months' rent on signing of the lease. Their husbands – both architects – designed the interior and helped with the refurbishing and equipment installation. There wasn't much to install, though: a sales counter at the back and a preparation counter with a small mixer and one oven in the front window. Finally, they hired a baker and a candy maker to make Treats' treats to Suzy's and Elizabeth's specifications.

They remember the day they opened very well. "It was December 20th, 1977, and there was a terrible blizzard outside. Our people were in the window making our treats, and the people were lined up around the block to get in. As they waited, they watched our baker and candy maker working on a marble slab and a counter top, and they bought."

Treats made a profit the first day it opened. It continued to make money for the two women entrepreneurs who developed the concept. Part of the reason for this is that they didn't stand still, as Suzy explains. "We started doing candies at first. We don't do them anymore, because everybody else started doing them. Now everybody is doing muffins, and we're moving into luncheon ideas, the munches and crunches." A munch is a small loaf that is highly seasoned and baked with the ham, cheese, pepperoni, tomatoes, or onions inside. The crunches are edible containers; instead of offering people deserts in plastic cups, they get edible dishes containing any kind of dessert filling they choose.

Some months after opening, Suzy and Elizabeth began to notice a change in the make-up of the people visiting the store. "Seventy per cent of the people were customers, and 30 per cent were trenchcoats. We knew the copy artists had discovered us," Suzy recalls, "because they wouldn't buy anything."

"They'd just stand there with their briefcases and watch us," Elizabeth adds. "They were lawyers and businessmen, who'd ask us a lot of questions. We knew if we didn't move fast, to protect ourselves, we'd lose a valuable opportunity."

One of the "trenchcoats" was Leslie Rupf, a professional franchiser with Zarex Corporation. "*He* found *us*," Suzy remembers. "We had come to realize that we could run miles with Treats, or somebody else would do it. We decided we better spread the idea ourselves. We had to think corporately. We didn't want to abdicate what was part of our meaningful lives, but we also knew that we couldn't do all the reorganizing needed for franchising ourselves, so Leslie offered a solution."

While Treats and Zarex jointly investigated national franchising opportunities, Suzy and Elizabeth expanded on their own. They opened a Treats store at the McGill University subway stop in Montreal, on the subway level of the Hudson's Bay Centre in Toronto, and in the College Park development at Yonge Street and College. None of this expansion required further bank debt. All the new stores were financed from the profits of the original outlet.

In 1979, the Zarex franchising plan was in place. Leslie Rupf and the Treats partners screened franchise applicants on the basis of what Suzy says were "people we could relate to and could relate to us. Those who could see us for what we are."

Prospective franchisees need money, of course – and a lot more than Suzy and Elizabeth started the company with – $30,000 cash, and a statement from the bank showing that they could borrow a further $50,000. The $80,000 lump gives a person a turn-key operation: all they have to do is turn the key to open the door and they're in business. Zarex handles the business side of the franchising – the finances, marketing, leasing of store space, selling, and advertising. The Treats partners are responsible for the concept and store operations – the food, merchandising, store design, staff training, and product development. Suzy explains: "Treats takes the lease, equips the store, supplies the recipes, and trains the franchisees and their staff. They get the original ingredients from us, to last one week. Then we put them in contact with materials suppliers with whom we have negotiated the best price. When we, as the head office, deal with a supplier, we get volume discounts, which an individual franchise wouldn't get. And we have control over quality. One supplier provides muffin mix made to our specifications."

Prospective franchisees have to be workers. "They can't just put their money in and sit there. We're looking for someone who has pride and pleasure in work. If the owner is not involved he doesn't understand the dialogue of the store. If he's not there to sense it, to read it, he can't serve, he can't satisfy. An owner has to be there to measure the needs of a store," says Suzy.

Some of the franchisees are women, some are men, and some are couples. The more successful franchise owners have opened additional Treats stores.

Neither Suzy Okun nor Elizabeth Volgyesi will admit to the size of their personal earnings from the Treats chain. "The day you call yourself a millionaire is the day you breathe out, the day you relax, and we've still got lots to do," they say. "If we had dreamed this, we wouldn't have done it. When we first talked about Treats, it just felt right all over. It felt right on the left foot, and it felt right on the right foot, then the left arm and the right arm," Suzy enthuses. "We didn't intend to whip the business world in shape. We went into it to have some fun. We have a lot of admiration and respect for each other. Really, we're like two kids looking for adventure!"

PHILIP CARROLL AND DAVID STEELE
Three Buoys

In January, 1982, Philip Carroll, David Steele, and Rob Jensen were on a ski weekend in the Rockies. Steele recalls, "We were driving through Sicamous, B.C., when we decided to look into renting a houseboat for the summer. We went to the marinas at Lake Shuswap and discovered, to our chagrin, that the houseboats were all booked up." Driving back home to Calgary in the car the three talked about the houseboat business. "Apparently, it had no advertising, no marketing, and the houseboats we saw looked fairly rickety, and yet they were all completely booked up. We said we should get into the houseboat rental business." Rob Jensen, a carpenter (with some boat-building experience), was working with his father in the construction industry. "If you guys can market them, I can build them," he said.

While most who dream of becoming entrepreneurs only talk about starting businesses, these three acted. The very next day they rented a farmer's barn at $50 a month and had a factory. Then they went to a marina advertised for sale on Lake Shuswap. The asking price was $125,000 with $5,000 down.

"We had $3,000 among us, which we offered the realtor," says Steele. "We said we could come up with the remainder in thirty days." Three boys had become Three Buoys and a business partnership had begun.

It was a gutsy undertaking. Steele and Carroll were each earning about $40,000 a year, one working in commercial real estate and the other as a financial consultant. In their college days they had worked well together in organizing university parties, but this was hardly the background to start a houseboat business. Steele admits that he had never even seen a houseboat until that fateful day in January, 1982.

Their business plan was straightforward. They would build a fleet of boats that would incorporate new features in the somewhat staid houseboat business and attract a new clientele to houseboating. Items such as water slides, penthouse suites, and stereo equipment were all part of their concept. Considering the fact that, even without those attractions, the industry as it currently stood was overbooked, their chances of succeeding seemed good.

"Raising the money, as might be expected, was tough," smiles Steele. The partners needed enough to cover both the marina purchase and the cost of building supplies. They went to about a dozen banks in Calgary and were turned down. But they kept trying. Finally they met a young chartered bank manager in Kamloops, B.C., who liked their story and lent them $180,000. They were also fortunate to win the support of their parents, who provided them with some of the required collateral.

Early in 1982 was a hectic period for the trio. Jensen and another carpenter they hired set up shop in the barn and started building two houseboats. Each cost about $50,000 to complete. Meanwhile, Steele and Carroll were still holding on to their regular jobs in Calgary and trying to market their houseboat vacation weeks on the side. Their marketing efforts basically consisted of manning a table at sportmen's shows, distributing some mimeographed fact sheets (office bulletin boards were a favoured medium), and doing a tremendous amount of talking. Friday at five signalled the beginning of a six-hour drive to Lake Shuswap for a weekend of pitching in at the barn.

After six months, both Steele's and Carroll's employers gave them an ultimatum: "Decide you're working for us, or quit and stay in the houseboat business." At this point they had only $30,000 of predictable revenue from rentals, but they took the plunge. Steele and Carroll quit their jobs and made the commitment to stay in the business.

Now that their fledgling enterprise had to provide the bread and butter, building more boats to generate more revenue was an absolute must. So Carroll and Steele came up with a pioneering innovation that would set the boat rental business on its ear. "We thought, why not sell our boats to investors as investments, and then manage the boats on their behalf," says Steele. Because of the tax incentive programs designed to stimulate growth in tourism and the marine industry, people buying boats in Canada were allowed a 100 per cent write-off over four years. At the end of that period Three Buoys houseboat buyers would own a solid, revenue-producing asset. The idea is similar to the one that helped Go Vacations expand into a major operation – evidence that when the time is right different heads will come up with the same apt invention.

They needed to line up investors, but their timing was bad. In the summer of 1982 interest rates were at 18 per cent and climbing. And the investors would be spending $70,000 to buy a houseboat from three twenty-two-year-olds they'd never heard of, who had no feasibility studies or demographics or anything more solid than a good idea and a couple of freshly built boats. Indeed, they had nothing beyond a typed-up "concept" package.

"In June, July, August, and September we spoke to about 150 potential investors who all said no," recalls Steele, grimacing. To make matters worse they had taken their last charter, interest payments were coming up, and they had nothing left in the account. During the summer Rob Jensen had left to pursue other interests, and construction had come to a standstill.

It was October and the two remaining partners decided to give it one last try. With $1,800 borrowed from a relative, they chartered a plane to take eight potential investors and their wives from Calgary to Lake Shuswap. It was a Saturday, and all eight investors gathered at the airport only to be greeted by a storm that forced postponement of the flight. The next day all eight cancelled.

Since the plane was already paid for, the resourceful pair spent the week corralling another eight prospects. This time Mother

Nature provided a glorious sunny day and the plane flew through the Rockies to land at the lake. "It was," recalls Steele, "the one day God shone on our business."

The weather, combined with a barbecue and cruise aboard the houseboat, convinced the investors. All eight bought houseboats at a cost of $70,000 each, including a $14,000 down payment. Three Buoys had turned the corner.

The same October, Steele and Carroll opened a new factory in landlocked Airdrie, Alberta, and hired fifteen builders. Over the next three months they sold $800,000 worth of houseboats and the fleet grew to twenty. Coincident with the winter construction was the marketing of the weeks of vacation time for the following summer. Three Buoys retained 25 per cent of the rental income in return for managing and maintaining the vessels. They promised each investor fourteen weeks of revenue at about $1,000 per week. The first summer they averaged seventeen to eighteen weeks of revenue.

While the building and marketing was going on the company was enjoying a fair bit of unsolicited media interest. A newspaperman arrived to have a look around the new factory, and before long TV stations were sending camera crews. "We'd captured a lot of imaginations," says Steele. "At that time, the recession was hitting Edmonton so hard, every day another business closed its doors. We were good news!" Publicity was also generated by such stunts as parking a houseboat, for everyone to see, in downtown Calgary, a manoeuvre they have since repeated in cities in southern Ontario.

So far so good. But the key decision in the marketing success of Three Buoys was yet to come. With all these houseboats under construction they set out to restructure the public image of a houseboat vacation. "We knew darn well that we would go out of our minds if we took a houseboat out for a week and only sat on it," says Steele. "That market was too small and we had no problem arriving at the conclusion that we wanted to create a vacation with much more action and fun."

So the partners took the biggest gamble of their brief career. In 1983 they built forty more houseboats at the Alberta factory and a huge hospitality deck that could hold up to 800 people at the marina. By throwing in jet biking, para-sailing, water-skiing, and then party nights, Three Buoys houseboats became the hit of

Lake Shuswap. In 1984 all the boats were sold to investors and all were fully booked. The partners decided to expand into eastern Canada to a waterway close to the densely populated areas of southern Ontario.

The Thursday, March 28, 1985, edition of the *Toronto Star* featured a colour photograph of a CN train on the front page of the business section. As the train snaked around a lake, rows of houseboats stretched literally as far as the eye could see. Three Buoys had hired an entire CN train to bring seventy-seven houseboats to Ontario; and it was a brilliant publicity coup.

The train had been given a send-off in Vancouver by Premier Bennett, who applauded it as the "economic renewal" train. It was the first CN freight to carry a major shipment of manufactured goods from the West to the East in six years. In Edmonton it stopped long enough for Three Buoys to receive a special award from Alberta's Minister of Tourism. One of their model houseboats was specially designed to meet the needs of the disabled and was equipped with a winch to lift bathers in and out of water, an elevator between decks, and an interior designed for a wheelchair.

As of the spring of 1985 Three Buoys had seventy-seven houseboats at a private marina at Oak Orchard on the Trent-Severn waterway north of Peterborough. Each houseboat comes equipped with stereo, penthouse suite, wet bar, gas barbecue, command bridge with a drive top and bottom and water slide (optional). All are now owned by investors, and by June, 1985, all had been booked for the months of June, July, and August. Three Buoys recently took its 1,500th weekly booking at an average price of between $1,000 and $1,200. "The really significant point," says Steele, "is that we have rented more weeks per houseboat now than when we only had two boats to worry about!"

Steele points out that investors today are not buying just any tax shelter. "That's why our houseboats are so popular. Buyers do get a 100 per cent write-off over four years but they also own a revenue-producing asset which enables each owner to keep about 50 per cent, after interest charges, of what the boat grosses." Since the boats are not primarily tax shelters but rather stable assets with good income potential over a long period of time, changes to the current tax incentive programs should not have any critical effects on Three Buoys' growth.

Asked what, if anything, does cause him concern, Steele responds, "Perhaps our biggest problem is deciding how much to take on. There are so many opportunities and the trick is to identify the ones you can handle and not overextend yourself." Steele also admits that it was a big change to go from carrying out the menial chores themselves, such as cleaning toilets and painting docks, to managing people. And he realizes that their biggest asset, and biggest liability, is their age. Most investors might be leary of investing in a business run by people in their early twenties. "But I'm firmly convinced that it was our youth that convinced the initial investors to go with us. We were full of energy and the buyers knew if anyone could pull it off, we could." They are both only twenty-five.

Head office is still Calgary even though their business is growing fastest in the East. Three Buoys expects to gross from $15 to $20 million in the 1985 fiscal year. The two partners, both unmarried, are leaving most of their money in the company although they recently went out and purchased two Mercedes-Benz 350 SLs. Their lifestyle is relatively unchanged by success, involving six-day weeks and as many sports activities as time permits.

Three Buoys is looking to expand to a total of eight marina sites in Canada. Two are under active consideration for the coming year. "We will expand further in Canada, and, yes, we have to look at the United States," states Steele. "But our future definitely is in the houseboat business."

Three Buoys is the perfect symbiosis of opportunity and entrepreneurship. Without the benefit of any market research, with no formal financing in place, money makers Steele and Carroll (who now runs the Calgary office) launched a business that may well make them tycoons of the vacation industry. When they stumbled across an opportunity in a very immature business that was just right for the Yuppie market, they acted without hesitation. They responded to adversity with some original thinking, transforming the houseboat rental business by offering a Club Med lifestyle along with it. But perhaps the single most important reason for this partnership's success is its innovative marketing. By selling the houseboats, taking over the worrisome chore of renting, cleaning, and maintaining them, and shaping the package to fit the needs of investors, Three Buoys found a steady cash flow that enabled it to grow and expand. The formula could well read: market plus desire plus innovation equals success.

BOB ISSERSTEDT, GUS GERMAN, AND TED GRUNAU
GEAC

There are six million volumes – including one rare copy of the Gutenberg forty-two-line Bible – on the shelves at Yale University, New Haven, Connecticut. Another four million books, many purchased with endowments from the legendary capitalists Rockefeller and Firestone, have collected at Princeton University in New Jersey since General George Washington was honoured there for his conduct in the War of Independence. Today, these two massive storehouses of culture and knowledge depend on foreign technology. Princeton and Yale use computers designed and built by General Education and Accounting Company of Canada – GEAC – a multimillion-dollar concern that grew out of the partnership of money makers Bob Isserstedt, Gus German, and Ted Grunau.

The computer is commonly viewed as the product of inventive America. Americans built the first computer, the UNIVAC, at the University of Pennsylvania in 1951. Today, they build and sell almost all of them. IBM alone sold a staggering $60 billion worth of computers in 1984. Honeywell and Hewlett-Packard shipped more than $8 billion in computers each. Control Data and Burroughs each rang up sales of over $6.5 billion. In comparison, sales at Canada's only mainframe computer maker are puny. GEAC's sales were just $61.4 million in 1984. But the projection for 1985 is for an increase of over 20 per cent. GEAC is growing exponentially, and unlike many of its American competitors, it is making a profit.

According to Chuck Williams, GEAC's president and chief executive officer, the company does not compete with IBM directly. "That would be suicide. Some computer companies have learned that to their sorrow. But IBM's very size and the magnitude of the marketplace create more opportunities to do things as long as you pick your slots and your niches. You can't be everything to everybody. You must understand operating in Canada, where you must pick your area carefully, and then do it very well." Williams knows the American computer giants because he once worked for one of them. He spent sixteen years with Hewlett-Packard. He also knows what mistakes other computer companies have made, because he was with MCM Computers Ltd. of Toronto as it headed for receivership.

"We're not selling computers, per se. We're selling solutions. We're in the automation business, not the computer business. We're not shipping iron out the door to compete with IBM's piece of iron. We would lose that battle, if that was the only thing we had to offer. We offer a great deal more than that."

The words behind the acronym provide one simple view of what the company offers: software and hardware for use in education and accounting. In the education field, GEAC designs computerized filing systems for university, college, and public libraries. In the accounting field, GEAC builds complete financial transaction systems for banks, trust companies, and savings associations. The company has diversified from those two product lines into systems for pharmacies, leasing companies, automated offices, and companies with bulk quantities of information that must be stored and easily retrieved.

Put simply, GEAC builds electronic filing cabinets with many drawers. The type of information to be filed doesn't really matter, whether it be account records of bank customers, titles and contents of books and names of borrowers in a library, prescription records and inventories in a pharmacy, or customer records at a car-leasing firm. The information is filed in a large GEAC mainframe computer. Any number of small desk-top computer terminals act like the drawers of the filing system, making information available to any number of bank tellers, librarians, pharmacists, or leasing agents.

There are GEAC desk-top terminals in hundreds of bank branches around the world – at Canada Permanent Trust, Avco Financial Services, Eaton-Bay Financial, Royal Bank of Canada, Vancouver City Savings, Bank of America, Bank of New York, Security National Bank, and even Banco de Central Consolidada, Venezuela. They're on counter tops in dozens of university libraries, including Princeton, Yale, Harvard, MIT, London, Utrecht, Leeds, Ottawa, Western Ontario, York, and Stanford.

GEAC's European offices are currently discussing the installation of national library networks with officials in Britain, France, and Italy, systems that would make available centuries of European culture to any village library with a computer terminal. GEAC's reputation has made the company the world's leader in the installation of library automation. The reputation is founded on the work of three men who knew how to make the most of the talents of others.

In 1970, there was no GEAC. The mini-computer had just been born. As Bob Isserstedt remembers it, "the mere mention of the word 'computer' back then would result in people throwing money in your direction!" Isserstedt was twenty-eight years old and an employee of the Huntington-Rockford Computer Company in Toronto. "That's where I learned how not to do everything. They attracted a lot of investment money from people wanting to cash in on the computer boom. Suddenly, Huntington-Rockford had all of this cash. The company spent it on a beautiful four-storey office building and a company jet. It went bankrupt in 1971."

The company had three assets that weren't worth much to the bankruptcy trustee. First, there was Bob Isserstedt, who had wanted to be a writer but didn't pursue it. He had studied math for a while at the University of Vienna, dropping out before he finished. He had walked blindly into Shell Oil Canada and been hired to learn computer programming even though he didn't know anything about computers, then quit in 1965 to join Huntington-Rockford. Second, there was Gus German, who became a consultant to the company after winning wide acclaim in high-tech circles for writing a computer language called "Watfor?" while employed at the University of Waterloo computer department. The third asset was a piece of paper that contracted the small Simcoe, Ontario, Board of Education to buy a computer system from Huntington-Rockford.

"Gus and I were totally broke when the company went under. We literally had about $25 each. But we talked the bankruptcy trustee into letting us have the Simcoe County Board of Education contract, because to them it wasn't worth anything," recalls Isserstedt. "Huntington-Rockford had planned to sell the Simcoe Board a dinosaur computer built by somebody else. Gus and I went to the Simcoe people and said, 'You don't really want a piece of hardware, you want a solution.' We convinced them that we'd be able to solve their problems, and all we wanted from them was a steady cash stream – no big lump-sum payment – just a regular income every month."

Gus and Bob together were paid $5,000 a month by the Simcoe Board. It might have seemed to be a big sum of cash, but the two men had to build a computer system with it and also turn enough profit to live on. While they'd worked at Huntington-Rockford, they had the use of a computer, which Hewlett-Packard was about to repossess. They approached Ted Grunau, who was Hewlett-Packard's general manager in Canada, and told him they didn't have any money. They did have a contract, however, and they promised to pay the computer off in a number of months. Grunau agreed. The transaction kicked off a relationship with Gus German and Bob Isserstedt that eventually led Grunau to join them as the third founding partner of GEAC.

German and Isserstedt also needed an office, but they didn't want to pay for it. So they rented the entire top floor of a building in Don Mills, Ontario, kept a corner for themselves, and divided up the rest to rent to other companies. It was a brilliant twist, which gave GEAC its first premises cost-free.

The Simcoe Board computer contract served as a badge of respect for the fledgling firm, and they were able to use it to win even larger contracts. The Peel County Board of Education, a much larger board west of Metro Toronto, became GEAC's second client. "We now had what I call two 'blue-chip' accounts," Isserstedt recalls. "The quality of our clients allowed us to lease equipment and get a line of credit at the bank."

For the first five years, GEAC didn't build anything. They sold human brainpower. They'd go into a library, for example, and design computer programs and systems for it using off-the-shelf equipment. They simply deployed the equipment to meet the unique needs of particular clients. By 1976, the company realized that the increasing sophistication of its computer programs was stretching the limitations of the general-purpose computers they were getting from other companies. That year, GEAC became a computer manufacturer.

Ted Grunau had quit Hewlett-Packard the year before and joined German and Isserstedt in their new effort. The three men each developed a list of contacts throughout the industry. Some they used to obtain parts and knowledge. Others were receptive to new career challenges, and were lured into GEAC to conduct the research and computer development program. This has been the founding partners' guiding principle: find and hire new talent as you grow.

"When you start a company," says Isserstedt, "you've got to be constantly looking for people who are better than yourself. You've got to look for greatness in other people. You've got to push people up the ladder. It's not hard to find good people. You develop a nose for it. You listen to the way they talk, the way they're solution-oriented. You've got to be wise enough to know you're stupid in certain things. You've got to realize that you can't do everything yourself, that there are people around who have qualities you don't have."

Sometimes, they'd trip upon new talent purely by chance. Bob Isserstedt remembers one of the many late nights in the GEAC office. "Gus was looking through a Hewlett-Packard publication which listed computer programs people had developed. Gus muttered a bit, and then said, 'I've found a genius!' He was talking about a Professor Michael Sweet at the University of Wales. I said, 'Let's phone him,' and we did. We figured we'd catch him at nine in the morning, their time, but a secretary said she hadn't seen Professor Sweet. He rode his bicycle to work, and often got sidetracked! He sounded like quite a character." When they finally reached the professor, they asked him to come to Canada to design computer operating systems. At first he agreed only to do some consulting work on a part-time basis. "He'd get on a plane at Heathrow on Fridays, work here all weekend, and fly back to Britain Sunday nights. About three of those weeks was all he needed. He quit at the university and came to work with us. He runs our research and development operation now."

Dr. Sweet's mandate was to develop products that would steer GEAC clear of the cutthroat end of the market. They knew they'd be swamped if they went head-to-head with manufacturers who turn out several thousand computers a day. Instead, they concentrated on specialized market segments. Their computer designs were tailored to meet the needs of individual clients. One could probably try to adapt any computer to a banking operation, for instance. You'd be better off using a computer that's designed just for banking.

Bob Isserstedt had seen other companies use their money badly and go broke. He and his colleagues were determined to spend wisely. They were paid salaries, but profits were plowed back into the company. That allowed new products to be developed without going to the bank, without mortgaging the company's future.

Isserstedt's personal theories about money and the entrepreneur developed from his experiences at GEAC and his observations and associations with other high-tech enterprises. "The worst mistake is giving new companies money they haven't worked for. Any firm that moans that government doesn't help them, I could kick them. If you take innovative management, people with determination and enthusiasm, but lacking in experience, and you give them money they haven't worked for, it's a recipe for disaster. There can't be any funny money. The growth has got to come out of profits. I believe in tough banks. Now, I might not have said that ten years ago, but I've seen so many companies get into trouble. I really think banks should be there to rap knuckles."

He points to the example of his father, who was an inventor. "He developed the auto-pilot while he worked for Minneapolis-Honeywell. When he left them, he opened a small engineering firm in Toronto, with ten or fifteen people. He never let go of the company. He didn't allow anybody else to control things. When he got sick, the company shrivelled up."

Reflecting back on the remarkable success of his partnership, Isserstedt returns to the theme of not trying to do it all yourself. "Starting a business is like driving a car. When you start it, you're in first gear. You've got to realize that you might not be capable of driving it up to second gear – or fifth gear. If you keep accelerating in first gear, you'll burn out the engine. That's why we've stepped back and let others run GEAC. We brought in Chuck Williams as president five years ago. He's taken the company to new heights. We keep our distance, but we also realize that a company in fifth gear might have to gear down a little when there's rough terrain to be covered, or the engine just won't work. That's where we come in."

Bob Isserstedt, Gus German, and Ted Grunau sit on the GEAC board of directors with Chuck Williams and Mike Bishop, their chief financial officer, but they leave the management of the company to the managers. The three founders are active in helping GEAC expand abroad. Isserstedt has moved to California, and German is now based in England. The company now operates facilities in Los Angeles to give better access to the United States market, and in London and Dublin to win contracts within the European Economic Community. But GEAC's manufacturing and research are still based in Canada.

"As long as a Canadian company has an international attitude and doesn't cover itself in maple syrup, as long as your people in England and the U.S. know that they have an equal chance of becoming president of the company, then you'll do well around the world," states Isserstedt. "Canada has an excellent reputation in high-technology. You'll succeed if you're good and you deliver a product that is good, on time, and on budget. That's what it is all about!"

Twelve years after GEAC was founded, the company listed its shares on the Toronto Stock Exchange. That enabled the firm to raise additional capital for expansion. That also gave a market value to the holdings of GEAC's founders and employees, who earn shares through a company stock-option plan. It is estimated that between ten and fifteen long-time GEAC employees became instant paper millionaires, due to the market value of the shares they had accumulated.

A strong founding partnership, employee ownership (20 per cent of the shares in GEAC are available to employees), research and development (8 per cent of revenues are plowed back into new products), specialization in specific markets, tight financial control, the aggressive pursuit of good talent, and the founders' trust in people to make the company grow: these are the elements that have made GEAC one of Canada's fastest growing and most consistently profitable high-tech entrepreneurial winners.

Part 3: Going It Alone

"It is the lone worker who makes the first advance in a subject: the details may be worked out by a team, but the prime idea is due to the enterprise, thought, and perceptions of an individual." Sir Alexander Fleming, the acclaimed discoverer of penicillin, made that observation in an address to Edinburgh University in 1951. Discovery, invention, innovation, and enterprise are solitary pursuits in the beginning, and many remain so. The originator of an idea or concept is inherently committed to see it through to fruition, even though partners, family members, investors, or employees might come to match his or her dedication.

The money makers who go it alone do so more by circumstance than by design. Their independence springs from their individual resolve to make life better for themselves. A young student develops a concept for increasing his summer vacation earnings from house painting during a moment of private contemplation. An electronic technician dreams up a retailing concept for computer parts while quietly working by himself in a University of Toronto back room. A mother uses the few idle moments she has at home while the children are at school to make the telephone calls that launch a unique manufacturing enterprise involving disposable clothing. Another entrepreneur defies conventional wisdom and challenges Canada's beer barons. A Vancouver woman thinks Canadians are more patriotic than they let on and starts stitching swatches of red and white together into flags.

Some people simply work better when they're alone. Some ideas must be tested by individual effort. Some enterprises require no more capital and investment than the time and dedication of one person. Some money makers succeed by themselves because their businesses are a reflection of their individual education and experiences, needs and desires, personal drive and ambition. Their solitary efforts benefit from the freedom common to all creators, who can, without the involvement of others, either fail or succeed spectacularly. The following pages detail the experiences of some who have succeeded by going it alone.

MELLANIE STEPHENS
The Kettle Creek Canvas Company

Port Stanley, Ontario, is a quiet fishing village on the north shore of Lake Erie. Every summer its population of 1,900 swells to accommodate the cottagers that come from such bigger places as London, thirty miles to the north, and even Toronto. It's also the stopping place for yachts cruising the Great Lakes. Most of the year it's a sleepy little town, outwardly not much different from many others in Ontario – no longer the centres of economic activity they were in the nineteenth century. This is a place to retire to, or grow up in, but not a likely place to start a multi-million-dollar enterprise.

Money maker Mellanie Stephens was born in Port Stanley and went to school there. She wasn't much of a student, failing her third year of high school and quitting after grade eleven. Then she travelled a bit, worked for a while as a truck gardener, even helping to sell the fresh produce from the back of a pickup. For a while she was a cook in a bush camp; she also spent some time as a retail sales clerk. Along the way, she learned to do a lot of things herself, and to do them well.

In 1976, at age twenty-six, while Stephens was between low-paying jobs and back in Port Stanley, she stumbled onto an opportunity that led to a sharp change in her material fortunes – and her lifestyle. The opportunity presented itself in the form of an expensive comforter she bought from a friend. A comforter is a quilt that's filled with down or some other light insulating stuffing. They are common in Europe; recently they've become fashionable North American bedclothes.

Stephens figured she could make comforters at least as good as the one she had just bought and could sell them at a nice profit. The first few sold fast. Soon she was swamped with more orders than she could handle at home, so she rented a small space as a workshop. The space adjoined a store for boaters and sailors.

When the store's patrons saw her at work sewing comforters, they asked her to make some utilitarian canvas bags – the kind you'd take on a day's outing. Before long, she'd saved enough money to open a small store selling items made from canvas.

Her original name for the business was The Kettle Creek Canvas Bag Company, inspired by the Kettle Creek that runs through town. But a friend wisely suggested that she eliminate the word *Bag*. She found a 300-square-foot store on the main street of town (and backing onto Kettle Creek), finished the interior with unvarnished pine to give it a Canadiana quality, and worked furiously to manufacture enough stock. But it seemed to be a losing battle.

"As opening day approached I was embarrassed about the empty space on some shelves, so I simply made up some canvas drawstring pants, since they were so easy to make," recalls Stephens. "By three p.m. everything was sold, but the clothing had gone first." It was the summer of 1978 and the Kettle Creek Canvas Company was in business.

Stephens quickly set up a system of using "cottage" labour to make her clothes. She purchased bolts of Canadian-made canvas (100 per cent cotton) and put it into simple patterns with the help of a small staff. Then local women, some of whom had previously worked only during the summers processing fish, were hired to sew the fabric into jackets, pants, and shirts. It was piece work they could do at home. Back at the store, the full-time staff sewed on buttons and provided the finishing touches.

Although the Kettle Creek concept has evolved over time, it took shape early in the development of the business. It can be summed up in four words: *simplicity, quality, casual,* and *handmade.* "My philosophy at Kettle Creek is to make a quality product, so that when people wear it, it makes them feel good," Stephens says. The *casual* and the *handmade* were reinforced by the original store setting with its rustic, pioneer flavour. The quality and the simplicity speak for themselves.

In the first two years the business grew rapidly and Stephens was able to finance any improvements and any increases in the size of her inventory out of operating capital. She learned the financial side of the retail trade as she went along: "I knew nothing about keeping books," she recalls.

It was in 1980 that she decided to make her move. The store

was doing well. She'd had a chance to test out various designs to see what worked and, more important, what sold. The time seemed right to franchise her concept, which would generate additional revenue for her company and provide a ready market for her clothes. "Part of our exclusivity comes from the fact you cannot find our clothes in a department store, next to a ready-to-wear rack. You have to go to a Kettle Creek store to buy our product."

Her first franchises were opened in Toronto and other Ontario cities. Franchisees paid no percentage of sales but they had to buy their stock from Kettle Creek. This meant the Port Stanley headquarters would have to develop into a major manufacturing operation.

But before this could happen she needed to finance the franchising push. "My accountants put together a proposal for me and we went through the humiliation of being turned down by financial institutions six times in ten days." Finally Stephens found a smaller bank that was impressed by her drive and gave Kettle Creek a significant term loan.

Her next step was to go to Fanshawe College in London, Ontario, and ask for their best graduate in fashion design. Like many successful entrepreneurs she wasn't afraid to bring in outside expertise. The young designer joined the company and helped the line expand from the original solid shades to stripes and plaids. Each successful new season has brought new designs; but quality and simplicity remain the theme.

The franchising effort was successful and soon Kettle Creek required a team of people to set up new stores. Part of their job is to provide each new location with a bright, warm, pine-walled decor – the perfect setting for buying casual clothes. In April, 1985, the thirty-eighth store opened, in Regina, and there are now franchises from coast to coast. Franchise fees now range from $5,000 to $50,000 depending on the size of the store and the population of the area. And the concept is so catching that a number of franchisees have invested in the parent company.

In 1984 Kettle Creek grossed $4.8 million in revenue, and it is projecting $7 million in 1985. "We've almost doubled our sales each year but that growth won't continue at the same pace," says Stephens. "We are looking at starting up in the U.S., but that will only make sense if we manufacture down there."

Today Kettle Creek's clothes are still all 100 per cent cotton. The line now includes fitted skirts, bomber jackets and jumpsuits for men, as well as sleeveless tops and drawstring trousers. Sizes are unisex from 1 (small) to 6 (extra large) and individual items retail from $10 to $80. Kettle Creek is so confident of its quality, it offers a 100 per cent guarantee on all items – complete satisfaction or your money back. And the clothes are all still manufactured by Stephens' stable of skilled local women, now numbering seventy, all of whom work out of their homes. The permanent staff who finish the garments now number fifty. The current store/factory is in a large former fisherman's warehouse just down the street from the original location.

After going it alone for the first few years, Stephens has now brought in a minority partner who does most of the merchandising for the chain. And she is actively considering inviting in another investor who would become general manager. "It would be nice not to have to deal with the day-to-day operations," she says.

Like most successful entrepreneurs Mellanie Stephens works very hard at her business, but she has managed to cut back to a fifty-hour week. Last year she even took a two-week holiday. She pours her earnings back into the business and draws only a small salary for herself. Her pleasures are appropriately simple. "I enjoy cooking, like to garden, and I love animals." Her 160-pound Great Pyrenese named Mainstreet can probably attest to that. Her only luxury, modest as it is, is a ten-year old diesel Mercedes, in mint condition. She still likes to make things herself. The desk in her brightly lit office overlooking Kettle Creek is handmade with a base from an old-fashioned sewing machine. "It was the first thing I ever made. I'm rather proud of it because the wooden top was laminated without the use of nails."

Stephens started small and learned about the market as she grew: "People are less inhibited these days and they want fun clothes which adapt themselves to the wearer," she says. From the first she insisted on handmade quality and has kept her products out of the large department stores. And she created a rustic retail image that suited her casual clothes perfectly.

Port Stanley is still the quiet tourist town it was in 1978 when Mellanie Stephens opened her first store. But now the old-fashioned grey-blue building that backs on Kettle Creek is the bustling hub of a growing clothing empire. Such success in a very competitive industry is impressive enough. Even more remarkable is its author: a young woman from an out-of-the-way place with little formal education and no training in the business, she has become a major money maker.

EUGEN HUTKA
Exceltronix

An Old World belief in the importance of property ownership allowed Eugen Hutka to begin his struggle for financial independence. The family emigrated from Czechoslovakia in 1966, when Eugen was eleven. The Communists hadn't allowed property ownership, so in Canada, property became one of the family's priorities. The Hutkas believed pleasures were to be earned. There were no hot cars or other teen-age frivolities for Eugen. He saved the money he earned at odd jobs through high school and in 1973 helped his parents purchase 100 acres of northern Ontario bushland for $12,000.

His schooling did not go easily, but, despite having to learn English along the way, he graduated from Western Technical Secondary School in Toronto and enrolled in an electronics course at the Ryerson Polytechnical Institute. His diploma from Ryerson landed him a junior position at the University of Toronto's computer and electronics department in 1977. He was paid only $10,000 a year, but he was self-confident enough to realize the job was an opportunity for better things in the future.

One of Hutka's responsibilities was to order electronic parts for the professors and researchers. University budgets are notoriously tight, and he became a superb bargain hunter, buying computer chips, circuits, and components at rock-bottom prices. He came to know parts suppliers throughout Canada, the U.S., and Europe who were keen to unload extra stock at cut rates. Every dollar he saved could be invested in fruitful research at the university but it didn't increase his salary.

In 1979, after two years on the job, his bank account was still empty but his mind was filled with the intricacies of the computer parts supply business. He decided to strike out on his own. He and his parents still had that 100-acre parcel of bushland up north. It had gained value over the years, and he was able to borrow $15,000 from the bank with the land as collateral.

Just west of his university workplace, he discovered a vacant store at College and Spadina. It was stuck between a hairdresser's and a travel agency. He rented the store, paid the first and last months' rent, and invested in shelves and fixtures and a cash register. That cost him $6,000. With the remaining $9,000 he did what he'd been doing for two years at the university: bought computer and electronics parts at discount prices. At this point Eugen Hutka had no money left, but he now had a small 1,200-square-foot store full of odd electronics parts. He named it Exceltronix.

Since he lived at home with his parents, he didn't need much income. He figured his store could last six months before he'd face bankruptcy. With no money for promotion, he depended on word of mouth. His first customer bought a telephone cord for $2.50. After a few weeks, the news got around that Exceltronix was selling computer microchips at low prices. Computer hobbyists from the university began to flock through the door. It turned into a near stampede during the winter of 1980, when the home video game craze took hold.

Manufacturers rushing to meet customers' demands for video units bought nearly the entire production of computer microchips from suppliers such as Intel and Texas Instruments. Hobbyists and small companies couldn't get microchips anymore, except from Exceltronix, which had established contacts with microchip makers in Japan and Europe. One year after Eugen Hutka had opened the door of his Exceltronix shop, sales revenues had hit an astonishing $500,000. He'd taken on four staff and had made plans that might make others shudder. In his own modest way, Eugen Hutka wanted to take on IBM.

Below the store was a litter-filled basement. Eugen and his staff cleaned it up and built some workbenches. Some of the researchers he'd bought components for at the University of Toronto designed computer circuit boards for him. Circuit boards are the guts of a computer, linking together the tiny microchips and other components that give a computer a mind and a memory. Hutka was already selling most of the parts that go into a computer, and a basement assembly line under his College Street store was a logical step in the evolution of his company. The boards sold rapidly to hobbyists, students, and researchers at universities and colleges, because they enabled people to design their own computer equipment at a much lower cost than buying ready-made equipment from the big computer companies.

By 1982, three years after Exceltronix opened its door, there were thirty people working in the crowded confines of the College Street basement. The street-level shop above had overflowed into the spaces used by the hairdresser and travel agency on either side, which put even more demand on the small manufacturing operation below. So, Hutka moved his manufacturing operations to an industrial mall in the Toronto suburb of Etobicoke and hired consultants from the universities to help design new products.

"We decided that we had to reinvest lots of bucks back in the business. We put everything extra into the development of new products. We believe that you cannot stop developing products. If you stop at one product, after half a year you become obsolete." That's Eugen Hutka's guiding philosophy. By 1985, his young company had fifty-five different products on the market, ranging from computer circuit boards to digital electronic signs. Those who use the Toronto or Vancouver public transit systems will be familiar with the Exceltronix signs – they are used by transit authorities in those cities to make passenger announcements.

The work force at Exceltronix now numbers sixty-five and sales have leaped to over $10 million a year. The firm has no debt but Hutka won't comment on profits, a private matter for a private company.

Exceltronix's boldest and most successful product innovation has been its own computer terminal. Since the company was already making the circuit boards loaded with microchips, Hutka simply hired a sheet metal shop, Metaltronics, to make the computer housings, and stocked a line of off-the-shelf monitor screens and keyboards. The whole package was labelled "Best Computer," and he boasts that it is entirely IBM compatible, as powerful as IBM's desk-top units, and less than half the price at $1,700. The package has a 300-day warranty, which is roughly three times longer than the warranties offered by the other computer houses. They're sold without a middle man, from Exceltronix's original College Street store and a second outlet in Ottawa. Stores are planned for Vancouver and Montreal and Hutka wants to sell franchises throughout the country. His product line is available only through Exceltronix outlets.

Hutka and his wife Andrea, who also works in the company, live comfortably, in a four-bedroom home overlooking Lake Ontario from the beach in Long Branch, not far from the Etobicoke factory. He reluctantly admits to one touch of opulence in his life now, a penchant for fast cars. He's particularly proud of a collectors' edition Corvette and a Lincoln. But he says he is far from becoming a millionaire – yet. His money is tied up in the business, to which he remains extraordinarily dedicated.

"People might think I was lucky. Sure, I was at the right place at the right time," he says. "But I didn't know it then. I gambled. It was phenomenally hard work. To this day, I've rarely had a weekend off. Andrea and I put in at least twelve-to-fourteen-hour days, including Saturdays, and we also work half of every Sunday." That may be unusual for most people, but it's not unusual for money makers like Eugen Hutka.

WAYNE METLER
Fantasy Sky Productions

Most Canadians are familiar with the blue balloon that floats across television screens in the commercials for Labatt's Blue beer. The balloon also turns up at innumerable outdoor activities across Canada, reinforcing the link between Labatt's Blue and good times. In fact, it has become so successful as a promotional gimmick that it now appears almost continuously at a host of weekend festivals and fairs year-round.

The money maker who designed and manufactured the hot-air balloon is Wayne Metler, the thirty-five-year-old president of Fantasy Sky Productions Inc. of Kitchener, Ontario. He has turned a love for the sport of ballooning into a flourishing enterprise that can make claim to being the only independent certified aircraft manufacturing company in Canada. (Balloons are classified as aircraft, and De Havilland and Canadair are not independent from government ownership.)

It started one summer weekend in 1973 when Metler was invited to the picturesque village of Aberfoyle, Ontario, for a ride in a friend's California-made balloon. This was his introduction to ballooning and it was a case of love at first flight. Metler knew immediately that "flying balloons was all I wanted to do and I was going to make a career of it."

At the time Metler's résumé would not have impressed too many corporate personnel officers. He was in his early twenties. He had attended several different universities, favouring courses in political science and philosophy, but had, as he puts it, "never stayed long enough to get a degree." He'd tried several different kinds of jobs, always working for himself, the longest stint as a freelance graphic designer, a skill he'd developed working in audio-visual projects while at the University of Guelph. To a casual observer he would have seemed a bit of a drifter, lacking in ambition.

In Ontario in the early 1970s there were no courses in ballooning, no formal training. You had to learn by doing. And you didn't need a licence. But first you had to have a balloon. "We flew, attempted a landing, and crashed the balloon," says Metler. "We repaired it, flew it, and crashed it again. It was by trial and error that I learned how to fly, as well as how to build and rebuild balloons. We just didn't understand that balloons should not be flown at all if there are thunderstorms anywhere in the area or if winds exceed a very calm ten kilometres per hour. We'd call the airport and be told conditions were fine for flying. Planes, yes. Balloons, not necessarily. We'd get up fine; coming down was the problem."

That original balloon was repaired so many times it had to be retired after a year, and in 1974 Metler set out to design and build his own. A tremendous amount of research went into the project, from the mathematics of structure and the intricacies of propane systems to the sources of materials. Not bad for a self-taught graphics designer with no engineering training. Once in possession of the new aircraft, Metler had no trouble at all hiring himself out as a commercial pilot under the name Fantasy Sky Productions Inc. "The sport was so new that as soon as word spread that a balloon and pilot were available, requests came flooding in," he recalls. This was 1975, two years after his first balloon ride.

On the road for seven months a year, Metler flew commercially for companies such as Re-Max Realty, Labatt's, and Air Canada. He appeared, with his Air Canada balloon, at the Commonwealth Games in Edmonton in 1978, the Can-Am Games in Florida in 1979, and numerous other locations throughout North America. Income from such jobs was in the range of $1,000 a day.

For the next three years Fantasy Sky remained primarily a company offering personal services – the balloon-flying skills of its founder and single employee. The popularity of his service enabled Metler to pay himself an adequate income and to invest the remainder in the building of several full-size prototype balloons. His ambition was now much more than simply to fly balloons for the rest of his life. The models were intermediate stages toward building what he now calls "the ultimate balloon." Fantasy Sky was going to become the first balloon manufacturer in Canada.

By 1982 Fantasy Sky had enough money in the bank to be able to apply for aircraft certification in the United States and Canada. This would mean Metler could manufacture and sell hot-air balloons of his own design that were guaranteed to meet very strict government standards on both sides of the border. The money was needed to cover the costs of engineering services, blueprints, justification documentation for both techniques and materials, the actual construction of a prototype, and testing. The whole certification process, from registering with the Canadian Ministry of Transportation and with the Federal Aviation Authority in the U.S. to gaining approval, took about three years and cost Metler $50,000. All of this money Metler raised through his pilot-for-hire company flying virtually every weekend of the year. It seems a large amount until compared, for example, with the $7 million or so De Havilland spent certifying the Dash 1. Nevertheless, the same steps must be taken whether you are a balloon builder or an airplane manufacturer. In 1982, Fantasy Sky's bid for certification was successful in both Canada and the U.S., and Metler was ready to manufacture for the marketplace.

Metler felt he could set up a profitable business in Kitchener. It was his home town, after all, and had been his base of operation since he started the company. But what was just as important, it was a location right in the middle of an industrial basin convenient to suppliers in Hamilton, Toronto, and Windsor and with reliable access to international sources of supply. He would be joining a very select club. At the time there were only five balloon manufacturers in the world. And he would be entering a small but growing market: there are some 6,000 balloonists around the world, two-thirds of them in the U.S. There are another 500 or so in England and France, and perhaps 200 in Canada.

Metler knew that 90 per cent of the balloons built today are used for pleasure, with only 10 per cent employed in the promotion of products. And, most important, with his eye on the U.S. market, he knew he had a price advantage. "My balloons sell for an average of $18,000 Canadian each," he says. "This works out to about 30 per cent less than U.S. manufacturers charge and it leaves me with a profit of about 50 per cent. I also build a product that I believe is well ahead of my competition in quality. You see, most U.S. manufacturers have been working with ten-year-old guidelines and, now that balloon technology has advanced, are having to retool. I could develop Fantasy Sky's newer recipe for aircraft manufacturing with state-of-the-art ingredients. I started right where the older businesses now want to be. So, for at least a while, they'll be playing catch up."

Fantasy Sky has developed its own engineering and design expertise in its 2,500-square-foot plant in Kitchener. The company works entirely with raw materials. For instance, material for the envelope (the actual balloon) is purchased in Britain, coated in the U.S., and then shipped to Canada. Wicker for the baskets comes from as far away as Taiwan. Most hardware is Canadian. Metler would prefer to use all Canadian materials but at present not everything he needs is available here. All the same, 25 per cent of the cost of each balloon is labour and they are, of course, wholly manufactured here at home. "The essential factor in balloon engineering is keying the size and weight of the balloon to the chosen payload. Whether a two-person model, a four or a five, it has to handle well in the air and have a long life. Balloons can last a total of 1,000 hours flying time, and the average private pilot may only be in the air forty hours a year. We build safety factors into each balloon based on the aviation industry's average of five to one. That means that every component must have five times the strength deemed actually necessary."

Metler now has three full-time and two part-time employees working for him. He concentrates on marketing his product through his appearances with his balloons on the road.

He says that he is targeting sales of thirty to forty balloons per year over the next three years. "The profit factor in each balloon is reasonably high and we feel we can meet our sales target in North America only." If so, his sales volume should approach $700,000 annually. Currently he works fifty to sixty hours a week and puts all of the earnings back into the company, taking only what he needs to live on. The promotional market is growing and Metler remains virtually the only commercial balloonist for hire in eastern Canada.

Fantasy Sky balloons operate on the simple theory of heating hot air. These days balloons can be ready for flight in fifteen to twenty minutes and stay aloft with the gas burner functioning about 15 per cent of the time. The balloonist's general rule of thumb is "land with a third of the fuel in reserve." For a two-person balloon in excellent flying condition that translates into an airborne life of as much as four or five hours per flight. And how high can you go? The world's record is 56,000 feet with oxygen (oxygen is needed for flights higher than 10,000 feet). Metler himself has reached 12,500 and would like to fly higher. "It really is an adventure every time you fly," he says, "because you're never really sure of where you're going." Each balloon ride is accompanied by someone following the flight from below in a car. The car ride is often as much fun, and as unpredictable, as the balloon ride.

Since all hot-air balloons are now certified aircraft, a pilot needs a licence to fly one. A minimum sixteen-hour instruction course with a balloon pilot is required to obtain a licence, and a fair degree of the instruction relates to a study of meteorology. Most flights tend to be in the early morning or late evening when the weather is calmer. Today, piloting skills have become phenomenal. In competition, when balloonists are given a target on which they must set down their balloons, often the winner is determined by a matter of inches.

Metler feels that the outlook for ballooning has, appropriately, nowhere to go but up. "There are a lot of people who still are unaware of the pleasures of ballooning and we have a growth factor in North American sales of about 25 per cent a year," he says. The sport also lends itself to media coverage; the CBC is currently working with Fantasy Sky in filming an hour-long feature film that will be shown on Canadian television in the winter of 1985-86.

The increasing international scope of the ballooning business was underlined at the New Mexico championships in 1985, which included a balloon team from China. Financed by Malcolm Forbes, the irascible balloonist and publisher of *Forbes* magazine, the Chinese team wore T-shirts throughout the competition with the words "capitalist tool" emblazoned on their chests.

With his cash flow under control Metler has no problems in obtaining his financing from a local chartered bank. The factory takes from sixty to ninety days to construct a balloon. The production crunch comes in the spring, with everybody wanting delivery in June. If his firm's growth continues on a steady path, he plans to bring someone in to administer it on a day-to-day basis. This will allow him to continue to fly in promotions while maintaining control over manufacturing. He still owns 100 per cent of the company.

At the moment Wayne Metler finds time to fly his beloved balloons for pleasure about twice a month; it is still his favourite form of relaxation. Besides spending most days, including weekends, overseeing the growth of his fledgling company, he is a keen devotee of squash and is a self-confessed fan of sports cars. And by the time this book is published, he expects to be married.

Wayne Metler has proved that the business of ballooning is anything but a fantasy. And he's come a long way since he took his first balloon flight on a calm summer afternoon. Like many entrepreneurs who go it alone, he figured out what he wanted to do, stuck to it, became a pro, and made it work.

CLEM GERWING
Alberta Boot Manufacturing Company

Making cowboy boots is only the latest venture in the life of Clem Gerwing, peripatetic entrepreneur and now a senior citizen who qualifies for the old-age pension. He says he never filled in the pension forms. Today, his Alberta Boot Manufacturing Company is Canada's number-one supplier of cowboy boots or, as he puts it, "boots for working cowboys, not drug store cowboys." In 1985, he expects to sell 10,000 pairs of them. Average cost: $200 a pair. The exotic leathers, such as python from Africa, lizard from Spain, and shark from Mexico retail at about $500 a pair.

It hasn't been easy, but money maker Clem Gerwing has come out on top. "The free enterprise system means you're allowed to make your own damned mistakes, so there has to be some compensation, called profit. You gotta be able to take the lumps if you want to make money."

Clem is one of twelve sons and daughters of homesteaders who were granted three sections of land at Lake Lenore, Saskatchewan, in 1903. "I was the oldest of the second half of the twelve kids – eight boys and four girls. My dad also raised grain, cattle, hogs, and chickens. I had to leave school after grade eight, to work on the farm, but I was able to go back later to finish high school at St. Peter's College, in Muenster, Saskatchewan. The school was run by Benedictine monks. Now, they gave us one tough education."

When Clem finished school World War II was beginning, so he enlisted with the Royal Canadian Air Force. He trained on Tiger Moths at Verden, Manitoba, and Harvards at Uplands in Ottawa, and flew Hurricanes in the 1st Canadian Fighter Squadron based at Sydney, Nova Scotia. Eight months later his squadron joined the Royal Air Force fighting the Japanese in Burma.

In November, 1945, six years after Clem Gerwing had enlisted, he left the Air Force and enrolled in an accounting course at Success Business College in Saskatoon. The next year, after he'd completed the course, he withdrew the $15,000 he'd saved during the war, borrowed $5,000 from his father and a further $5,000 from the bank, and bought the local hardware and farm implements store in Aberdeen, Saskatchewan. "It was a good business, but I didn't find it very challenging at the time. There was a town every nine or ten miles along the road, and every town had its farm implements store." He sold the business after five years and, with the help of the Veterans Land Administration, bought a section and a quarter (a section is 640 acres) near his father's farm at Lake Lenore for $25,000. "That was 1951, and you ask any western farmer about 1951. The crop never came up. We toughed it out until spring. We had a bit of money left from the store, and like all farmers, we somehow managed to make it through."

He had the farm for ten years. "I'm sure they were the worst ten years ever in the West, even worse than the thirties. The first year was too cold – we had frost for five of the ten years – and for nine of those ten years I bought hail insurance. The one year I didn't buy hail insurance, hail destroyed my whole crop!"

With a growing family and poor crops, Clem needed an income from somewhere, so he exploited his wartime flying skills as an instructor at the Regina Flying Club. In 1957, he bought a two-seater Cessna 140 trainer and established his own flying company, Parkland Airways, at Melford, Saskatchewan. Revenue from flying lessons generated enough profit to buy more aircraft, which he chartered out for fish and game patrols and electric powerline inspection. Then he bought a Piper Pawnee equipped with crop-spraying gear, which brought in more dollars from local farmers.

"By 1963, I was in my forties, and the government insisted I have twice-yearly medicals to keep my commercial pilot's licence. I figured they knew something I didn't know, so I decided I needed a change." He'd sold the farm two years earlier for $75,000 and now sold all but two of his planes, a new Cessna Skyhawk for the family and a recently purchased Piper Super Cub for crop-spraying. That was the business he continued when the family moved to Calgary. When Clem bought into a farm implements business there, he turned over the crop-spraying to another pilot. But after four years he became restless again and sold his interest in the implements company. For the first time in his life, he wasn't sure what to do next.

After some months of prospecting, he came across the footwear wholesaler, G.F. Bletcher Ltd., which was up for sale. "I think I paid $329,000 for it – $100,000 cash, and the rest was borrowed from the Bank of Nova Scotia." The company supplied independent shoe stores, mostly with Canadian-made shoes and boots. When he bought G.F. Bletcher, the firm grossed $700,000 a year. Under Gerwing's ownership, it went through a series of good and bad business cycles, caused by changes in the shoe business and the economy. In 1969, after less than two years as a shoe distributor, Gerwing's sales had rocketed to $1.6 million. He needed more space for expansion, so he bought the former Western Grocers' building at Tenth Avenue and Fifth Street in Calgary. He also opened a chain of five Village Cobbler stores in the Calgary area. But by the mid-1970s he was competing with growing national shoe store chains that bought directly from the manufacturers – overseas manufacturers. The competition was nearly overwhelming. By 1982, only one of his five stores was still open, and revenues at G.F. Bletcher had shrunk to just $500,000.

But Gerwing had been fighting for four years to keep the company alive. In 1978 he sold the Western Grocers' building for $1.2 million and moved to rented premises across the street to save his money. The same year he lost his cowboy boot supplier in Quebec when it switched wholesalers, so he began to import Vacquero boots from Mexico. Imports seemed the only route to salvation. Dozens of Canadian shoe manufacturers had closed because they couldn't compete with inexpensive foreign shoes. Although the federal government imposed import quotas, the foreign product forced the Canadian companies to operate within small price margins.

By 1978 an outsider might have concluded that Gerwing's 1967 investment was imprudent at best. Yet, the ingenuity of an entrepreneur cannot be quantified. There are no accurate ways of predicting the creative outcomes of entrepreneurial endeavours. While everybody else was closing shoe and boot factories and putting thousands of Canadians out of work, Clem Gerwing decided to swim upstream. "One day I added up how much money we'd been shipping out of the country. It added up to millions of dollars!" This was too much for this money maker. "I said to myself, 'If a Canadian has a mind to do it, he can do it better than anybody in the world.' It might sound old-fashioned, but I'm a Canadian, and I wanted to do something here, for us. I decided we'd make boots in Canada."

Gerwing's business and patriotic instincts merged with the interests of another Calgarian, Karl Meyer, originally from Germany. Meyer had settled in Calgary on the mistaken understanding it was the centre of Canada's footwear industry, because so much leather came from the region. He set up a machine in a basement and Meyer's Jaguar Shoes started making moccasins, which were very popular in the sixties. But by the mid-seventies the fad had faded, and Karl was contemplating retirement.

Enter Gerwing, who bought Meyer's equipment for $40,000 and moved it to his newly rented premises. Two of Meyer's sons, Albert and Herbert, joined Gerwing as operations managers. From 1978 to 1980, as the rest of his business struggled, the new Gerwing manufacturing operation grew slowly with mocassins and slippers.

But Gerwing wanted to make boots. "The key to a good boot is a good last. The last is the wooden form around which the boot is moulded. We worked closely with the United Last Company in Cambridge, Ontario. We must have gone through fifty changes before we developed a good-fitting last. Once you've got a good last, a professional grader can develop all of your sizes. We ended up with the best-fitting boot in all western boot manufacturing. They fit better than any. We really built a better mousetrap." He insisted that the boots be made entirely of leather and set up the production line accordingly. Leather for the boot lining was bought from Dominion Tanners in Edmonton. Leather for the uppers and soles came from Ontario and Quebec. And so was born the Alberta Boot Manufacturing Company.

At first he met resistance from Canadian retailers. "The toughest thing in the world was convincing stores to sell Canadian-made boots. They told us to come back another time, when we had proved ourselves in the marketplace." This didn't phase Gerwing. "We did an end run around them. We opened our own store, right here in our building in Calgary. Today, it's the biggest boot retail store in Canada. And we've also opened outlets in Regina and Saskatoon. We're planning more, but I won't tell you where until we've done it."

One city that isn't on the list is Toronto. "I just can't figure that city out. I spent a few days there, trying to find a place to put a store. But the city didn't make any sense to me. I didn't know where a logical place would be for a boot store."

Gerwing also associates Toronto with a bad business experience. It was during the urban cowboy craze. All sorts of new stores popped up in Toronto to sell to the city's urban cowpokes. Everything went fine with the first few orders – they were modest in size and promptly paid. "The third order would be a whopper, more than $10,000 or so. We thought their credit was good from the first few orders, so we'd ship out the boots. We never got paid, never saw the boots again, and never heard of them again either." The post office wasn't much help in trying to track down the delinquents, saying the forwarding addresses were "privileged" information. "And there's no point trying to sue, because the only ones who get rich are the lawyers! When the banks move in, they might get ten cents on the dollar. Suppliers like us get nothing. There's such a crazy system in Canada. Everything seems to be there to protect the crooks. "The urban cowboy craze was the last lesson I needed to learn – never fall for a fad."

Gerwing complains that keeping employees is a problem, even in post-recession Alberta, where the unemployment rate is said to be woefully high. His words are echoed by others in this book. "People who come in here for jobs often demand too much. They're very militant. Let me give you an example. Last week we had a fellow who wanted to wear headphones to listen to music while he worked. Our supervisor told him that the Labour Department doesn't allow that, because he has to be able to hear when he's running machinery, for his own safety. He was also told to tuck in his shirttails so they wouldn't get caught in the machinery. He did what he was asked the first time, all right. But the next day, he was found wearing the headphones with his shirttails hanging out again. So, we asked him to follow safety regulations again. This time, he threw down his tools and called us every name in the book and walked out on us.

"I can't understand that mentality. When I was twenty or thirty years old, I was damned happy just to have something to do. People didn't carry on like that when I was younger. I just don't believe people should be able to give up perfectly good jobs and go on the dole. Everybody knows people do it all the time, but the politicians and the media seem to be the only ones who never notice. It's a very sore point with me."

He also complains of a shortage of skilled labour despite all the shoe factories that have closed in Ontario and Quebec. "You know, I've had a job ad posted with Canada Manpower for two years now in Ontario and Quebec. Two years! I'm looking for people who can work with lasts and can handle a welting machine. There are supposed to be lots of those people around. I haven't had one single job application in those two years! Those jobs pay $25,000 a year. If I'd been able to get those people, I could have doubled my production of boots. You know how many more jobs that would have created? I'm going to get those people, but I'm not getting them in Canada. I've finally got permission to bring them in from other countries.

"I'm sure that at least 10 to 15 per cent of all the people who say they're unemployed could be working today, if they really wanted to."

Despite these problems Clem Gerwing is making money – just how much, he's not saying. His family's future is secure and life is satisfying. His wife, Hedy, after raising six children, has added a new subsidiary to the family firm – an antique furniture sales division operating from the same building that houses the Bletcher footwear wholesale company, the Alberta Boot Company, and the retail boot store. His eldest son, Tim, who graduated from university with a degree in commerce and gained additional business experience at IBM, is now general manager of the boot company. The family companies employ forty-five people.

Clem is now sixty-five, but it doesn't look as though he'll be retiring for a while yet.

PAUL CORMIER
La Mine d'Or

Paul Cormier readily admits his jewelry store in the quiet city of Moncton, New Brunswick, is not yet a gold mine. But, he notes, "I've got over 5 per cent of the retail jewelry business in the province, and I'm looking at franchising my concept." Not bad for a twenty-eight-year-old who's been in the business only six years.

Cormier was not cut out for university life. Working as a waiter at a French restaurant in the evenings while attending the University of Moncton in the daytime, he met a jewelry wholesaler who allowed him to borrow a few pieces to test out his selling skills. He took only ten minutes to sell his stock to a bridge party at his mother's home and was able to pay back the wholesaler with a small profit for himself. It seemed he was destined to become a money maker.

With a $5,000 loan from a local banker he went to Montreal to buy a selection of chains, pendants, and rings. Then he had some business cards printed and concentrated on selling one to one. La

Mine d'Or was in business. All thoughts of a university degree were set aside.

"I sold at Tupperware-style parties, in beauty salons, in hospitals and offices at lunchtime, wherever I could find a gathering of people," recalls Cormier. After a few months he rented store space in the basement of a building on one of Moncton's main streets at $200 a month, but the first few months were free – he'd made a deal to redecorate the 150-square-foot space in lieu of payment. Then a new bank manager requested he begin repaying the original $5,000 loan. "That would have meant giving up my only working capital and doing so pre-Christmas, just when it made sense to add inventory." Cormier went to speak to the bank, and born salesman that he is, came away a few hours later with double the money.

In time, his growing sales volume brought with it a new problem. Some manufacturers refused to sell to him because of his limited credit, and because, as the new boy on the block, he was providing regular customers with additional competition. Unphased, he set up his own wholesaling company, Eastern Jewelry Ltd., which allowed him to buy direct from the manufacturer and sell to La Mine d'Or. With the problem of supply solved, Cormier was able to concentrate on selling.

At first it was a struggle. "I worked a minimum of eighty hours a week and did everything. I even learned how to do minor repairs. But I believed that personalized service, the careful selection of quality inventory, and *very* competitive prices would be a winning combination." As business grew, he was able to qualify for manufacturers' volume rebates and could pass those savings on to customers. His overhead remained low – he was still his only employee. As the suppliers came to know him, they offered good advice.

In the fall of 1979, one piece of advice from a manufacturer led him to take his biggest risk to date. The advice was "buy gold, the price is going to skyrocket." Cormier returned to his bank manager and this time borrowed in excess of $100,000 for the gold purchase. Shortly thereafter he was able to finance the purchase of the entire building that housed his basement store, which he then moved into a 2,500-square-foot space on street level. He turned part of the rest of the building into an apartment. "I worked constantly anyway," admits Cormier. "And I do think that living right upstairs from the shop was a key ingredient of success. I'm simply there whenever I'm needed." The purchase of the building increased the company's assets as well as its visibility and its acceptance in the community. And a stable location would help repeat business – if the gold tip proved true and he still had a business to repeat.

But as yet no giant leaps in prices had taken place. He decided to take a rare vacation. He even determined to avoid newspapers for a few days. When he did pick up a paper, he read both that Russia had invaded Afghanistan and that gold prices had more than doubled. He quickly sold a good portion of his gold stock for an instant profit; the remainder he added to his stock in the store. By selling at current prices, Cormier made a healthy profit.

La Mine d'Or started as a discount jewelry operation, with low overhead. Soon it had enough volume to make as much, if not more money, on retail sales – benefiting from the extra margin due to volume discounts. Competition among the more than 100 jewelry stores in the province is fierce. But the store's physical size puts it in the top 5 per cent of the country. Sales were $1.4 million last year and in 1985 should reach $1.5 million, in the top 8 per cent of Canada's independent jewelry stores. Jewelry stores in New Brunswick average from $300,000 to $500,000 in sales per year.

With expansion and success has come the inevitable challenge of hiring and managing a bigger staff. Today he has ten full-time employees and fifteen part-time employees, most of them students. "I have very good people in the key positions, including a certified watchmaker with thirty-five years' experience, but you have to stay on top of your people in this business," says Cormier. "Unfortunately, too many prospective employees think that life today should be easy, and a lot of people aren't prepared to work." But he has learned that he can't possibly do everything himself and last year he was able to cut back from eighty to sixty hours per week. In 1985 he achieved a real breakthrough with an occasional fifty-hour week.

This doesn't mean Cormier has reined in his ambitions for La Mine d'Or. He has now expanded into the giftware business and claims to have the largest selection of Royal Doulton figurines in the Maritimes. And he is seriously considering franchising his concept: quality name jewelry at reasonable prices made possible through high volume sales. If he does, he'll start slowly and stay in eastern Canada, at least at first. "The national chain stores are hurting down here. But I can multiply my buying power through a chain based in Moncton. Local people prefer the security of dealing with locally based businesses."

La Mine d'Or was obviously helped by the fact that Cormier is a local boy. But that doesn't fully explain his success at entering a mature, competitive market. He was able to combine a natural knack for selling with unmitigated hard work. He understood the value of building trust among customers. And he was willing to take risks. "I've always tried to be shrewd about risk-taking and not spend what I haven't earned, and I believe you have to have complete confidence in yourself and in your ability to learn. You have to deal fairly with people – customers, suppliers, everyone. And you have to have the endurance of a prize fighter and, I think, the same absolute single-mindedness about winning."

ROBIN DEVINE
Classically Yours Automobiles

"Get up, get out, and do it" summarizes the philosophy of a thirty-year-old Toronto money maker by the name of Robin Devine. Operating out of her modest home just east of the Don Valley Parkway in the heart of the city, this dynamic young woman has sold over $9 million worth of automobiles over the last eight years. She firmly believes that anybody can be her or his own boss and become financially independent. And she has kept proving her point, with used cars, new cars, and replicas of classic cars. Now, in what seems like a big departure, she's promising to do the same with grandfather clocks.

"I was always taught to value whatever I had," says Devine, president of Classically Yours Automobiles Ltd. "I was able to save enough money to invest in the stock market at age sixteen. It seems my instincts were already belying my working-class upbringing." At age twenty she learned to buy and sell cars for a profit, concentrating on more exclusive models such as Corvettes and Audis. She watched the want ads in the local newspapers and checked out the finance companies' repossessed cars. She bought the ones she knew she could sell at a healthy mark-up, making $500 to $1,500 per car. "The simple fact is that certain cars use up their depreciation value quickly, then after that they begin to appreciate." Her success at this first venture entrenched her love for the automobile. And at age twenty-two she looked for a way to enter the business full time.

"I had heard about the Checker car, which everyone equated with the taxi. The person who had the franchise for Canada was here in Toronto so I approached him and told him I could sell his cars. He really didn't believe me," recalls Devine, with a smile. "And I never heard from him for six months. One Sunday morning I got a telephone call and I was told to come by and see him that week." The deal she struck was very simple. She had to put up $5,000 to become a partner. In return she would split the net profits fifty-fifty with the franchise owner. She would also get a hefty sales commission on every Checker sold.

And so Robin Devine set about reshaping the image of the Checker. She approached newspapers and magazines with her story and found them ready to write about the unusual spectacle of a woman selling the Checker car. *En Route*, Air Canada's in-flight magazine, did a feature, as did the *Financial Times* and *Financial Post*. Local television and radio stations were also willing to run short pieces. "We really turned the Checker into a reverse status symbol," she recalls. Because of its roominess and reliability, it had primarily been used by courier agencies and taxi companies. But it was ideal for the executive with a family, who wanted a car that wasn't likely to be in every neighbour's garage. The car was priced around $18,000 but could cost as much as $25,000 with options. Duty was high because Checker was not part of the Auto Pact.

Because the car was expensive (this was 1977) she sold all of the options at cost. "We also tested out each car and on delivery I told every customer what was wrong with it, if we found anything amiss." She kept her costs down by having no staff and by using her partner's garage to service the cars. The Checker cars were not renowned for their paint jobs and often had to be repainted before being sold in Canada. Testing and delivery took place simultaneously. A driver merely went to Michigan and drove the car to Canada.

Then in 1982 the Checker Automobile Co. decided to go out of business. It was faced with union demands it couldn't handle, and it could not afford the cost of a massive retooling. So it merely shut its doors and today supplies replacement parts only. "It was a tough blow. Particularly since we had built up a very saleable business which was worth about a half million dollars. The day after the announcement, it was worth nothing."

To add insult to injury, the last Checker that Devine was able to buy was seriously damaged in an accident in Michigan while it was being ferried to Canada. "What a day," she recalls. "When I saw the car, the very last one we could buy, I screamed out loud at the shock." However, the customer was willing to wait while it was repaired in Canada. Perhaps he realized that he was also purchasing a unique piece of automotive history.

At twenty-seven years old, Robin Devine had to begin all over again. Now married to a Metro Police sergeant (who has a master's degree, speaks eight languages, and will soon have a novel published), she looked for work in the automobile industry. She quickly discovered that the car manufacturers were singularly unimpressed by her outstanding sales record; they were more concerned with the fact that she had quit school after grade twelve plus one year of community college. "In effect the major car makers told me if I wanted to work for them, I would have to start at the bottom, although one well-known manufacturer was willing to hire me if I would move out of Toronto." Although Robin Devine did not articulate this, she was also demonstrating that most entrepreneurs find it difficult working for a large corporation.

So she set out to start afresh in another enterprise. "I was introduced by a friend to a man in the replicar business," she recalls, "and I loved it. We merely made a mould from an original 1952 MG TD and were able to form a fibreglass body from it. All of our car bodies are put together by hand. It's so simple, anybody could do it."

Her chartered bank gave her a credit line in twenty-four hours, convinced by her record with Checker, and she found a garage that would serve as a car dealership. Thus equipped, she set up Classically Yours Automobiles, which is an elegantly simple operation.

The replica MGs are built on a Volkswagen beetle chassis and use Volkswagen engines, both readily available. She has a manufacturer outside Toronto who makes the cars on order, and she re-sells them to corporate clients for $15,000. Unlike the

Checker, which was aimed at companies but which she mostly sold to individuals, she has concentrated on the corporate market for most of her replicar sales. "A replica MG is such an attention-getting car that it's perfect for incentive and sales contests of all kinds. One Simpson's store had to reprint the forms it had in a shopping centre contest because of the attention this car created."

She quickly realized that car sales would not be sustained through the retail market and concentrated her efforts on informing corporations about the car's availability, and its attention-getting appeal. "I'm no expert on marketing, but I do follow some simple rules," she states matter-of-factly. "First of all I price the car fairly, probably somewhat below what some of my competitors charge. By keeping my overhead down, I can still make a good profit." She calls up companies directly, puts her car in parades and in shopping malls, and does a limited amount of advertising in magazines. She says the magazines bring results (she won't reveal which ones she uses). Rather than tie up money in a demonstration, she takes prospective customers to the nearest display car, which is usually in a shopping mall.

In exactly two years of running Classically Yours, Robin Devine has sold over 200 cars for over $3 million. Currently she is negotiating with an importing firm in Japan and has her fingers crossed that she will shortly be able to start shipping cars to the Orient, a delightful twist on the usual North American automotive story.

Although her love of cars got her into her own business to start with, Robin Devine's marketing approach, and her ability to find profitable enterprises that incur very low overhead, ought to work with other products, such as the one she has just begun importing into Canada. "I had seen this marvellous grandfather clock I wanted to buy, but found it a bit too expensive. When I get a hunch, I act on it, and so on a whim I called up the clock manufacturer in Europe and asked if he was interested in selling directly to Canada. He was, so I got on a plane, visited him, and he gave me the rights to market his clocks in Canada." She laughs with pleasure when she recalls the meeting. "All I had to show were the press clippings of my selling Checker cars and the replica MG, but it was enough." She's now awaiting confirmation of orders for the clock, which she has already presented to a number of major Canadian retail outlets. "Believe it or not," she says, "but I think that selling grandfather clocks is going to be a bigger business than either the Checker or replica MG." She still operates out of her house.

Unlike most money makers, Robin Devine does not admit to working long hours and six or seven days a week. "In fact, I work less than a forty-hour week," she says, "but your mind is always on your business. My customers, too, can call me anytime."

Mr. and Mrs. Devine recently acquired a new Audi to accompany their 1973 Dodge Dart and the MG replicar. Their leisure pursuits are modest. "I like to cut the grass and I enjoy roller-skating," she says.

When asked whether or not she planned for the future, Devine could only smile. "Next year I have no idea what I will be doing." She will admit to a concern for the ordinary citizen. "It peeves me that all of the seminars run on business, accounting, financing, etc. are all aimed at established people," she says. "Why doesn't someone set up self-help seminars for the poor? They're the people who are most in need of improving themselves." Nevertheless her success has convinced her that anyone can start a business in Canada. "You don't really need money or special connections. Just get up, go out, and do it!"

Robin Devine was able to turn a fascination with cars into a profitable enterprise. Although she claims it was simple, it was her vision and determination that made it work. She made her own markets by reshaping the image of the Checker, and then by helping to establish the replica automobile as a prestige gift item. One key to her success was certainly keeping her costs down – no office, no staff, no overhead – which allowed her to keep the price of her products very competitive. Her challenge at age thirty will be to stay small. But she's shown the courage to strike out on her own and the ability to adapt to different marketing situations.

ANTON DISSANAYAKE
Alpha Bytes Computer

"If I had twenty-four hours a day to work, I could create gold mines. There are tremendous opportunities in Canada, opportunities for everybody, for anybody who is willing to work hard." The words belong to Anton Dissanayake, the founder, owner, and president of Alpha Bytes Computer Corporation. He has ten employees who work computer keyboards in 1,000 square feet of rented industrial space in Markham, Ontario, which is known as the silicon suburb of Toronto. The area is home to a number of computer firms, including the Canadian headquarters of IBM and the offices and factories of Canada's GEAC Computer Corporation.

Alpha Bytes is a small business, but Dissanayake created it through dogged determination, and he firmly believes his young company will become a winner on an international scale. Nobody gave him a thing, and that's why he can't tolerate grumblers. "People have to get off their butts. Lots of people phone me for jobs, but they don't really want to work. So many are basically lazy. If you really want to work, things will start to happen. It doesn't happen in one day, but it'll happen. I started with zero. Now, I've got something."

Dissanayake grew up in Britain, where a staggering 80 per cent of all young people still do not go to university. In Canada, by comparison, more than half of all secondary school graduates go on to college and university. Social, economic, and class pressures in Britain still conspire against higher education. Although Margaret Thatcher's economics made Britain the fastest growing European economy by 1985, the relatively low level of Britons' education will hamper economic progress and understanding for many years to come.

So Anton Dissanayake was in the minority among Britain's young people when he graduated with a Bachelor of Science degree in London in 1971 and landed a job with a computer consulting firm, Buckley and Kelling. Seven years later, the firm transferred him to Canada. One of his first contracts was with Columbia records. He was to design a computerized payout system for royalties owed to recording artists. Columbia was so impressed they hired him away from the consulting firm. He stayed until he felt there was no more room for advancement and joined Morguard Investments, where he ran the firm's computer department.

"Micro-computers were just starting to happen. I wanted new challenges. So, in 1980, I set out on my own. At first, I sold computers and software out of my home in Thornhill (north of Toronto). I didn't need any money to start that business because I was really just a middle man. I had contacts and I knew the business from my previous jobs. Knocking on doors and selling computers generated an income."

At the time many people were selling computers and software. The field was crowded and competitive. Dissanayake felt success lay in doing something differently. "I wanted to find a use for computers that hadn't yet been developed by others. I looked at using computers in doctors' offices, lawyers' offices, retail stores, small businesses. I finally found one. Opticians and optometrists didn't have a good computer system available. I decided to go after that business. I learned everything I could about it. I lived on selling general-use computers, and in my spare time I studied the optical business. I just went through the phone book to find people who could help me. I found an optometrist and an optician [to work as consultants], and together we designed a computer system they could use. After a few months, we developed a working model and took it to an opticians' convention in Toronto, just to get opinions. We realized then that we'd come upon a vast, wide-open market for the product.

It took him more than a year of fourteen-hour days to develop a product upon which to build a business. Part of his time had to be spent selling computers so he could support his wife and children. Finally he was ready to test the system at a store near his home in Thornhill. It was a busy location, and he and his co-designers were able to work out the bugs in six months.

By the middle of 1984, he was ready to enter the market. "We called the system 'Alpha-Optic,' and what it needed then was publicity, publicity, and publicity. We'd made contacts at the opticians' convention and got an ophthalmic supplier in Clinton, Maryland, to market the computer system in the U.S. We also landed a job designing a billing system for the Ontario Association of Optometrists. That helped spread the word for us and gave us credibility in the business. By late 1984 we'd sold more than a hundred systems! Now, we're into the United States in a big way. We're working with Imperial Optical down there, and that could tap a very large market."

Alpha Bytes had been in business as a designer and supplier of customized computer systems for less than a year and Anton

Dissanayake was already claiming to be the best in the business, to have eliminated the competition in the optical field. At his newly rented quarters in Markham, his staff have now developed a second customized system for dentists, called "Alpha-Dental." The company won customers in Europe when Dissanayake accepted a $15,000 grant from the Ontario Ministry of Trade to join a European trade mission. It's the only government money he's ever accepted.

"We take only enough money out of the company to live on. Everything else goes back in. I mortgaged the house, the car, everything I had to start this. The rewards are when you see that you're making something happen. There's lots to do out there. We're going to keep developing new software computer products. I can't believe the opportunities that are out there."

Dissanayake won't discuss company revenues or profits. But a hundred systems sold in the first half year, at about $3,500 a copy, gives a good idea of where this thirty-five-year-old money maker is headed.

RUTH SHAW
Covent Garden

When you step inside Covent Garden on Toronto's Yonge Street a mile north of the famous "Strip," it's like walking into a sun-bathed greenhouse, although the only natural light comes from the glass front of the store. Yet it's chilly inside. That's how it must be to allow the row upon row of cut flowers to retain their freshness and appearance. Each group of flowers is neatly labelled with the store's triangular design label – a hand, holding a stem of baby's breath, on a mauve background. The store's symbol is also emblazoned on the stylish mauve awning that juts out into the street. Inside, ginger, rubrum lilies, frescia, aster, allium, peonies, and baby's breath represent only a small sampling of the flowers within arm's reach of the customer. There are no coolers here, *everything* is out in the open. This is no ordinary flower store.

Money maker Ruth Shaw, the owner and manager of Covent Garden, came to Canada from England ten years ago and has had a varied career ranging from modelling swimwear to producing television commercials. In 1981, in her late thirties with two young children, she made her first stab at business ownership. "I was in a waiting room and read an article in *Forbes* magazine that said there would be a cut-flower boom in the 1980s, that the European attitude toward flowers was infiltrating Canada. So my husband and I visited one of the new flower stores in New York where customers had easy access to the flowers. It was nice, but I thought we could do it better."

She and her husband, who is a consultant in accounting, sold their house and used the proceeds to launch the business. It cost about $100,000 to open Covent Garden, half of which was obtained from a local bank, with a guarantee provided by the Federal Business Development Bank. And in April, 1982, Covent Garden was open for business. "We were living at risk for a while, but that's what it took to get here," Shaw says today. "I contend that entrepreneurs are willing to follow their rainbow, no matter what. If you really believe in what you're doing, you will be less likely to seek out the rest of the world's opinion and be disheartened by it." Such independence of vision served her well as she learned the flower business and refined her marketing approach. When the store opened she did everything herself.

The concept for the store evolved very simply. "I merely looked at the competition. It took no sophisticated research to realize that the average flower store is somewhat antiquated in its marketing approach. The flowers are usually shut up in a fridge, there are no prices posted, and the selection is very limited." Grocery stores that sell flowers in the open with price tags aren't cool enough and the quality usually suffers.

Covent Garden makes its flowers totally available by making the store, in effect, one large cooler and by inviting the customer to step right inside. Equally important, Shaw offers the rare, quality flowers that one seldom sees, like stargazer or Dutch daisies. And she prices them by unit so that customers can buy by the stem. Even the rare blooms become an affordable choice. "It's important that people be able to touch and feel the product. Buying flowers is an emotional experience. As a matter of fact, it's an emotional business. We're really trying to make people happy."

Ruth Shaw's marketing sense led her to hire a designer to develop the store's mauve motif, which individualizes its labelling, stationery, and packaging. The look was so effective that Covent Garden's graphic design has won a Design Canada award. She also developed her own method of arranging the flowers in a looser, more natural way that departs from the formal arrangements of established florists. When a customer has made his selection of flowers, they are wrapped in a triangle of transparent plastic, sealed with the Covent Garden label, and presented with instructions on flower care tucked neatly inside the package.

Like many other successful entrepreneurs she places a high priority on quality and service. She's at the wholesaler at four in the morning to get the best selection for her customers. She buys Ontario flowers whenever she can but relies on more readily available imported flowers from Holland, Italy, and even Hawaii. "In Covent Garden you are always on show. We have a perishable product and really only three or four days to move it out of the store. I have researched the subject and we have developed a very strict methodology for flower care. Each one must be individually stripped and conditioned. Quality and style must never be compromised."

Today Covent Garden has seven full-time and three part-time employees and Shaw's role has changed from that of owner-salesperson to owner-supervisor. The business has also evolved. "When we opened, we figured we would be strictly cash and carry. But a business takes on a life of its own. We found we needed to be more flexible and so we decided to extend credit. A lot of corporations have discovered us and we now do arrangements for parties and special company events." She was recently asked to speak at a Flowers Canada convention about marketing, and is pleased by the fact that her competition has come to accept her as a talented, if avant garde, team member.

Covent Garden has achieved twice the average revenue Statistics Canada reports for a first-time flower store. In the first two years, sales volume doubled and Shaw confidently predicts a volume of $1 million in the fifth year. Life was not all smooth sailing, however; there were quiet periods during 1983-84 when cash flow was a problem. In hindsight, she says she would have preferred to find private financing for her venture.

When asked to state what she does in her leisure time, Shaw was quick to reply "sleep." She and her family enjoy bike riding and she delights in cooking, especially after visits to Toronto's St. Lawrence market. For the most part, though, she keeps her eye on the store, working six days a week.

Covent Garden's new approach to the art of selling flowers is spreading. One franchise store has already opened in Vancouver. However, Ruth Shaw feels she would like a little more operating experience before she sets up a full-fledged franchise system. "When we do, we'll need to do it in a big way, and do it right."

JIM BRICKMAN
Brick Brewing Company

"I've always wanted to market my own product, I didn't want to re-invent the wheel but I wanted a product that was relatively recession-proof, had a high profile, and was easily introduced. I felt that beer was that product." The words belong to Jim Brickman, founder of the Brick Brewing Company in Kitchener, Ontario. Although it's too soon to tell just how successful his company will be, Brickman has already proved that there's room in the Canadian beer market for a company that plans to stay small and concentrate on quality.

Brickman's background is marketing. After graduating from university with a B.A. degree in English and psychology, which he somewhat unkindly describes as a "complete waste of time," he went to work for an advertising agency in Toronto. He worked as a copywriter and became involved in the premium-incentive business. In simple terms this involves using premiums and incentives, such as sweepstakes contests, to entice consumers to buy a product. In 1976 he left the agency and set up his own premium-incentive business, called Brick Promotions, which is still active in Toronto.

While at the agency Brickman had also learned about the general marketing strategies of its many clients in the packaged goods industry. He had developed a strong interest in package design and even began playing around with designs for his own label on a premium-shaped bottle of beer. By the time he started out on his own, Brickman had formed some pretty firm opinions, not only about marketing but about the marketplace itself. "Sure, I know how competitive the beer business is. But from

1978 to 1980 I saw two things emerging. First, there is a trend toward specialty, high-quality products, such as the popularity of Häagen-Dazs ice cream. Second, consumers are starting to think that maybe big isn't so great. Smaller, specialty operations can build a loyal customer following."

But Brickman was only willing to follow his instincts so far. He hired outside professionals in marketing and research to test his opinions, to discover if there was indeed a market to support a small business, to find out if that business should be located (as Brickman thought) in a smaller community, if it should market a premium product, and if that product should in fact be beer. The evaluations made by innumerable focus groups proved him right. In fact, all age groups tested agreed that if the beer delivered good taste, they would support the premium product of a local, community brewery. It was time to do some serious market projections and undertake full-scale feasibility studies for different locations.

While these studies were being done, Brickman was running his company and learning all he could about the beer business on the side. He visited a number of breweries around the world and talked to brewmasters and owners of independent breweries like the one he wanted to open. Canada then couldn't provide him with a parallel for study but sixty-one breweries in twenty-two foreign countries over a period of six years did.

His biggest initial challenge was to determine the optimum size for his brewery. It had to be big enough so he could make his product efficiently and sell it at a profit, small enough to keep quality high. The operation he decided on would produce 52,000 hectalitres or 110,000 cases of beer annually.

For the brewery's location Brickman cannily chose Kitchener/Waterloo, about an hour's drive southwest of Toronto. Because of its annual Oktoberfest, the town has become known as the beer capital of southern Ontario. "It's a good community with a beer-drinking tradition, and there are a lot of Europeans there," he observes. He guessed that the local people would follow the European habit of supporting the local brewery. Choosing a name was the next problem. "Brick" was not his first choice for the enterprise, but it turned out to be the name most favoured by consumers in focus-group testings. Now he needed a building to turn into a brewery. The one he finally chose, on

King Street in downtown Waterloo, had plate-glass windows in the front through which the huge brewing kettles would be seen by passersby. It would cost $780,000 to renovate, but it would create a strong image for the new company.

Raising the funds to construct the brewery was a major task. It was budgeted at approximately $2 million and, as Brickman points out, "all the money is put down on day one." Using income from Brick Promotions, he spent over $100,000 on engineering and to have his accountants help him prepare a projected statement of income and expenses for the banks. The big question was, could a small brewery manage a $2 million debt?

He saw approximately forty banks, including some with venture capital divisions. Meanwhile, he received invaluable financial assistance from the Ontario Development Corporation, which approved his concept within twenty days. Eventually, thanks primarily to the thoroughness of Brickman's projections, the result of seven years of work, the venture capital division of a major chartered bank put up most of the funds. He persuaded several investors to join in as well. "It was a close call, I have to admit. My situation was such that had the project been turned down, I would have been bankrupt."

It was July of 1984 when he finally had his financing in place, in time for a pre-Christmas launch. This and early spring are the times "when consumer interest peaks and you have a fighting chance." But he had less than five months to renovate the building, install the equipment, work out production kinks, and start brewing. When the renovations began Brickman was still searching for an expert brewmaster. After interviewing thirty-five candidates he found the man he wanted, not surprisingly a native of Germany. He also hired a top-flight engineer with some experience in the brewing business to oversee construction. The brewery was completed in the fall of 1984 at a final cost of about $100,000 over the $2 million budget. By early December, Brick's beer was ready to come flowing out of the production line and into the storage tanks.

The first bottling of Brick beer took place on December 18, 1984. The slim brown bottles bore a stylish label bearing a reproduction of the brewery facade – "our billboard," as Brickman puts it. It was no coincidence that the date was also Jim Brickman's birthday. Brick beer was an instant success, and, as forecast, soon captured about 5 per cent of the Kitchener-Waterloo market. The major breweries, who own the Brewers' Warehousing outlets in Ontario, hospitably allowed Brick beer to be sold through their stores in the region. Today, less than a year after opening, Brick beer sells every bottle that's made.

In fulfilling his desire to produce a distinctive product, Brickman has made no compromise on quality. He uses the finest quality ingredients and even imports his hops from Germany. Brick beer is a truly premium lager, aged for the maximum period legally permitted in Ontario. From the initial brewing to bottling takes a total of twenty-eight days. Each step in the brewing process is carried out traditionally and, as the label says, the beer is "brewed with no preservatives."

Early in 1985 a strike at the major Ontario breweries proved a bonanza for the young company, as for other small brewers such as Amstel. People lined up from as far away as Toronto for Brickman's suds. "We limited sales to one case per customer and we were sold out in forty-two minutes." Refusing to compromise on quality by shortening the aging period, the upstart brewery did not sell another drop during the week.

The brewery's major problem today is guessing the point at which consumer demand will level off. Brickman has already raised $190,000 for one expansion and can now produce up to 150,000 cases annually, but there is little room for more in his current operation. He emphasizes that he has to stay small to succeed. "One thing the major breweries can never do is to appear small. But I can and in today's marketing environment, that's an advantage." He also knows that he doesn't have the ability to compete with the majors on a larger scale. "They've been great to work with, and even welcomed me into their association, but it would be suicide for me to try to compete head on with them across the country. But there certainly is room in this country to open several small breweries in other communities," and he doesn't rule out the possibility.

Brickman projects revenues of about $900,000 in Brick's first year, $1.5 million in its second, and $2.9 million in its third. "Despite the up-front costs, we may make a profit in our first year," he says. Not bad money-making for someone who recently turned thirty-two.

Brickman is still a bachelor, still lives in Toronto, and still runs Brick Promotions while commuting back and forth to Waterloo (he sometimes stays overnight with a relative). He drives a four-year-old Porsche with Brick 1 on the licence plate. (It is symptomatic of this man's drive that he registered the name "Brick" long before a high-profile furniture retailer with the same name moved into Ontario.) His typical day goes from seven a.m. to seven p.m. but he admits to going to bed early at night. He might fit in a casual game of golf at a nearby course, but not often, since he works about six days a week. His brewmaster oversees operations and supervises the six full-time employees (six more part-time employees are used during bottling operations), but being on-site is important for a developing business, so he spends as much time there as possible.

Jim Brickman can derive considerable satisfaction from seeing his careful projections come true. He entered a very mature and highly competitive business and created a new market out of the old. The major brewers have introduced premium beers with success in Canada over the last few years, but few can compete with a small brewery producing a premium beer for local consumption only. Brick beer should be around for many years to come.

DOREEN BRAVERMAN
The Flag Shop

Canadians are not noted for the flag-waving brand of patriotism, but one woman in Vancouver, British Columbia, has built a thriving business by following a hunch that we are more patriotic than we let on. The Flag Shop has two retail outlets, one in Vancouver and the other in Calgary, and it has expanded into a flag-making business that will gross $2 million in combined sales in 1985.

Money maker Doreen Braverman is a former telephone operator, receptionist, school teacher, advertising alumna, a recent recipient of an MBA, and mother of two successive families. She is obviously an uncommonly intelligent, energetic, and capable person. Her career as an entrepreneur began in 1976. At the time she was forty-four years old. "I had managed to put together $17,000 to buy a small premium and incentives business called Vancouver Regalia. It had only a few boxes of flags but I liked the idea of selling them. They make such a positive statement." She traded the regalia in the store for more flags and decided to simply concentrate on flags and decals.

Braverman correctly realized that there is a substantial market for flags beyond the obvious buyers. "Boaters are a happy lot," she observes, "and they like to fly flags." So, too, do service stations, shopping malls, and municipal governments, not to mention provincial and federal governments, which need a steady supply for buildings as well as for celebrations. She is also the supplier to the B.C. government for Expo '86. Corporations are increasingly ordering flags imprinted with their own logos, and today this constitutes the bulk of her customized business. Her product line also includes flag poles: standard indoor poles are kept in stock, outdoor poles are made to order by a manufacturer.

After its opening the Flag Shop quickly discovered that it needed a reliable, steady supply of flags. It also wanted to reduce the time required to fill custom orders, up to ten weeks when ordered from manufacturers in eastern Canada. So, in 1977, Mrs. Braverman purchased for very little money a silk-screening business that had gone bankrupt. Out of her profits she was able to finance the purchase of the building where her store was located in downtown Vancouver. With the help of a British Columbia Development Corporation low-cost mortgage for $175,000 she was able to add 5,000 square feet of space for the silk-screening operation. All of a sudden she was in the flag-making business.

"Learning how to screen and print flags was not difficult," recalls Mrs. Braverman. "We had the equipment, artists, and seamstresses to do the work. But finding good foremen was not easy and even the printers were used to working with a different set of priorities." The recession slowed her fledgling manufacturing business, but she experienced no such problems on the retail side, recording healthy sales increases virtually every year.

The Flag Shop's "bare bones" marketing process is deceptively simple. Braverman put together a direct-mail catalogue that colourfully presents a variety of its products, listing prices. "We wanted to keep advertising and marketing costs to an absolute minimum and first tried to figure out who would buy flags. We used sales slips to tabulate information about our regular clientele, for instance, and now we send our catalogue to the purchasing agents of government offices, churches, gas stations, you name it. Today our customer list numbers over 15,000 people." Direct-mail business is still a significant portion of total sales. Her contacts in the advertising business help her reach her corporate customers with the "flag-as-logo" product.

In the early days Mrs. Braverman earned the funds she needed for expansion; today the banks supply her with a credit line. But echoing Covent Garden's Ruth Shaw, she says that if she had to do it over again she would look for partners with equity capital. "There are lots of people around with money and you're better off working with private capital than with bank loans." She also freely acknowledges the importance of mixing with her peers in the Vancouver community. "I joined the Board of Trade, and groups such as the Canadian Manufacturers' Association helped me greatly."

Today, with forty employees, half of whom are in manufacturing, Braverman still works on average a six-day week. She rises at 5:30 a.m., reads the *Globe and Mail*, and sees her seventeen-year-old daughter off to school. Most days, she's in her office at 8:30 and stays there till 6:00 p.m. She's also in the store on Saturday because "it's a day to get things done without being interrupted by telephone calls." Of her current lifestyle, she says, "I love every minute of it."

Recently, the Flag Shop decided to franchise its retail concept and Doreen Braverman now has new worlds to conquer. Her second retail outlet opened in Calgary in 1981, weathered the recession, and is doing well, despite not being in the best location. She plans to move it further downtown where it will benefit from traffic off the street. "If you can be profitable selling Canadian flags in Calgary, you can do it anywhere," observes Mrs. Braverman. Her franchising formula is carefully laid out. She is looking for owner-managers with $20,000 to invest in the business and she will take a 5 per cent royalty on sales, 3 per cent of which will go toward advertising. The first ads for the Flag Shop franchise are now appearing in the *Financial Post*. But her horizons are not limited by geographic boundaries and she freely admits, "I'd like to have a Flag Shop in every major city of the world."

PAUL DOYLE
Go Vacations

"Go Your Own Way, Worldwide" is the slogan of Go Vacations Limited, a Toronto-based company that now serves vacationers from around the world by renting motorhomes and houseboats across North America. Under the crafty management of thirty-six-year-old money maker Paul Doyle, this company has become one of the largest renters of recreational vacation vehicles (popularly known as RVs) in the world. In 1985, Go Vacations and its growing list of vehicle owners (for whom it manages and rents motorhomes, houseboats, and yachts) will gross about $10 million.

Few would have predicted such success for Doyle as a teenager. He was asked to leave two high schools in Toronto and quit after grade eleven. Always a bit of a rebel, he objected to such rituals as the Lord's Prayer and singing "God Save the Queen." Nevertheless, he did not lack scholastic ability. He completed and passed grades twelve and thirteen on his own, then took a degree in only two years at York University, majoring in fine arts and psychology.

After graduation he worked as a high school teacher and took a job renting and selling camping trailers in the summertime. It went so well that in 1973 he decided to leave teaching and make a full-time job of RV retail sales. "My parents believed in me so I was able to start with $15,000 borrowed from a bank, with their home as collateral. In the first year I sold tent trailers and was able to gross $50,000 and put all of the money back into the business." With this early success under his belt, he rented a small house on a highway in Thornhill, a suburb north of Toronto, and watched his sales expand to include motorhomes and larger trailers. His front yard doubled as a sales lot. Go Camping (as it was then known) even bought out a competitor who had the Winnebago franchise for Toronto.

He had thirty people on staff when the recession came along in

1979. One of the first businesses it hit was recreational vehicles. Sales volume fell to 30 per cent of normal and Doyle was left with too many vehicles sitting unsold on his lot. "It was a time of high interest rates, skyrocketing gas prices, and nobody was buying. Life was miserable."

Looking back, Doyle can see it was adversity that moulded the company to the shape it has today, not an uncommon story among successful entrepreneurs. "We looked at the vehicles sitting on our lot, our bankers were giving us a hard time, so we thought, why not rent them out?" Without knowing it, Doyle was laying the foundation for a worldwide enterprise in a very new market.

His plan was simple: sell vehicles to individual owners (generating an instant profit); then invite the owners to hire back the company to rent the vehicle, service it, and keep track of it as it went from one vacation destination to another. In effect, the RV owner would have started a business, making some of his expenses, such as interest cost and insurance, deductible. Since the owner would be able to use the vehicle whenever he wanted, it looked like a very attractive investment. So events proved.

In 1980, the first summer of the new business, Go Vacations rented out seventeen vehicles and Doyle sensed success. Reasoning that the falling Canadian dollar would make a Canadian vacation especially attractive to Europeans, he flew overseas and contacted the people who put together wholesale travel packages. He showed them attractive photographs and offered several simple vacation packages. In turn, they put him in their brochures and the results were immediate. In 1982, one year after the transatlantic sales trip and with the fleet expanded to seventy vehicles, Go Camping rented to Europeans 70 per cent of the time.

Adapting to a new market meant some changes. "I had to hire a multilingual staff. Our brochures on how to use our equipment had to be printed in several languages, German, Dutch, French, and so on. And I had to expand the number of destinations offered." Ex-employees opened offices in Calgary and Vancouver, a full-time marketing rep was hired in Europe, and the push was on.

"We decided to really go for it the following year," says Doyle, "and we opened dealerships that today have spread to Whitehorse, Anchorage, Winnipeg, Ottawa, Montreal, and Halifax." Go Vacations opened up dealerships in the United States as well, covering major cities such as New York, Miami, Denver, San Francisco, Los Angeles, and a number of other locations.

The company learned a number of hard lessons during this period of rapid expansion. The fifty-fifty partnership arrangement worked fine with some dealers, as long as the dealership made money. But predictably, a number of the dealerships were headed by poor managers, and Go Vacations had to make up the loss. So Doyle started selling full franchises with trademark rights and charging a management fee on rentals. But there were still problems. Some people who bought franchises and purchased vehicles from Go Vacations' manufacturer weren't cut out to be salesmen. "It was impossible to take a non-salesperson and give him a guarantee of success. We're far more careful in our selection of franchisees." He now looks for people with some sales track record.

Today Go Vacations is a continent-wide chain operating approximately 1,000 motorhomes and has expanded into houseboats and yachts, with a fleet of fifty vessels on vacation waterways in British Columbia and Ontario. An expensive computer system has been installed to keep track of reservations, and there are employees on duty at the head office from five a.m. to nine p.m. "We like to confirm a vacation request within an hour if we can," says Doyle. Head office has a staff of twenty-five people and each franchise has an average of ten on the payroll. All told, Go Vacations has 325 employees in North America.

The company also contracted with an RV manufacturer to build its own fleet of green-and-white vehicles, under the "Elite" brand name, incorporating the most desirable features sought by vacationers. Many of them have built-in furnaces enabling year-round use.

Finding buyers for the growing fleet of rental vehicles has not been particularly difficult for Go Vacations, but it has not been easy to keep all of the new owners happy with the revenue generated. "The fact is, not all destinations are equally popular and some vehicle owners do better than others." To overcome the inequity, Doyle has come up with an inventive and sophisticated package for investor participation in his company. On December 12, 1984, investment dealers introduced a prospectus for the

"1985 Go Vacations Limited Partnership." For a chosen fee an investor can purchase a unit that is applied by the corporation to the price of a recreational vehicle. The vehicle becomes part of a fleet utilized in unspecified locations according to demand. The scheme has attractive tax advantages and investors are paid a percentage of rental profits. They also receive "Go Dollars," which permit them to rent a vehicle at any Go Vacations dealer for 10 per cent of the standard cost. The first offering of units was snapped up and a second is planned for fall 1985. According to Doyle, investors receive three benefits: "generation of income, tax deduction benefits, and use of a superb vehicle."

With his company rapidly reaching maturity in North America, Doyle is actively looking further afield. "It's fun competing in the international market. And our next step is to set up franchises internationally. Australia, New Zealand, Europe, and the Far East will all, one day, have Go Vacations franchises. To our clientele and investors, we will be able to offer a destination virtually anywhere in the world."

GREIG CLARK
College Pro Painters

Sure indications that the long Canadian winter is coming to an end are the bright yellow "College Pro Painters" signs sprouting up on front lawns across the country. Money maker Greig Clark, the thirty-two-year-old former business student who has revolutionized the home repairs business, is modest about his accomplishment. "It was a simple observation to make. Painting was a horrendously unorganized business. Estimates were unprofessional, often written on a cigarette package, and they varied greatly from company to company." His idea was simplicity itself. He would hire college students for the summer, the period of peak demand, train them to handle the work, and put in place a management system to locate customers and ensure that each project was carried out professionally.

In 1971, while taking an Honours Business Administration program at the University of Western Ontario, Clark discovered his summer earnings would leave him $1,000 short of the amount he needed for the following semester. So he decided to try out his theory that he could compete in the painting business. He went to a Canada Manpower Centre, hired some students for just above minimum wage, and put them to work on jobs he located by simply knocking on doors. This test took place in Thunder Bay, Greig's home town. He gave proper though still-informal estimates, priced competitively, made sure his painters showed up on time, and checked that the task was carried out to the customer's satisfaction. Greig Clark's summer earnings went from $3,000 in the first year to $7,000 in the second to $12,000 in his final year at Western. After graduation in 1974 he took a year off to travel around the world and started to put together a manual for the operation of College Pro Painters. Drawing on the knowledge he had acquired at school, he developed a chronology for starting a business and systematically attacked every topic from "Business Plan" to "Close Down" in what would become his corporate bible.

His preparations were downright scholarly and, unlike many money makers, Clark admits he approached the idea of going full-time into his own business with caution. "I wanted first to test the idea of having someone else run the business for me. I hired a manager and in the summer of 1975 I test-marketed the concept in London, Ontario. The trial was a failure and I lost money. I was of the school of thought, however, that believes an absolutely key administrative challenge is the careful examination of all the elements of success – or its opposite. And so," explains Clark with a smile, "I had just what I needed: an early failure to take a good hard look at and learn from."

What Clark discovered were the essential qualities of a good manager. He must be a self-starter, an adept decision-maker and problem-solver. Clark also learned that he needed to improve vastly his communications and sales tracking procedures. His London manager, for instance, had reported his weekly bookings to Clark by telephone. But his revenues didn't match the reports. The problem proved to be in the interpretation of the word "booking," the manager using it to describe leads and Clark understanding it to mean definite future commitments.

In 1975 Clark put College Pro on hold and took a position in the brand management group with General Foods. He stayed there for two and a half years. "I learned a lot, particularly that if you have a systematic approach to marketing you can solve most problems." And so the College Pro manual's marketing chapters came to include information on the preparation of an advertising plan on target groups, and on consumer benefits including substantiation of any claims made.

In the meantime Clark got married, and even though his wife was earning a good salary as well, they moved into a modest basement apartment and pocketed most of their earnings. "The first few years were tough when we adopted a lifestyle not followed by our peers. But we needed our money to further test the College Pro system." The following summer, 1976, he set up a trial in London and one in Mississauga. This time London succeeded and Mississauga failed. The value of finding good people to manage each outlet was clearer than ever.

Undaunted, Clark refined his system and set up a plan for outlets across Ontario, all in areas dominated by single-family dwellings and family incomes substantial enough to support his enterprise. Then he looked for managers. "I put an ad in the university newspaper with a big headline that said 'Make $7,000 This Summer and Run Your Own Business,'" he remembers with amusement. "I thought it would be like offering free dope at an Alice Cooper concert, and that I would be overwhelmed with replies. I received zero response." He realized the students did not find the offer credible and that he would have to recruit his managers himself. The following summer, while still at General Foods, six outlets were operational – London, Etobicoke, Mississauga, Kitchener, Thunder Bay, and the Rosedale area in Toronto. They all made money.

That was all Clark needed. In 1977 he quit his job and went to work on College Pro full time.

The size of College Pro's achievement can be measured today by the fact that, in 1985, there are 270 outlets involving 4,000 students across North America, including the states of New York, New Jersey, Pennsylvania, Massachusetts, and Vermont. "Outlet" is the term used for what is basically a geographic area. All are overseen by managers living within their own jurisdiction and working out of their homes. Managers function as independent franchisees, responsible for their own profit or loss and paying a percentage of sales – a royalty – to their corporate mentor. The College Pro head offices at Bathurst and Eglinton in Toronto have, in turn, a linear management structure. There is a Canadian president, then vice-presidents and general managers with regional responsibilities. The U.S. president operates out of Boston. Both presidents report directly to Clark, now chairman of College Pro Painters Ltd. Profit-sharing and a policy of bringing highly skilled and intelligent people together in an atmosphere where they can flourish are attracting more and more part-time employees who later pursue permanent College Pro careers at the corporate level.

"Every year I need 270 managers plus staff to run our outlets," says Clark. "And even though we have many students and managers returning to work for us throughout their college careers, I still spend about 50 per cent of my time on matters of recruitment." He spends every weekend from January to April recruiting and training students on campuses across the country. It takes three weekends of training for the average manager. These courses are complemented by quarterly seminars conducted by specialists from places such as the Harvard Business School on topics such as Time Management or Leadership Skills. The company manual today covers every topic from estimating, selling, and production to personnel and accounting, and has spawned a number of imitations.

"I believe our small business training program is the best in the world," states Clark firmly. "We're training people to run their own small businesses and our best people seem to get picked by the major recruiters on campus such as Procter and Gamble." One of College Pro's more successful managers built his own franchise business on the side while working at the company.

Key to the company's success is the system of setting targets for the managers and employees. "Everyone knows where they're trying to go. In fact we spend 25 per cent of our time helping our people set clear, measurable goals." Clark's systems training at General Foods has been put to good use at College Pro.

Clark has a ten-year plan to double the size of his business and believes this will actually happen over the next four to five years. He would like to expand into many more U.S. locations. He welcomes competition: all it does is make you better "and, happily, it hasn't cut into our growth at all. The only thing that has really annoyed me is that one of my competitors actually used my manual and changed the company name."

Within College Pro a so-called Acorn Planning Committee has

been set up to examine new business proposals; it is one of the reasons the company provides services such as shingling roofs and replacing eavestroughs in addition to painting. Clark sees the company evolving into more than a venture capital corporation. He prefers to dub future activities "business facilitation."

College Pro made Greig Clark a millionaire by age twenty-nine, but he is not particularly impressed by his achievement. "Happiness brings success, it's not success which brings happiness," he says. He works virtually seven days a week but does enjoy travelling with his family, visiting countries in South America, as well as Egypt and Greece. And, belying his conservative nature, he likes to invest in real estate.

Greig Clark was able to make a marriage of convenience between a ready and talented pool of seasonal labour and a market that was immature and unsophisticated. He has also distinguished himself as a corporate manager, having learned to support his employees, develop their skills, and draw on their ideas. "Innovation has to come from other people in the organization, not just one." With almost religious zeal, he says he wants to help make the talented people who work for him independently wealthy. If anyone can do it, it is this entrepreneur who has turned a college job into a $20-million-a-year enterprise.

BARBARA CALDWELL
Cleanwear

In 1976, money maker Barbara Caldwell's only business plan was to be in business. Her "assets" were those of the typical suburban homemaker – a house with a hefty mortgage; a car in which to chauffeur her two young sons to hockey and baseball games; a tight budget with no money for babysitters or daycare; experience at a variety of full-time and part-time secretarial and bookkeeping jobs; and a telephone. The telephone calls she made while her kids were at school became the investment that launched Cleanwear Ltd., with gross sales in the 1984-85 fiscal year of $1.5 million, a staff of thirty-two, and a 6,000-square-foot factory in Scarborough, Ontario. Says Caldwell, "I believe if you want to do something in life, you've got to get off your duff and do it."

Barbara Caldwell grew up in Winnipeg, but her parents sent her to the "Mother House" in Montreal. "It's one of the best secretarial schools around, run by the Sisters of the Congregation of Notre Dame. I was one of only six non-Catholics to go there. The education was superb." She got an office job with Domtar in Montreal on her graduation in 1963. Three years later, she was married and moved to Toronto. "I thought I'd never work again. My mother didn't work. I thought that was the way it was. When the boys were born, there wasn't time for much anyway. They were just seventeen months apart, and raising them was a big job. But we found that money was tight, and I got a part-time job with Stathmos Scale in Markham. It was just two afternoons a week, and I viewed it as my R & R time – rest and relaxation time."

Her boss was himself raising a young family. "I felt he was an extraordinary individual, because he told me my family came first. When the kids needed me, he insisted my place was at home with them, and he was very understanding when I couldn't make it to the office."

But this return to the work force whetted her entrepreneurial appetite. She enrolled in the Certified General Accountants Program and kept at it part-time for four years. Her plan was to open an employment agency in Markham. "There were a lot of young mothers in the town then, a lot of new houses, and so many of them thought I was lucky to have a part-time job. I thought I could match companies in the area with these people, and I thought it was important to have my own business. That's because women who have to work outside the home for somebody else must suffer stress unlike anyone. At least, if you run your own business, you can set your own hours, you can be there if the kids are ill with the mumps or whatever."

Barbara's husband Ross had a business distributing sanitary clothing to the medical and food industries. While continuing her part-time job and her accounting studies she helped him with the bookkeeping and learned about his industry – what products were in the marketplace, who made them, and who bought them. Before long she spotted a market niche for disposable clothing. Hospitals, drug companies, and food processors concerned about bacteria escaping the cleaning process had to sanitize reusable clothing. How would they react to clothes cheap enough to throw away?

Caldwell established her business in disposable clothing without a penny in September, 1976. She simply started calling hospitals and a variety of companies that manufacture products under strict sanitary conditions and asked them what they needed. "I'd never sold anything in my life. I had no idea if I had any skill at it. I just got in and said 'I better do this.' I worked from the phone in the basement for two or three months, just trying to get appointments with people. One man, I remember, asked me why I wasn't at home minding my kids. I literally burst into tears. Then anger set in. 'You stinker,' I thought. That kind of comment turned out to be a great motivator."

All she needed was a letterhead. She did her own typing and carried no stock. She asked the people she called up what they needed. If they placed an order she went to suppliers and bought the item wholesale. Whenever she talked someone into an appointment, she would borrow samples from a supplier. "I often wondered why people bought from me. To a certain extent, I guess people had nothing to lose."

Caldwell found that most people were encouraging and willing to take a risk with her. "Today, they giggle at me and I get pink in the face. Gosh, I had a lot of nerve. But I was given a lot of help. I told people that I didn't know what exactly they needed, but that I'd find it." That led Caldwell into manufacturing. Her customers had product specifications that weren't being met by her suppliers, so she decided to make what she couldn't buy. This required her first big investment, after half a year in business. It was a sewing machine – a professional model made by the Juki Company in Japan – purchased for $1,200. She hired a sewing-machine operator, and Cleanwear Ltd. began manufacturing its own line of disposable bouffant caps.

In short order, Barbara needed second, third, and fourth sewing machines. In September, 1981, five years after making her first sale, she moved the company out of her Markham home and into 600 square feet of rented industrial space in Scarborough. "I felt like I was mortgaging my soul. The rent was $425 a month, and I paid the first and last months' rent up front. Everytime I made another step towards growing bigger, I got that panicky feeling that goes with taking a chance. I still get it to this day, and right now I'm negotiating to move into 13,000 feet of industrial space!"

One of the secrets of her success seems to have been her willingness to seek advice. From the beginning, she made no secret of her ignorance. When she moved Cleanwear to Scarborough, she contacted the Federal Business Development Bank, a federal government agency best known for backing loans to small business. The FBDB also runs a program identified by the acronym CASE, for Counselling Assistance for Small Enterprise. CASE maintains a stable of professionals with experience in innumerable businesses. Many of them are retired, and many others once ran their own companies but no longer play an active role. Through CASE they offer their services at a nominal fee charged to the enterprise seeking their counsel.

"I've used CASE a number of times," Barbara explains. "The first person to help us out was named Moe Partick. He'd been in the garment trade forever. He must have been shaking his head when he saw our operation. But he was extraordinary. He gave me lots of advice. He was a tremendous contact.

"Right now, I'm using a consultant for strategic planning. I also get advice from our customers, and from our competitors. People are really very helpful. I've never found any of the ugliness out in the business world which other people tell me is there."

In spite of Caldwell's cashless beginning, she had needed little financing to build the company. Only in 1981, five years after she started, did she seek money from the bank. The revolving line of credit she negotiated then for the expansion into the Scarborough warehouse has never been increased. Caldwell says she just hasn't needed the money. Revenue from sales has always been sufficient to support the company's growth.

Most of Barbara Caldwell's thirty-two employees are sewing-machine operators. In spite of frequent reports of garment-industry shutdowns and unemployment, she has difficulty finding skilled people to sew for her. She acknowledges that the industry had a reputation for exploiting its people, but she does not think that is true any more. Cleanwear sewers can earn in excess of $8.00 an hour – a base rate of $5.75 an hour, plus a productivity incentive that amounts to between $1.00 and $2.50

an hour. And in August, 1984, Caldwell sought advice from the Profit Sharing Council of Canada, which helped Cleanwear implement a profit-sharing scheme for employees. She says it adds another 5 per cent to employees' paycheques.

No garment manufacturer in Canada has it easy. "We have to compete with stuff from Taiwan. In Mexico, they pay people $4.50 per day! We have to sell to hospitals in Canada that are on strict government budgets, and are conscious of every dollar they spend. I believe we win our contracts because we offer service. We're right here in Canada, and we can react to customers' needs quickly. And I've found that our customers prefer to buy Canadian-made products, even if they cost a little more. I also think we're competitive because we're small, and our overheads are low."

Cleanwear's disposable clothing is manufactured with a polyethylene fabric, called Tyvek, developed by Dupont. A paper-thin version of Tyvek is used to make envelopes for courier companies, because the Tyvek is extremely tough and nearly impossible to tear. And building-supply companies have recently developed a Tyvek house wrap, which serves as a tough combination vapour barrier and insulating material for new homes. It is also being used in bookbinding. Caldwell uses a thicker, drapeable Tyvek stock for Cleanwear's disposable clothing. White is the most common colour for hospital and manufacturing uses, but she is buying coloured Tyvek cloth to develop new clothing products.

"We've developed a line of ski wear and sports clothes with it. We think it'll be great for children, because they grow so rapidly that parents won't mind so much when their clothes don't fit any more. Our products are cheaper and therefore easier on the family budget. We also think our sports clothes will be attractive to companies as a promotional item. They can be custom-made and be cheap enough to give away."

She recognizes the need to develop new products, realizing the company needs to diversify in case free trade with the U.S. becomes a reality. She's amazingly objective on this thorny subject. "It could hurt our current products and markets, but it could lead to new products and new markets, too."

Barbara Caldwell calls herself "an oddball" because she is one of the few women who own and run factories. "Initially, I think being a woman in manufacturing was an advantage. There was a certain curiosity factor. I don't think I've ever been discriminated against, except for that one man on the phone in the beginning. The banks have never been a problem. They can see that we run a good shop. We keep good records for them to see. We keep the banks well informed. No banker has ever asked me to get a co-signer on a loan. I think the banks are getting smarter about women. We're being recognized as good business managers."

She has some theories about why women succeed in business. For one thing they are less inclined to take out a big salary. For another, "they're less inclined to drive expensive cars. They aren't pushed to display their success as much as men feel they are. Women can learn more easily, because people don't seem to mind when they show they don't know much about business. We can ask more questions."

Like many entrepreneurs she's developed strong views about the role of government in business. "I wish governments would do more to encourage profit-sharing with employees, to encourage productivity. We better, by gosh, do something about productivity, or we'll be in the soup! Governments should encourage people to get into business. Those of us who are in business don't want the government's money. They should spend it on education. They should help empty nesters who have outdated skills."

For Barbara Caldwell, being a money maker means more than making money. "Small business is the way to go. It's really exciting, a real adventure. I get a little evangelical. It's just great to have the opportunity to grow people, to develop the people we have. What in life can be more rewarding? For me that's where it's at – people development." She cites with pleasure the example of some immigrants from Vietnam whom she recently hired. "They started at the bottom. Now, they've become sewing-machine operators, and they'll go higher in the company."

Barbara Caldwell says she could probably make more money working for someone else. But that's not the point. "I'm certainly not rich from this. But the more people who get out there and try things, the more business is made to work, the better it'll be for our young people."

Caldwell's vision extends beyond the confines of her current enterprise, enabling her to anticipate changes in the marketplace so she can meet the challenges of foreign competition and changing customer needs. She makes Cleanwear today. She might make sporting wear tomorrow. And the day after that, who knows?

Part 4: Whizzes

Every successful money maker in this book is a whiz at something, because every one of them is doing or producing something new or making something old differently. They might have developed their own market niche with a product or service that was never available before. They might have discovered a way of providing a widely available product or service at a higher quality or a lower price. Or perhaps they succeeded by adding an original twist, a new style, an unusual marketing concept, or a different, more attractive design to something already on the market.

However, from all the whizzes in this book, we have selected some for being special, not because they are making any more money or are more successful, but because their products or services are notably different. Some of these money makers wave the Canadian flag in outer space. Others print paycheques for tens of thousands of Canadian workers. Another wrote the Canadian bible on payroll law. Some provide systems ensuring that we get responsible medical care. And one has dedicated himself to providing many of us with good food and good cheer. It's an entrepreneurial melange of music, pasta, microchips, balance sheets, and robot arms. Yet all are the products of extraordinarily original minds.

Many of these whizzes engage in activities usually labelled as high-technology, yet not one comes from Silicon Valley North, the Ottawa suburb where the Mitels, Systemhouses, and Bell Northern researchers reside. One of them – SPAR Aerospace – is in Toronto's so-called Silicon Suburbs. Two others – BDM and Develcon – are found on Canada's Silicon Flats, in the area around Saskatoon.

We make special mention of high-technology because it tends to isolate an economic activity from the mainstream of Canada's

154

business life. We suppose electrically driven inventions were also isolated when they were injected into the steam age. Our high-technology whizzes are taking computer microchips and injecting them into the mainstream of Canadian life today. High-technology is no longer a separate industry relegated to small regions of the country. Instead, it is a synonym for change, for doing old things differently and usually better. So BDM, Develcon, Comcheq, Linear, and even SPAR are not high-technology companies in the way they have been described in the past. They are companies run by whizzes who are changing not only the character of our industrial society, but the style and quality of life itself.

KEN ORD
Graf Bobby's, Gran Festa, and Others

Money making and food have been part of Ken Ord's life for fifty years. He started washing dishes in a restaurant in his native Britain when he was fifteen years old. He came to Canada in 1957 to work for Versa Food, the giant catering and institutional food service. In 1970, at age fifty, after he'd risen to the position of vice-president of operations, he left Versa to become an entrepreneur. That year he opened his first restaurant, the ninety-seat Graf Bobby's on Wellington Street, across from the O'Keefe Centre in Toronto. He invested his savings, borrowed money from the bank, and the risks he took quickly paid off. Soon Ord expanded into the basement of Graf Bobby's, where he opened Vines, now a popular Toronto wine bar. A couple of blocks south, beside the old St. Lawrence Market, he established the original Fish Market restaurant in a vacant turn-of-the-century warehouse. Fresh seafood was readily available from vendors' stalls across the road. The concept attracted investors who backed Ord in expanding with more Fish Market restaurants in Ottawa, Windsor, and Brampton, Ontario. He wasn't through, however. Across from the first Toronto Fish Market, he rented space in the basement of the St. Lawrence Market and opened the Market Grill, a Chicago-style chophouse that got its fresh vegetables and garnishes upstairs.

Dreams of restaurant ownership must be the most commonly

recurrent money-making fantasy of the human species. Surely, almost every structure with some semblance of a roof and four walls, from Sooke, B.C., to St. John's, Newfoundland, has been scrutinized by aspiring restaurateurs with visions of bustling crowds of hungry, thirsty patrons, begging for that last table, even if it is beside the kitchen door!

Big dollars can be made serving every imaginable type of cuisine. There are many success stories, Ken Ord's included, but many more restaurant failures. About 10,000 Canadians invest their savings in new restaurants every year. This leads to the opening of 2,000-3,000 establishments annually. Of those, 80 per cent will fail. It takes determination and forethought to become a money maker in the food and beverage trade. Knowing the odds and the market is essential.

As Ord is quick to point out (he is now a consultant), "There is no point to opening just another restaurant. You have to have a new idea, something that will add to the local scene, something we haven't got. There are restaurants that have opened only as restaurants, with no raison d'être. There are lots of seafood restaurants, Italian restaurants, Chinese restaurants. You must be different in some way. The concept is important.'

"A number of clients have approached me with ideas to open restaurants, and I've told them their idea wasn't new enough to make it pay off. It's hard to say how you know if a restaurant will work. I've been in this business a long, long time. You get a feel for it. Sometimes, it'll work because a new neighbourhood has opened up, like the Beaches in Toronto. That's where neighbourhood places work, not destination places like you find downtown. Market research is important. You've got to know who will come, what they'll spend, what they want. The menu must be good. If your food isn't good, you'll fail. You can only fool people for a short time."

The Canadian Restaurant Association (CRA) estimates that there are 52,000 restaurants of every description in Canada. That includes hamburger stands, taverns, fast-food kiosks in shopping malls, hotel dining rooms, factory cafeterias, and upscale cabarets and dining establishments. Nearly a quarter of all restaurants are chains and most of them are franchises.

In 1984, Canadian restaurants sold a staggering $16.8 billion in food and drink. This CRA chart might be helpful for those hoping to earn a small piece of those industry earnings:

Percentage of national food and beverage sales by restaurant category

Licensed, full-service restaurants	28.0%
Unlicensed, full-service restaurants	18.6%
Institutional, including military, hospitals, airlines, prisons, factories	17.1%
Take-out food	7.8%
Taverns	4.8%
Caterers	4.8%
Food service in hotels, motels, and campgrounds	14.1%
Vending machine sales	1.1%
Department store cafeterias	1.6%
Other retail establishments, milk stores, grocery stores	1.5%
Drive-ins, motor parks	.6%

The CRA projects that the dollar volume of food sales will grow by 6.4 per cent in 1985, and roughly 6 per cent in 1986. Some of that will come from an average 4 per cent increase in menu prices, the rest from increased restaurant sales. In 1984, the average Canadian spent 33 per cent of the food dollar in restaurants (adding up to about $11.50 per week) and the remaining 67 per cent on food prepared and eaten at home. The trend toward eating more in restaurants has flattened after a dramatic surge over the past twenty years. In 1964, only 16 per cent of the food dollar was spent in restaurants, but the increase to 33 per cent stopped in 1979, and the CRA sees no evidence of that share changing in the near future. That means new dining establishments must be competitive enough to attract customers from existing businesses. During the 1982-83 recession, people did not eat less, nor did they measurably change the proportion of food eaten in restaurants. They did, however, change the nature of the food consumed to save money. For the home, they bought generic, no-name brands and cheaper cuts of meat; in restaurants, they ate hamburgers more often and steaks less often.

Ken Ord is one entrepreneur who understood the market and made it work for him. In 1980, ten years after he set out on his own, he had an almost perfect track record in creating and opening interesting and successful restaurants. That year, when he turned sixty, Ken sold everything. He hoped to enjoy his wealth in semi-retirement. But people kept calling him for advice and he became one of the country's leading restaurant consultants.

Then, in 1984 he saw an opportunity he couldn't resist. "I saw it in Italy. There was nothing like it in North America. It's the kind of place where people can have parties and have a ball. I had to try it!"

Gran Festa is the name of the new restaurant. Like the Fish Market it is in a converted warehouse, this time across the road from the new Toronto Convention Centre. It is immediately next door to the Whaler's Wharf, a long-established and popular seafood spot, but Ken Ord knows his business, and a competitor next door didn't seem to phase him. He knew he had a good idea.

You can't choose what you'll eat at Gran Festa. Ord offers one nine-course fixed meal of Italian food for $12.95. "Italian food is in. A lot of people don't like to make choices, though. They like their host to say, 'relax, I'll bring you something you'll like.' " The menu features a ten-item selection of antipasto, a broth of chicken and angolotti noodles stuffed with cheese, hand-made guitar string pasta covered with tomato and cheese sauce, roast lamb and potatoes, salad, lemon ice sherbet, and figs.

While people eat, three musicians walk among the tables – an accordionist, a violinist, and a saxophonist – to get the fun going. "They play everything from 'When the Saints Come Marching In' to 'O Solé Mio!' Everybody starts singing and clapping. It's become a very popular spot with groups. We get lots of office parties, birthdays, service clubs, curling groups. And there are lots of people who just come as a couple, and then return a few weeks later with a group of friends."

Is Gran Festa the last word in restaurants? Has every idea been exploited? "Not at all," Ord states emphatically. "There are still lots of good ideas around. You have to be sensitive to what works and what doesn't."

Ord has sage advice for anyone contemplating a foray into the food-service business. "It's show business. You have to want to do it." And you've got to have adequate financing. "If your food is good, but you don't have the financing, you'll fail. Most people don't have much money left when they open the door. The average restaurant won't return any money for a year. If you're lucky, you might start seeing some money after six months. The more cash you've got, the better chances you have. Too much debt means too much interest paid, and that's a drain." He points out that because the restaurant business is so risky the banks are very reluctant to lend money. "You can give them everything, all your chattels, everything you own, and they'll still often say no."

Ord figures that a good restaurant costs an average of $3,000-$4,000 per seat to open. "A 100-seat restaurant can cost $350,000 to $400,000. From there, the more seats you have, the cheaper it becomes, because you save costs when you're working with a larger place. Apart from the chains, the true entrepreneur starts by himself, either because he is known in the field, or because he has risked a lot of his own money. These are the people who can really change the scene, they can really bring something new to the restaurant scene."

If they do everything right they may beat the averages and have a genuine money-making success. The average net income for a restaurant is 11.4 per cent of gross sales before interest payments and equipment depreciation. So, if you go in with a load of bank debt, your profit margin can be very quickly gobbled up. The average Canadian restaurant earns $500 net income per seat per year. The average owner-operator works between seventy and ninety hours a week to earn that.

Ord stresses the vital importance of finding the best staff and managing them well. "The good waiters know the good restaurants, and they'll come to you if you've got a good reputation and a good concept. Waiters are entrepreneurs. They know how to treat customers. They know how to turn over tables. A good waiter can make at least $100 a night. They hustle. They know how to squeeze in another group of customers, because there's no money to be made if a group of people sit around and just drink a few liqueurs.

"This is an insecure business. The bosses are often insecure. And when they're insecure, it makes the staff uncomfortable, and they leave. The staff wants to be directed properly and taught what to do, and then left alone to do their jobs. They don't want to have you on top of them all the time, but then they shouldn't be ignored either."

Ken Ord's success is proof that statistics only offer the broadest outline of this difficult business. They'll tell you that you're probably headed straight for bankruptcy if you're spending 99 per cent of your sales on advertising, or that you ought to think carefully about hiring a band and putting on a full staff for Sunday nights, statistically, the slowest night of the week. There is no such thing as an average restaurant. Every establishment bears the imprints of its creator. You're wise, though, to consider some professional advice from a restaurant consultant such as Ord before you sit down at the canvas to become the Picasso of the restaurant trade. In this business, like most, even the most talented creator can use the discipline of experience.

WILLIAM LOEWEN
Comcheq Services

Anyone who has ever run a company or worked in accounts payable knows that one of the most bothersome tasks is handling the payroll. Making sure employees are paid on time, and in the proper amount, is a fundamental responsibility for any organization. If the function is not performed without error, the ramifications can be serious. At best, late paycheques cripple morale. Paycheques that bounce drive employees away.

In 1968, money maker William Loewen was thirty-eight years old and leading the quiet life of a chartered accountant working for a medium-sized firm in Winnipeg. His job was secure and the future looked comfortable. Today Loewen is the president of Comcheq Services Ltd., a company that has parlayed his payroll expertise into a successful enterprise and made Winnipeg the payroll-processing capital of Canada.

"I knew all the steps for processing payroll well," he recalls, "but there was no effective and complete system available in business. Most companies left a float of funds in a payroll account at a bank, for which they received no interest. An in-house department was kept busy issuing cheques and balancing the books. I believed that businesses could benefit from the availability of an outside service that would take over both of these functions. It was the completeness and uniformity of the system I had in mind that made it marketable." The service he had in mind would collect payroll funds from clients, bank them together in a single account large enough to earn interest and affect some of the cost of processing cheques, complete individual cheque forms for distribution to all employees, and balance each company's payroll account. It was a system that put the nuisance of both processing cheques and administering the bank account outside a company.

To test the idea he simply wrote to fifty firms and asked if they would be interested. In a one-page letter he outlined the benefits of his service and explained his intention to pool all the payroll funds into one interest-earning account. He pointed out that volume-buying of cheque forms and other supplies would translate into lower costs for individual companies. He also promised to produce T4 slips and gave them an idea of the fee structure for the service. In a word, he offered them more service for less money. Fifteen companies said yes.

Loewen decided he had to spend some time with a computer. "I spent four months writing programs so that a computer could run the system. Hence the name Comcheq. I wasn't a computer programmer but I got some help. Today we still function with the same basic method, although obviously we have fine-tuned it." By happy coincidence, in 1968 the right computer technology had just become available to support his idea. With the advent of the IBM 360 series and the computer language COBOL, there existed the resources necessary to make the system streamlined. On-line time could simply be bought through the computer utilities. Five years earlier, he likely would have been stymied.

Now he turned to his other main challenge. With fifteen positive reactions to fifty mailings the idea seemed more than viable. But prospective clients needed to know that their funds would be absolutely secure. So Loewen allied himself with the Fidelity Trust Company of Winnipeg. Being a local firm, they were very approachable. Since the idea was Loewen's they met his $5,000 investment with a $10,000 investment of their own and a fifty-fifty partnership began. But Comcheq's role would be more limited than Loewen had originally envisioned. He would prepare cheques drawn on a Fidelity Trust account and signed by a trust company signator. He would oversee the process, but Fidelity would guard the funds. It was a workable solution for getting started.

With security taken care of, Loewen had to convert "we're interested" responses into "count us in." He vividly remembers counting the number of cars in downtown Winnipeg company parking lots. Where there seemed to be enough employees, he made a cold call. The normally introspective accountant found this no easy task.

"It was really tough to get companies to come with us at first," admits Loewen. "We started in June, 1968, and did not get the first account until December 1. By the end of the year we had three accounts." He now was faced with the crossroads decision of his career: should he commit to Comcheq full time and quit his "safe" job? Three accounts hardly provided security for a chartered accountant who was also the father of five children. But Loewen took the plunge and went to work at his desk in a corner of the Fidelity Trust office.

It was April of the following year before Comcheq landed its fourth account. But in June two more companies signed up and the small trickle became a full-sized stream and, eventually, a roaring river. Today 2,500 companies employ Comcheq's services across Canada and the firm handles over 3,500 different payrolls.

Soon he was able to open his own office, but he was still walking over to Fidelity Trust to have the cheques signed. This situation grew increasingly unworkable as the company expanded to other cities, some of which didn't have Fidelity branches. "Processing payrolls requires a lot of direct client contact and fast turnaround. You just have to be where your clients are." For some time Comcheq continued trying to arrange banking through local trust companies, but after four years of growth it became apparent that the company should indeed be all that Loewen originally had imagined – it must run its own payroll account.

Creating its own trust account permitted Comcheq to build up an asset that today stands at $39 million. It also permitted the company to expand wherever it wanted. Today the firm has offices in Montreal, Toronto, Winnipeg, Calgary, Edmonton, Vancouver, Halifax, Quebec City, Ottawa, London, and Regina and employs a total of 180 people.

Needless to say, handling a firm's payroll account in trust demands very conservative investment policies. In the 1985 fiscal year, for example, Comcheq will process payroll funds totalling about $2 billion. "We have a rigid policy overseen by our bankers and auditors, and we report to our clients annually. We also keep our account at a chartered bank," says Loewen. The company's growth is testimony to prudent management and to the value of providing a quality, reasonably priced service.

"In essence our system takes the work off the client's hands for about ten cents more per cheque than if the client were dealing direct with a bank. We charge about seventy-five cents per cheque and I estimate that a client would pay sixty to sixty-five cents alone for paper and bank charges. This doesn't take into account staff time to run the department. We simply use the revenue generated from the interest in the trust account to reduce the cost of services to the client. And we do all the work."

When asked to pinpoint some of the problems he has had to deal with Loewen is quick to finger marketing. "You know, we are an accounting and service-oriented business," remarks Loewen. "We weren't trained to sell, so we had to learn how, and it wasn't easy. We now have a full-time person doing the job and it's going very well." Comcheq is also helped by the fact that client referrals have become an important source of new business. And the company has now been around long enough so that when executives who are used to the Comcheq system move to other companies, they invariably take it with them.

Competition from the chartered banks was swift, within six months of Comcheq's initiation. Loewen was not surprised by the competition and says it has had a positive effect. It awakened potential customers to the need for such a service. "The bank's branch network means they can pick up a lot of business, but over the last three or four years we think we're gaining on them." Quality of service is what makes the difference to a client.

But changes are coming to the payroll-processing industry. The advent of the micro-computer has improved the collection of information from Comcheq's clients. And on the payment side, there is a clear trend toward the direct deposit of a paycheque in an employee's bank account. With its eye on providing more service and maintaining a competitive edge, Comcheq is moving into serving individual employees by developing a system that will permit them to pay bills by phone using their telephone at home or at work. By dialing the proper number, a digitalized (electronic) voice will prompt a customer to enter the financial information by using the numbered dial tones. A pilot program using 100 households is already under way in Winnipeg. It could mean the end of the monthly household ritual of stuffing cheques in envelopes and mailing them.

Today, Bill Loewen and his family own about 60 per cent of Comcheq, which is privately held. Employees also own a portion of the shares. He still works hard, travelling often to Comcheq's offices across Canada, but he also has time to relax. He and his wife enjoy the rich cultural tradition of Winnipeg and are frequent visitors to the symphony and ballet. He's an avid gardener and they both like to travel for pleasure – when business permits. Occasionally he can mix the two.

"We just had the year-end meeting of Comcheq in London, England, and we've been able to use venues such as Paris, Bermuda, and on the S.S. *Norway* in the past. We also use a variety of resorts across Canada. But it's great for our employees to be able to combine a vacation with their work. And back home in Winnipeg, we are all excited about the purchase of a new head-office building. It's a beautiful three-storey structure built in 1907. It also happens to be right across the street from where I first started out with nothing but a desk in the corner and a key-punch machine. How's that for coming full circle?"

NIGEL HILL AND GEORGE SPARK
Develcon

It started with the story of a travelling salesman and a computer "whiz kid." In 1973, Nigel Hill, an expatriate Briton who'd immigrated to Canada in the sixties, was selling electronic parts in western Canada for Allan Crawford Associates of Vancouver. One of the regular stops on his sales circuit was the office of Professor George Spark of the Faculty of Electrical Engineering at the University of Saskatchewan. Spark was what is known as a tinkerer. He's happiest at a bench littered with capacitors and transformers and micro-circuits, trying to solder them all together into some dazzling invention.

By the early 1970s, many universities had a number of mainframe computers with roomy data banks. But Spark wanted the

164

computers in his faculty to be able to share their knowledge with computers in other faculties, some of which were housed in buildings several miles away. Neither Nigel Hill nor any other electronics supplier had cost-effective equipment available that would make this possible. So Spark went to work at his electronics workbench at home.

He hand-built two short-haul modems, devices that allow computers to transmit data by telephone lines over distances of up to thirty-five kilometres. Spark's modems did it for one-third the cost and four times the speed of the costly devices offered by other companies. The University of Saskatchewan bought the prototypes from Spark immediately and this enthusiasm led Spark to ask salesman Hill whether more of his modems could be sold elsewhere. Hill contacted a number of the mainframe computer users he'd dealt with over the years and found that there was vast potential for such a product. Both men had saved what they thought would be enough money to live on and start their company, so they quit their jobs. Their self-confidence had been bolstered by the University of Saskatchewan's quick acceptance of the prototypes and the positive response Hill received in his survey of prospective customers.

Spark built the modems in his garage and Hill set out to sell them. This simple corporate arrangement was reflected in the name they chose for their company – Develcon – a contraction for Develop and Construct.

At first, everything seemed rosy. Hill sold a few modems and they took on two employees to help them. But neither man will forget that payday in 1974 when they didn't have a penny left in their bank account. They had to get cash advances on their personal VISA cards to pay their staff. It could have become the kind of bad habit that corporate disasters are made of, because Hill and Spark had to resort to such desperate tactics a number of times that first difficult year. They burned up their personal savings and juggled payables and receivables until they had enough business to warrant expansion. But the banks wouldn't lend them the money. However, they were able to entice the Federal Business Development Bank to purchase a minority interest in Develcon.

In 1975, with the help of the FBDB investment, they were able to move into their own business premises, a 500-square-foot space in the corner of an industrial mall on the east side of Saskatoon. The University of Saskatchewan allowed them to use their computers for product testing, and the university's support added credibility to their marketing program.

By 1980, new partners, such as Doug Freestone, who'd worked with Spark at the university, and Mike Peacock, an accountant who lived in England and who'd known Hill since boyhood, added additional cash to Develcon's equity pool. Freestone became vice-president of research and development, and Peacock emigrated from Britain to become the vice-president of finance. A fifth partner, an American named David Kane, joined the group and established a subsidiary in Philadelphia, Develcon Electronics Incorporated. Kane and Hill launched a North American marketing drive, while Spark and Freestone developed products.

Develcon's "Dataswitch" was hailed as a breakthrough in intelligent data switching in 1978, and a more recent product, "Develnet," made it possible for large companies to link together as many as 16,000 computers, terminals, and printers into one coherent network. They rapidly attracted clients from the *Fortune* 500 list of largest companies in the world. The National Aeronautics and Space Administration uses Develcon products to link together all of its sophisticated computer equipment at the John F. Kennedy Space Centre. The U.S. Senate employs Develcon communications gear, as do the Toronto Stock Exchange, most of the telephone companies in Canada, the federal Ministry of Communications, General Electric, Hughes Aircraft division of General Motors, and even Hewlett-Packard, a giant computer company itself.

Eight per cent of Develcon's substantial revenues are invested in research every year. The federal government's Enterprise Development Program has made grants available for the development of specific products, such as the Dataswitch. But the Federal Business Development Bank is now out of the picture. Spark, Hill, and company bought back the FBDB's holding in 1982. That same year, Develcon went public with its first share offering on the Toronto Stock Exchange, raising $4.8 million. A further $17 million in equity capital was raised in a second share issue in January, 1984.

George Spark has stepped back from the company's day-to-day

operations to devote his time to electronics research. Nigel Hill has assumed the presidency. Develcon still maintains a close relationship with the University of Saskatchewan, which continues to help the firm with product development and supplies the company with fresh talent from its pool of graduates every year.

There are several hundred thousand businesses in Canada. In 1984, fewer than ten years after its founding, the company had revenues of $20.3 million and could well do $25 million in 1985. Develcon has no debt and a cash reserve of $7 million in the bank, plenty to meet the payroll of its 320 employees. In 1984 Develcon was the sixteenth fastest growing company in the country. It all started when a travelling salesman met an electronic whiz.

DENNIS COVILL
Nautical Electronics Laboratories

A few miles from Nova Scotia's picturesque Peggy's Cove is Hackett's Cove, noted for high-technology rather than tourism. It is the home of Nautical Electronics Laboratories Ltd., world-renowned for its expertise in solid-state marine and aeronautical beacons and solid-state radio transmitters. Nautel, as the company is known, has a payroll of 100 people and is the largest employer in the area.

In 1969 Nautel's founder and current chairman, Dennis Covill, was forty-five years old, "too old it seemed to be launching a new venture." He had a good job as chief engineer at a Nova Scotia branch plant of an English engineering firm, EMI-Cossor, which made military transmitters. But that year he and partner Pat Tiani decided to create a customized research and development company. Head office was the basement of Covill's home in Hackett's Cove; there were then no plans of getting into manufacturing.

But before long, the fledgling company came across an opportunity to bid on a tender put out by Canada's Department of Transport. It called for bids on the construction of aeronautical radio transmitters in solid-state form (without tubes). No such product then existed and many larger companies, such as Phillips, called it an impossibility. But the founders of Nautel were convinced they could develop the new beacon. "Rather than saying it couldn't be done," says Covill, "we tendered a bid which, in effect, gave the Department of Transport what it asked for." After a long process, during which the unknown company had to satisfy delivery questions posed by the Treasury Board, approval finally came through for Nautel.

Covill says the company's major problem in the early stages was simply a lack of money. It had to provide a bank guarantee to the federal government for the original contract and would soon discover the pitfalls of doing business internationally. "Whereas domestically bills are usually paid in thirty days, some foreign countries took four or five months. The banks helped, but it was never easy. Eventually we learned to take precautions such as arranging export insurance, requiring letters of credit, and shipping overseas in batches that were progress billed." But in early 1969 problems with foreign customers were still a few months in the future. Nautel still had to pass its first test. To do so it persuaded three other engineers to leave EMI. These were John Pinks, George Close, and David Grace. Among them the newcomers managed to raise about $35,000 to contribute to equity.

That first year Nautel built a plant and developed a successful prototype that was delivered on time, within budget and at a profit. Hackett's Cove provided a location close to Halifax and a pool of labour particularly well suited to the painstaking tasks of assembling high-tech transmitters. Many of the local people are former fishermen, skilled at using their hands. Shortly after delivery of the first order, the Department of Transport ordered thirty more.

The solid-state beacon is more reliable than the beacons it replaced and uses considerably less power. These factors made it attractive to many countries around the world. The firm's first attempt at expansion was into the United States, but the Americans were reluctant to import a high-tech product. "They generally see themselves as the high-tech nation and prefer to do things themselves," says Covill. "So, again in 1969, we set up a subsidiary in Bangor, Maine, which continues to meet our demand there. We also avoided paying duty. And to the Americans, we're American." Nautel's two main American customers were the U.S. Coast Guard and the Federal Aeronautics Association. Sales have continued to grow and the company now has thirty employees in the States.

In 1970, a worldwide marketing push began in earnest. As a result Nautel now has commissioned agents working for it around the world, and in the U.K. a firm was licensed to market the new product.

The beacons today are designed for both aeronautical and marine navigation and provide a signal that planes or ships can use to determine if they are on the correct course. Aircraft, for example, have direction finders tuned to the beacon's frequency. When the direction finder picks up the call sign of the beacon it enables the crew to pinpoint where the aircraft is in relation to it.

Back in Hackett's Cove, Nautel expanded its facilities and continued with its research and development (by the end of the 1970s its annual R & D budget had nearly reached the half-million-dollar mark), all the while manufacturing the new beacons in a variety of sizes with price tags from $4,000 to $50,000 U.S. Then, in the early 1980s, it stumbled across a new opportunity. "Having no tubes, our beacons lasted longer and required little maintenance, desirable attributes since many of them were in remote areas. We thought, why not apply the same principles to the field of A.M. broadcasting? We knew we could make radio transmitters that were super efficient and consumed far less electricity." In fact, Covill surmised, station owners could cut their power transmission costs by half.

In 1982, the world's first solid-state ten-kilowatt A.M. transmitter went into operation in Antigonish, Nova Scotia, immediately attracting worldwide attention. Shortly thereafter, Nautel landed a large contract to supply the small transmitters to New Zealand. Early in 1985 CBC Radio in Halifax came on the air with the world's first fifty-kilowatt transmitter. Nautel now has orders for $2 million worth of the king-size version.

Today Covill spends most of his time in charge of research and in training engineers. The rest of the original founding group looks after the marketing and manufacturing. David Grace, who took over the title of president from Covill seven years ago, oversees the marketing side. There is a full-time marketing manager for the broadcasting product line and Nautel has a professional marketing program in place that includes spending money on trade shows and advertising. Over the years the budget has had to be quadrupled to give the company a fighting chance in an extremely competitive field like broadcast technology.

Dennis Covill is proud of the fact that Nautel has never ended a year, since its incorporation in 1969, without a profit. And by the early 1980s, his company had close to 50 per cent of the free world market for its specialties, the rest divided among fifteen or sixteen competitors. As of this writing, the value of the original 4,050 shares had risen from $10 to over $450 a share. Equally impressive considering the country-wide recession of a few years ago, Nautel has never laid off anyone through lack of work.

Unlike most who venture into a new market, Nautel was fortunate in finding a federal government contract that helped it to develop its unique product and its solid-state expertise. But this would never have happened had the five original principals not displayed some courage in deciding to set up their own business and forgo the security of employment with a multinational company. Ownership of the company still resides in the founding partners, and in 1985 sales are expected to reach $8.9 million. Chairman Dennis Covill is unambiguous in giving his money-making recipe: "Be absolutely determined to succeed," he says.

DOUGLAS BARBER, WALTER PIECZONKA, AND ROBERT SIMPSON
Linear Technology

In November, 1973, Dr. Wally Pieczonka, Robert Simpson, and Dr. Douglas Barber were turning silicon into prototypes of electronic microchips in a Hamilton laboratory of the Canadian offices of the giant American multinational, Westinghouse. The name Westinghouse is best known for appliances, although the company's business interests include production of giant electrical generating stations, defence systems, and other large-scale engineered products. However, Pieczonka, Simpson, and Barber were developing a product smaller than the tip of your smallest finger. They managed to squeeze an audio amplifier, which works on the same principle of the amplifier in a home stereo, onto a tiny silicon chip measuring less than two millimetres square. It seemed to be a perfect device for use in hearing aids.

Westinghouse, having carved out its successful niches in other product lines, chose not to pursue this microchip development. Dr. Pieczonka remembers that the unit he worked in at Westinghouse had been "a money drain, a cash sink, and it didn't fit in Westinghouse's corporate strategy and product plans." But Pieczonka and his colleagues believed their tiny audio amplifier had merit, that the product could be marketed at a profit. They decided to start their own company, so they approached Westinghouse and found management there to be very supportive.

The establishment of a new company, however, would require a substantial investment, and Pieczonka, Barber, and Simpson were employees. Their salaries had been dedicated to financing family life – mortgages, car loans, kids' clothes. There just wasn't much opportunity to assemble the capital with which big businesses are made. The three men pooled their savings and whatever credit they could manage to come up with a total of $45,000. That was about the price of a small family house in 1973, but a piddling amount compared to the half billion dollars in business Westinghouse does in Canada every year. Undaunted, the trio contacted friends and business associates and found two investors willing to put up an additional $45,000. They polled fellow workers at Westinghouse who were interested in joining the new venture and found eight of them willing to invest a total of $10,000.

They now had $100,000 out of the $300,000 they and the accountants at Westinghouse figured was needed to open the new business. Westinghouse's support proved invaluable. The big company helped convince the Ontario Development Corporation – a government agency – of the export potential of the audio amplifier microchip, and it matched the investors' pool of capital with a $100,000 loan. The federal government was also approached and advanced a further $100,000 under the Industrial Research Assistance Program. The trio now had their money, but no company and no product. Product rights had to be negotiated with Westinghouse.

Westinghouse agreed to sell all product rights to the new company for $200,000 and agreed to accept payment over a period of four years. This allowed the new company – now named Linear Technology Inc. – to conserve its $300,000 cash pool for business development. Westinghouse added another plum, by allowing its offspring to operate from Westinghouse premises!

Pieczonka became president, Barber the vice-president and general manager, and Simpson, the vice-president of marketing and business development. They inherited twenty staff from Westinghouse. "The parting from Westinghouse was very amiable," says Pieczonka. "They take great pride in being the midwife. Our operation was at the point of turnaround at Westinghouse. We would have become profitable there as well. When we went out on our own, we were well positioned to take advantage of the market. Mind you, we were lucky. There was luck in the timing. And there were risks, but we diminished them with good planning and good management."

All but one of the major hearing-aid manufacturers are outside Canada. That meant Linear had to be export-oriented from the very beginning; the Canadian market alone wouldn't justify a production line making hundreds of thousands of audio amplifier microchips. Simpson headed up the marketing campaign, and he called on hearing-aid makers in the United States, Europe, and Japan. At first, the orders were small. The hearing-aid companies seemed to be testing Linear for reliability and quality. The first year's revenues were respectable, however, at $500,000.

Pieczonka found Japan to be the hardest market to break into. "They're very nationalistic. They'd rather buy from a Japanese company, even if it costs them more. They're loath to buy imports. We spent six years negotiating with the Japanese. But they will buy from you if you can show them that you have a clearly superior product. Breaking into foreign markets is tough. You've got to persevere, do a lot of work. Canadians are very well regarded overseas. In many ways, foreign companies are more willing to deal with us than the United States. It's what you sell that counts, though. Customer service, credibility, confidence in your product, thorough testing – that's all very important."

Linear Technology Inc. has recorded 30, 40, and even 50 per cent annual increases in sales. In 1984, the company balance sheet showed revenue of over $10 million. In 1982, the owners listed their shares on the Toronto Stock Exchange to help clear off debts and raise capital for expansion. It meant that no single shareholder would have majority control of the company, but that had never been the case. "Control by one individual or group could actually get in the way," explains Pieczonka. "The present ownership situation is something like a minority government. We have to look at issues from all angles, and it's worked very well for us."

Indeed it has. The company is now the world's largest maker of hearing-aid amplifiers, with 60 per cent of the Western market. Forty per cent of its sales are in the U.S., 35 per cent in Europe, and the remaining 25 per cent of sales come from Canada, Japan, South America, and the Middle East.

Linear now operates two factories in Burlington, Ontario. It left Westinghouse's premises late in 1974 and paid off its debt to Westinghouse in three years, a year ahead of schedule. Staff has multiplied by a factor of ten, to nearly 200. Linear now has sales and service centres in Virginia, Indiana, New Jersey, New York, and Ohio, and it has established a design and marketing relationship with Sanshin, a Japanese hearing-aid company.

Twenty per cent of company revenues are devoted to research and development. Dr. Pieczonka believes "You've always got to be scratching around. You've got to pick niches and slots in the marketplace. You've got to specialize. We can make microchips for computers, but that would be suicide, because so many companies in the world, much larger than us, have been doing it for years. The computer market is flat right now. But since we're specializing, we still see plenty of opportunities. We are custom microchip makers, and we believe the whole electronics area is going to custom or semi-custom chips. We're developing two new product lines. We think there are big opportunities in building devices for radio frequency communications. Wireless communications will be the next big trend."

Linear is also working with the 3M company in the U.S. on the development of hearing-implant systems to help people who are completely deaf. But it could be years before an effective system is discovered.

The money makers at Linear Technology say it would have been very difficult to start the company without government help and without the co-operation of Westinghouse. Yet the founders' international view, their expertise in leading-edge technologies, their ability to spot market opportunities, and the fact that they had their own money and futures on the line have combined to make Linear one of Canada's outstanding high-tech performers.

DALLAS HOWE
BDM

Dallas Howe likes to tell the story of his meeting with an executive from a large national drug store chain in Toronto. Howe's company was marketing a newly developed computer system for pharmacists. "Our first installation is in Fysh's Pharmacy in Moose Jaw, Saskatchewan," Howe told the Toronto mogul. The response was a bemused smirk and the suggestion that Howe come back when his product had proven itself.

"We design, engineer, and manufacture in Saskatchewan," says Howe. "But if we want to sell in Ontario, we sometimes have to send our stuff to our U.S. sales offices and ship it back to Canada. The Americans don't worry about the origin of a product. They know if it is good or not. An executive from a big American company didn't laugh at Moose Jaw. He flew up to the city, had a look at our product, and bought it." It is an all-too-familiar tale to Canada's money makers.

Dallas Howe is a farm boy. He grew up on his father's wheat farm outside of Regina, received a Master's degree in mathematics from the University of Saskatchewan, and spent a year working toward a doctorate in computer science at the University of Toronto. Then he got a job back at the University of Saskatchewan with a team working on research in biomedical engineering for a salary just over $8,000 a year.

Howe was in his mid-twenties and he found the work interesting, but he didn't see it in his future. When a half-section of land, 320 acres, came up for sale next door to his father's farm, he decided to buy it. It cost him about $100 an acre but with his modest university income and the money he would earn by growing wheat, he qualified for the mortgage. He worked at the university in Saskatoon during the week and farmed on weekends. Howe looked upon his farm – small by prairie standards – as a fall-back position.

In 1973 the mini-computer had just hit the market, providing the first affordable opportunity for hospitals to consider the computerization of their records. Since the university didn't have a computer department then, Howe and his colleagues working in biomedicine were asked by the government of Saskatchewan's Ministry of Health to design a computer system.

The computer design work went well, and the Saskatchewan government had the systems installed in the province's hospitals. Medical staff could put all patient records and drug and treatment information into an electronic filing system. There was no longer any need for mountains of unwieldy documents, which were difficult to retrieve and could easily get lost. The pushing of a few buttons on a computer terminal instantly provided a detailed summary of a patient's medical history.

The story of the Saskatchewan system found its way into medical publications around the world, and the attention resulted in a parade of experts from the U.S. and elsewhere visiting Saskatchewan to have a look. Many of them wanted to buy. Trouble was, there was nothing for sale. "Provinces can be so provincial," observes Howe. "They wanted their own system to serve Saskatchewan hospitals, and that was it. They had no mandate or interest to do otherwise. I pointed out to them that there was a great opportunity here, but they didn't see the benefits of exports or the commercial value of what we developed."

The subject was hotly debated, during lunch breaks and after-hours beers in 1973, among Howe and two of his colleagues, Blaine Homeland and Murray Pask. They thought up a company name, the first initials of each man's given name, Blaine, Dallas, and Murray – BDM. The initials remain, but only Dallas Howe persisted. Homeland directed his energies into academic work and is now the vice-president of the University of Saskatchewan, helping to make the university one of Canada's leading training centres for high-tech entrepreneurs. Murray Pask left the university to become a very successful grain grower in rural Saskatchewan.

Howe continued to work in biomedicine. Between his job and his grain farm, by 1974 he had saved $20,000. That year he used the money to start BDM Information Systems Ltd. It wasn't a lot to start a company, but Howe felt he could afford to lose it, because he could always go back to farming. He rented some office space in Saskatoon, hired a secretary, and started working the phones. What he was selling was his knowledge, the expertise he'd acquired doing basic research and development.

"Selling was easy, actually. We were among the first to put computers into hospitals, so customers came looking for us," Howe remembers. "A Boston company, Spear Medical Systems, was trying to develop the same kind of computer program, so they came to us. The Americans are good at searching out people who have something to offer. We were able to win a development contract with them worth $5,000 a month. It gave us cash flow and meant that our company could carry on."

Spear marketed BDM computer products in hospitals across North America. Then an even larger market developed when Spear was acquired by the multibillion-dollar medical supply conglomerate, Becton-Dickenson Ltd. But Becton-Dickenson didn't stay with the business. "Large corporations sometimes find they're in too many lines, so they sold Spear to Litton Systems. But Litton didn't want to keep Spear's marketing network for medical computers, so we were able to take it over."

In 1979, Howe opened his own sales and service centres in the U.S. and Canada. He believed clients ought to be able to reach BDM at any time to get rapid service. It was a good business notion, especially when clients are in a field such as medicine. Howe set up a twenty-four-hour toll-free line. "Toll-free lines weren't available in Canada at the time, so we spent a lot of money for a dedicated line from the U.S. border to Saskatoon. The 800 number gave us a major corporate image."

The development in the early 1980s of even smaller computers, the table-top micros, meant BDM could put its patient record systems into smaller facilities, such as neighbourhood pharmacies. BDM's retail pharmacy system sells for $20,000-$30,000 a store. It provides complete prescription management, automatically printing labels and patient receipts, providing patient profiles, prescription costs, inventory control, and third-party billing. Pharmacies in Saskatchewan that use the BDM system plug their local neighbourhood computers into the Ministry of Health computer in Regina every evening to bill the government drug plan directly. The pharmacy receives payment for its prescriptions instantly.

BDM does for computer systems what architects do for houses. It designs everything, and constantly supervises and monitors everything it installs. The components to build the systems are purchased like bricks and mortar from firms such as Texas Instruments, Control Data, and CADO/Contel Corporation.

Howe has now started a second computer company, Advanced Data Systems, to develop computer products for other disciplines. He retains 100 per cent ownership of BDM but employees of Advanced Data share ownership with Howe. Together, both firms employ sixty people. In addition to the expected assortment of computer professionals, five pharmacists are employed to ensure that the BDM product lines fill their discipline's requirements.

Rapid expansion poses some problems. Howe doesn't have any trouble finding people with the required technical training, but he does have a difficult time finding the right kinds of management people. "The government might put a lot of emphasis on training people for high-tech jobs. But they don't concentrate enough on training managers. What we often face is hiring experienced management people and teaching them the technical skills. Or hiring technical people, and hoping they can acquire management skills."

Howe has hired the odd temporary employee under government-sponsored employment programs. However, he proudly emphasizes that he has never accepted government money or grants to build his two companies. "The first three or four years, it was hand-to-mouth. Our contracts just covered our expenses. I suppose the farm gave us the confidence to keep going, because we knew it was always there. I was doing both for many years, running the company and farming. If I look back now, I wonder where I got the energy." His wife, Sandra, was certainly a big help. She works as financial controller of the company. And somehow they found time for their two children, now eleven and fourteen.

In considering the rapid rise of his companies, Howe returns to the importance of going to the United States. "It seems to me that Canadians come up with great ideas, and then sit around and talk about it, and dream up all kinds of reasons why it won't work. Then, of course, it doesn't. The Americans talk about it for a while, and then they invest in it and make it work. We've been dealing with Americans from the beginning. There's nothing to be intimidated about in the U.S. We're very comfortable doing business with them. Right now, we're working with Prudential, one of the largest insurers in the world. They want to get into more medical services, and they want our systems to help manage everything."

BDM began with three dreamers. But it took one particular whiz to turn the dream into reality. Howe's original partners must occasionally think wistfully of what might have been. In Saskatoon today, observers are convinced BDM means "Best in Data Management."

DIANA FERGUSON
Berwick Ferguson Payroll Canada

In the late 1960s Diana Ferguson was a struggling young Toronto singer who wrote her own material, occasionally landed a gig, and earned her living at jobs in accounting and payroll. She had quit school after grade thirteen to pursue her singing career; having worked as a bank clerk, the transition into accounting, then payroll, was a natural one. But her first love was still show business. "I took one final fling at twenty-five years of age and went to the U.K. to make my way in the world as an entertainer," she recalls, "but it didn't work. I returned to Canada, got married, and tried to start a family." When she discovered that, for medical reasons, she would be unlikely to have children, she decided to concentrate on a career in business.

She got another job in payroll and discovered that not a lot had changed. "I was so concerned by the lack of any comprehensive information source that I decided to research the subject myself and that simple decision led me to be considered as an expert by some companies. If I was indeed going to live up to my reputation, I needed to systematize my knowledge for quick reference."

"Most companies had an appalling lack of knowledge of payroll law and there is a myriad of ever-changing federal and provincial regulations affecting efficient payroll management. Neither did they seem to have a very thorough understanding of even simple matters like overtime or vacation pay. But where could they turn for guidance – for employee education or up-to-date information in understandable language, for legal advice?

178

There was no single source of expertise, though the need for one was mushrooming from coast to coast." This time she decided to do something about it. She would make herself into Canada's payroll expert.

She cleverly called the company Berwick Ferguson, a combination of her maiden and married names, because of its ring of establishment stability. Over the next two years, financed by her husband's earnings (he works for IBM), she wrote the basic manual that has formed the foundation of her money-making success. "I wrote the document around the needs of the companies. Everything is distilled into simple language," says Ferguson. "Section by section, I cover everything from taxable and non-taxable earnings to standard deductions, medical plans, and maternity leave. The peculiarities of each province are outlined with, of course, particular attention to Quebec where so many differences are encountered."

In 1977, with her three-ring binder of information clutched underneath her arm, she contacted several companies who told her that, yes, they would probably be able to use such a document. So Ferguson put together a simple pro forma statement, an estimate of the amount of money she would need to start a business and of her projected income. With this in hand, she visited her local bank manager, who obliged with $10,000 in start-up capital – provided her husband co-signed the note. "I really didn't mind the requirement because, after all, I had no track record and little collateral," Ferguson says. "Frankly, I think more women have to learn to seize opportunities, like men do. But the experience really provided me with the discipline of determining how much money I would need."

She got herself an auditor, incorporated a company, then went looking for clients. "Basically the money I borrowed was to pay printing costs. So I printed up the minimum number of manuals I felt I would need and kept the master copies for easy updating. I also had a sales brochure printed." Now she was ready to market her product. Initially she decided to charge $100 for her service.

She figured any company in Canada with over 100 employees was a likely candidate so she purchased a Dun & Bradstreet mailing list and sent out her brochure to about 8,000 businesses. She had conservatively based her projections on a positive response of 2.5 per cent or 200 acceptances; instead, she received 480. "I knew I had a business," she recalls.

Ferguson moved her operation out of her house into a small office and hired her first staff. Like many other entrepreneurs she found the transition from loner to manager not as easy as she had anticipated. "It took me a while to realize that employees do not look at the company through your eyes. No matter how capable your employees may be, the fact is it's not *their* company, so they usually do not put the same care and energy into everyday tasks as you do."

Ferguson soon solved the problem of motivating her employees. She installed a healthy profit-sharing plan. In 1984 her ten employees earned an 18 per cent bonus over normal annual salaries and in 1985 it will amount to almost 30 per cent. Although she has retained ownership of 85 per cent of the company (her husband owns no shares), the remainder is held by two employees. These moves to give employees a stake in the company's success help imbue the entire establishment with a spirit of teamwork. "In a company like ours, everyone does everything. We get the job done and we don't let a hierarchy stand in the way."

Berwick Ferguson Payroll Canada Limited now charges almost 5,000 companies an annual fee of $235 for the installation and maintenance of Canada's authoritative manual on payroll procedures. The manual is updated fourteen or fifteen times a year to take into account changes in provincial and federal regulations. As well, she offers participating companies a consultation service using her own staff experts. Her consultants have eighteen months of in-house, in-depth training. "We have about a 98 per cent rate of solving problems."

The frequent changes in tax law and new Revenue Canada or provincial regulations have prompted Berwick Ferguson Payroll to introduce payroll administration seminars at an introductory and an advanced level. In 1984, the company gave thirty-two seminars attended by an average of twenty-five people. A recent special seminar on the subject of terminating employees was attended by 720 people.

Diana Ferguson's desire to take the mystery out of payroll procedures prompted her to push for the creation of a non-profit group in 1979, known as the Canadian Payroll Association. It has

180

helped educate people about payroll procedures across the country and works for better interaction between employers and tax authorities. Ferguson sets a good example in this area, having developed a strong liaison with federal and provincial regulators. And she currently serves on an advisory council of the federal Department of Employment and Immigration. Berwick Ferguson's voluntary move to bilingualism has also contributed to very affable relations with contacts in Quebec.

Now Berwick Ferguson Payroll is expanding into the more complex United States market. Marketing is conducted from Toronto and an administrative office in New York City, with a research staff, masters the intricacies of fifty-one different taxing authorities. This means more manpower to keep the manual up to date. There is also more competition south of the border. "The U.S. will take time, but there is still nothing like our product down there," observes Ferguson. "We are prepared to put some money behind our effort and we think we will succeed. In fact, we gathered investors and have just recently spent several hundred thousand dollars on the acquisition of a U.S. prospect list."

In Canada the company is looking at providing specialized services to small businesses (with fewer than 100 employees). An owner/manager employers' manual for Ontario is due out this fall. If it succeeds, it will quickly be introduced to the other provinces.

Ferguson is fond of recalling the time during the recent recession that one company tried to eliminate the manual as a cost-cutting measure. "But when the employee responsible for payroll was offered the nominal annual salary increase of a few hundred dollars, she politely requested that her pay remain the same, but that the Berwick Ferguson Payroll manual be reinstated. In the end I believe she received both her raise and our service."

Berwick Ferguson Payroll's annual renewal rate for its services is at 92 per cent. Most firms that don't renew are usually those lost through takeovers, mergers, and bankruptcies. In the seven years since the company's first sale, its manual has become the bible of the payroll industry, and its expertise has made it the Canadian authority on payroll law and procedures. All that adds up to projected revenue of more than $1 million in 1985.

Eight years of hard work have left Diana Ferguson philosophical about her success. If anything, being a woman has made it easier. "When I'm negotiating a credit line with my bank manager over lunch, he often grants my request and he still picks up the cheque. Often, when I go to a conference I am one of the few women present. It's an easy matter to seek out the brighter people there and learn from their experiences."

Ferguson still works hard (averaging twelve to fourteen hours a day), but on weekends she and her husband journey to their cottage in Haliburton to swim and sail and get away from it all. In the winter they enjoy cross-country skiing. Their house is totally paid for, and the latest arrival in the family is a Porsche.

Ferguson has this advice for other entrepreneurs. "Hire to your weaknesses. Examine yourself, determine what you're not good at doing, and hire people who can fill the gaps." This money maker started out by becoming very good in a field where experts are few and then used that expertise to meet an almost universal administrative need. Like William Loewen of Comcheq, she saw a real need in the payroll area; lacking his formal training she taught herself to be a payroll whiz. Her success in Canada may or may not be duplicated in the U.S., but it is clear the simplicity of her product has found a warm corporate welcome.

WILLIAM JACKSON, LARRY CLARKE, AND ROLAND DODWELL
SPAR Aerospace

Astronauts might be the celebrated media stars of the space age, but the technology that makes their missions possible is the real champion. Canadian technology from Toronto's SPAR Aerospace has been part of every manned American space flight since Mercury first dabbled in the fringes of space more than two decades ago. Then, the SPAR contribution was considerably more modest than the multi-jointed manipulator called the Canadarm, which waves the flag for Canadian technological achievement every time a space shuttle goes into orbit. In the 1960s, NASA bought SPAR's so-called STEMs for the antennae on its manned spacecraft, including Mercury and Gemini, and the Apollo missions to the moon.

STEM, like NASA and SPAR, is an acronym. The STEM, or, Storable Tubular Extendable Member, was developed by SPAR when the company was the Special Products and Applied Research division of the De Havilland Aircraft Company. The STEM design is simple and brilliant. It works on the same principle as a carpenter's roll-up tape measure. As you extend a carpenter's tape, the metal curves slightly, which gives the tape rigidity and strength. The STEM takes the idea further. As the metal extends, it forms a hollow tube.

De Havilland didn't have much use for the STEM technology or the other products being developed by its SPAR division because De Havilland's primary business was and is building aircraft. In 1968, it decided to dispose of SPAR.

Instead of letting the company die, a small group of De Havilland employees, convinced that SPAR's technologies had a future, "mortgaged their lives and sacred honours" to make it an independent enterprise. The words belong to Christopher Trump, a long-time consultant at NASA and currently a SPAR vice-president. "They had very little money of their own, so they put new mortgages on their homes, borrowed what they could, and assembled $300,000."

Three men were central to this takeover of SPAR. William Jackson was the most senior of the trio. Jackson was Toronto's first flying weatherman in the 1930s and one of the first two dozen workers to join De Havilland of Canada in 1939. He was one of the first to test the all-wooden Mosquito bomber before it entered World War II. Christopher Trump describes him as an eternal optimist who blithely risked his life savings in SPAR. "It was the aviation business and we knew what we were getting into," Trump quotes Jackson as saying. He could always go back to flying if he lost everything on SPAR.

Jackson got to know the second of the founding partners when a young lawyer named Larry Clarke joined De Havilland as contracts manager in the early 1950s. Jackson and Clarke worked together on the building of Bomarc missile sites in northern Ontario and Quebec. The third man was Roland Dodwell, an accountant and investment expert who smoothed over many of the considerable financial difficulties they encountered starting their new company.

Although their initial $300,000 ante would seem a respectable sum by most entrepreneurial standards, SPAR came complete with research and production facilities and a staff of 250. They needed more cash, and that meant some door-knocking.

One of Larry Clarke's friends was Tim Beatty of the investment dealer Burns Brothers (now Burns Fry). He told them they'd need more up-front capital before they could raise any funds on the stock market. So Beatty and some associates pooled a further $100,000 and then helped the SPAR partners launch a public offering of shares. This gave them enough to pay $1.8 million for the firm and have some cash left in the bank to cover operating expenses.

Beatty was once asked why he'd risked his own money in a venture that had been of little interest to a company as large as De Havilland and whose future rested on a rather exotic combination of skilled people and futuristic inventions. "The person doing the asking," was Beatty's reply. "That's the only question in any investment of this sort." Clearly, Beatty found Jackson, Clarke, and Dodwell to be an impressive team.

In 1968, the newly independent SPAR had two unique products – the STEM, and an infrared sensing device that held promise as a detector of smouldering forest fires before they flared into raging blazes, and as a surveillance tool for navies. The young company also inherited a repair and overhaul shop for aircraft components and instruments. None of that was enough to generate the cash flow for SPAR's considerable payroll. The fastest way to bring in more money was to acquire another business. SPAR took over York Gears Ltd. of Toronto as a comfortable fit with SPAR's existing aircraft maintenance work, and it gave SPAR the additional clout needed to win a major contract with General Electric to supply accessory and power gears for aircraft engines. The acquisition almost drained what remained of SPAR's original cash – but it quickly brought in badly needed revenues.

That year – 1969 – the SPAR team put in eighty-hour weeks to prove to GE that they could deliver the gear products on schedule. Everyone knew a reputation for reliability would be invaluable to them. The deadline was met and GE was clearly impressed, as were other clients of the young company. In its first fiscal year, SPAR had gross revenues of $5 million and a profit of $40,000.

It was an auspicious beginning, but it wouldn't last without the aggressive development of new product lines. The STEM technology, developed in association with the federal government's National Research Council, had already proved itself in space. Now SPAR developed it into the Sparlite, which could be mounted on the roofs of emergency vehicles to raise a flashing warning light high in the air. The company's infrared expertise led to production of the Hot Spotter, used by firemen to detect fires between walls of buildings. Later, the infrared technology won SPAR large contracts with both the Canadian and U.S. navies, which wanted instruments to detect vessels at sea.

But what propelled SPAR to a $200-million-per-year corporation was its space technology. Although STEM made wonderful satellite and spacecraft antennae, there wasn't enough of a market. And there was no hope of competing with a giant like the $4-billion-a-year Hughes Aerospace, a major satellite builder. "It would have been an exercise in futility," says Trump. "So we decided to co-operate with them, to work with them. There was a lot of aerospace expertise under the bushel in Canada. The Alouette made Canada the third nation in the world to put a satellite in space, and it worked three times longer than its design life of three years!" When Canada began the Anik satellite program, Hughes in California was the prime contractor on the project. By working with Hughes, SPAR picked up expertise and experience, so that by 1979 the Canadian government made SPAR the prime contractor for the Anik 'D' series of satellites.

The Anik 'D' program was worth nearly $80 million, and it gave SPAR the credibility to bid on large international contracts. Brazil made the Canadian company the prime contractor for its $125 million domestic satellite communications system. SPAR's long-time partner, Hughes, gave SPAR a contract to provide subsystems for the Intelsat VI series satellites. RCA hired SPAR to provide systems for the G-STAR satellite.

According to Trump, "The Brazilian scene was fiercely competitive. Our major competitor there was Aerospatial, the French government company. To prevail in that market means you've come of age, that you have a high-quality product, the price is competitive, and that you can deliver on time, which is of course the essence of any business, but especially in advanced technology."

Because of the STEM antennae system and its satellite work, SPAR established close contacts throughout the U.S. aerospace community. When the Canadian government offered to assume a role in the U.S. space shuttle program, SPAR seemed a logical choice to do the work. Four Canadarms have to date been delivered to NASA at $100 million apiece. Trump sees it as only the beginning. "If you look at the way a space station might be put together, it is in effect a modular device. You'll need something, a crane-like device, the Canadarm, to put the modules together. You would see an extension of our remote manipulator system technology being used in the construction of a space station."

The Canadarm technology, in addition, has led to earthbound contracts for SPAR. Ontario Hydro asked the company to build remote manipulators to handle highly radioactive materials in its nuclear reactors. Other applications are possible in the burgeoning field of robotics.

These contracts are the result of an intricate development chain within SPAR. An extendable antenna leads to more sophisticated satellite work, which in turn leads to remote space shuttle arms that provide the know-how to build nuclear station equipment. That kind of evolution is only possible with a massive commitment of talent and resources. Today, one-third of SPAR's work force of 2,000 are engineers and scientists. Funds equal to a quarter of SPAR's annual budget are dedicated to research and development. Christopher Trump offers this advice for firms engaging in high-technology business: "The technology must be market driven, there must be a market for it. Don't take on too much and then fail to deliver. Emphasize quality and price. Specialize. Keep small. Define your markets."

Keep small? SPAR's gross sales in 1984 were $190 million. In the first three months of 1985 alone, the company rang up sales of $58 million, a 33 per cent increase in just one year. The idea of keeping small is expressed in the decentralized nature of the company's organization. SPAR is divided into a number of different operating divisions and laboratories. Each concentrates on particular specialties and product lines. Satellites are built in Ste. Anne-de-Bellevue, Quebec, Canadarms and remote manipulators in Weston, Ontario, infrared defence and detection systems in Kanata, Ontario, aircraft gears and transmissions in Toronto.

186

Antennae and other deployable structures for space and ground applications are made in Carpinteria, California, and communications systems in Santa Maria, California.

Trump says that "With teams of one hundred or two hundred, you keep an edge. You keep a sense of working on something that's 'ours.' And within a broadly designed charter, these divisions go to it. Define your market. Hone your technology. And at least for the moment, we see that as one way of avoiding the pitfalls that do occur in this business."

In fifteen years, SPAR has jumped from a relatively modest offshoot of De Havilland Aircraft to number 286 in the *Canadian Business Magazine* survey of Canada's 500 largest corporations. Return on the money from SPAR's founding partners and investors has hit an impressive 40.7 per cent. Assets have mushroomed to over $125 million. All of this means that SPAR is ideally positioned for a large share of the estimated $50-$75 billion that experts believe will be spent on commercial satellites by the year 2000. The company has the technology and the resources to play a major role in the construction of orbiting space stations. Its infrared sensing systems allow SPAR to bid on parts of the multi-billion-dollar space and ground-based defence systems being planned in Washington and Ottawa. And in addition to all of those opportunities, SPAR has budgeted a further $750,000 over the next three years to investigate artificial intelligence, which the company believes will have major applications in robotics, both in earth- and space-based industry.

SPAR's achievements have helped establish Canada as a player in high-technology's major leagues. By successfully competing in the marketplace it has provided a fruitful outlet for the nation's academic and government research communities. By establishing its own labs and manufacturing facilities, it has provided challenging opportunities for talented Canadians, who might otherwise have sought futures abroad. And by its outstanding success, SPAR has proved that entrepreneurialism and pure scientific research can be meshed for the benefit of all.

Part 5: Visionaries

Visionaries are sometimes idealists; often they seem impractical, even a bit eccentric, as they push and pull the marketplace far beyond its present bounds. By being at the progressive fringes of the market, they create its leading edge. Often, their visions fail to become reality. But when they succeed, they succeed magnificently – as some of the money makers in the following pages demonstrate. They are further proof that starting a trend is more effective than following one, though some of them must wait longer than they would like for others to follow the trends they attempt to set.

One of our visionaries plans to revolutionize the food-growing industry in North America, perhaps even the world. Another hopes he has solved the problem of what to do with used computers. Yet another is proving, contrary to popular wisdom, that fine wines can be made in Canada. And yet another, Frank Stronach of Magna International, has spent his life developing a business philosophy he believes can help solve the problems confronting modern society – a philosophy that has worked spectacularly for his corporation. And one was simply driving through a small southern Alberta town one day and the next was back to begin bottling "the purest water in Canada." Visionaries have seen things others haven't. They've followed the rainbow.

GEORGE MOORE
Hydrogrowers

George Moore finds one ritual of Canadian life distressing. The midnight border crossings of the Canada-bound salad convoys from the hothouse southern U.S. states might seem an immutable fact of our northern lives, but Moore sees no reason to remain resigned to the cycles of the seasons. He believes it is possible to grow fresh fruit and vegetables throughout our harsh winter. He has developed a system of year-round farming that could free us from our dependence on an estimated $3 billion in imported fresh produce a year. Moore is a revolutionary who finds no comfort in the knowledge that December's cucumbers are ripening in sunny California.

Money maker Moore describes himself offhandedly: "I am a round peg in a square hole. I studied natural science, history, and oceanography. I spent much of my life in the military, in security and intelligence systems for the Royal Canadian Air Force in the U.K. and Europe. I sank a schooner off Newfoundland while doing science studies. I crushed my spine. I've consulted for museums and science centres. I've been involved in historical reconstruction. And I don't really know how I got started on this food project. It was nothing but a stumbling process. I'm a generalist, a maker, not a poet."

By the summer of 1985, Moore had $8 million to invest. Just seven years earlier he and his partner, Philip Macdonald, started their company with just $8,500. "Philip was at our place one night, and we pounded on this mouldy kitchen table of ours, and we swore to build a business that would do a million a year over that table." In 1984 George Moore and Philip Macdonald did just that.

The Moore-Macdonald partnership created Tiercel Digital Limited, which specializes in the development of automated communications equipment. Moore won't be more specific about their clients or the exact nature of the work they do for them, because he says his clients expect confidentiality. Nevertheless, the firm generated enough cash to allow Moore, Macdonald, and a more recent business partner, Gerry McIntosh, to invest in research and development of Moore's brainchild, the hydrogrower.

The story really started in 1980, when the partners made a simple analysis of the imported food Canadians eat. The three entrepreneurs spotted a huge market opportunity: 92 per cent of the lettuce Canada eats is imported from the south; spinach tops, 96 per cent; cantaloupe, 95 per cent; broccoli, 89 per cent. Green, red, and rainbow peppers, cucumbers, and bokchoy come across our borders in similar quantities. They knew little about how they might pursue that market opportunity, but they immersed themselves in a lengthy process of education and experimentation until they developed an ideal winter growing system.

Their goal was to provide everything a plant needed to grow in a hostile, high-latitude environment. In other words, they wanted to harvest green vegetables throughout the Canadian winter. They chose to concentrate on broad-leafed vegetables, because they grow rapidly and seemed the most adaptable to the growing system they were beginning to evolve. From 1980 to 1985, they experimented with bell jars, greenhouses, light bulbs, plastics, insects, countless plant nutrients, and, of course, plants. They drew upon the expertise of university scientists and agricultural experts around the world.

On the surface, their growing system looks like an immense window, planted on the ground, as if it were the top of a 500-foot by 60-foot underground greenhouse, which it is, in a very general way. Their "cultivation chambers," as they call them, are constructed by excavating a trough six and a half feet deep, 500 feet long, and 60 feet wide. The trough is lined with moulded composite plastic walls and floor. The roof is made of a double layer of a translucent polymer called Tedlar, developed by the Dupont chemical company for the surface of solar-heating panels. Tedlar is unique because it screens out ultraviolet, yellow, and green light from the sun and permits only red and blue light to pass through – the only two elements of the spectrum that are essential to plant growth.

The cultivation chambers are completely sealed, and they contain no soil whatever. They are equipped with an air-supply system that is particularly rich in carbon dioxide, the breath of life for plants. A plumbing system feeds the chamber with a bath of natural ground water enriched with minerals and other nutrients. Since the chamber is in the ground, it remains warm – below the frost line the earth's temperature stays between 50 and 60 degrees Fahrenheit winter and summer. During cold nights, a low energy heat pump supplements this natural heat source. The entire growing environment is monitored by computers, which automatically adjust the air temperature, the carbon dioxide levels of the air, and the flow and mixture of nutrients. Moore and his associates are certain their farming system will work, because they have been growing small numbers of experimental crops during the five-year developmental process.

Plants begin their lives when the seed is inserted in trays lined with rock wool that is soaked in nutrients. The seeding is done by an automatic planting machine in a germination chamber – a smaller version of the chamber described above. When the first leaves sprout above the rock wool, the trays are attached to a very slow-moving track in the large cultivation chamber. The track speed is determined by the growing speed of the plants. For instance, a head of romaine lettuce might take twenty-five days to mature, so the track takes twenty-five days to move the plants from the chamber's entrance on a 500-foot journey to the exit at the far end, where they can be harvested and brought to market. This system ensures a daily harvest, year round. Every day, new trays of young plants enter the chamber, and every day, mature plants are harvested.

Human beings never enter the cultivation chamber, unless maintenance of the growing systems is required. Then, they must wear special protective apparel so that the growing system won't be contaminated by fungi or other diseases that could harm the plants. Since the cultivation chamber is sealed, nothing should get in, meaning no insecticides, fungicides, or other chemicals should need to be used. Outside, as a precaution, selected species of plants that are known to repel insects are planted around the chambers. If insects do get through the screens and other barriers, parasites that prey on the interlopers will be introduced. Should any first aid be required to save the plants, only organic chemicals will be used.

"Our first rule is prevention," says Moore. "Most plant diseases are borne by insects and people, so we'll keep them out. Fungi and diseases grow in a hot, humid atmosphere, so we'll keep the cultivation chambers cool and dry, with no free-standing water. We'll use Mother Nature in as many ways as we can to protect the plants. We refuse to carry on blindly with deleterious chemicals when it can't be proven that they're not harmful!"

The plants are harvested with their roots intact. "Once you cut the root off a plant," George comments, "the plant begins to die. We'll ship everything while it is still alive, with the root still embedded in a doggy bag of nutrients. I've had lettuce in my fridge that has stayed alive, and even produced new leaves, three weeks after I put it in there. Imagine going into a supermarket and being able to pick vegetables from the counter that are still growing! You can't get anything fresher than that. And you won't get any waste, because none of the outside leaves will have shrivelled up and gone brown. Imagine what that means to restaurant chains and food processors, who lose millions of dollars a year because they have to throw so much away. They'll be able to use every bit of the plants we provide!"

This food-growing system is enticing for other reasons. Farm workers won't be required to stoop all day when they're harvesting the crop. The system uses only one-tenth the amount of water needed to feed plants growing in open fields, because nothing soaks away and little evaporates. Growing times for vegetables can be speeded up considerably since optimum growing conditions can be created.

The cultivation chambers can be constructed almost anywhere because of their elegant design. Moore and his colleagues assemble the chambers with prefabricated modules, which can be snapped together until the 500-foot-long hydrogrower is complete. These ten-foot by thirty-foot modules will be moulded in an assembly plant, now under construction in Milton, Ontario. They will be shipped with all plumbing, heating, air, and nutrient supply systems installed. Because of their manageable size they can be shipped anywhere in the world.

Moore expects a 500-by-60-foot cultivation chamber to produce a minimum of 4 million heads of lettuce a year. Hence, a typical farm might consist of four of these chambers, for an annual harvest of at least 16 million mature plants. But he believes that further research and refinement of the computerized growing system might double the yield. That means that just twenty of these farms would satisfy the entire fresh lettuce needs of Canada – over 600 million heads a year!

A four-chamber farm is expected to cost about $20 million to construct, and George and his colleagues believe such a farm would pay for itself in just over four years, based on the low-yield scenario of 16 million mature plants harvested per year.

This visionary enterprise is still not a money maker, however. Hydrogrowers Corporation was incorporated on January 31, 1984, when Moore and partners felt the system was ready to go commercial. So far they have invested close to $500,000, most of it funds generated by Tiercel Digital. "Hydrogrowers inherited four years of research and conceptual work. It was obvious, though, that we needed a whole whack of capital. A German company offered full financial support, but we're Canadian. This is a Canadian solution. We were born here. We're going to do it here. If the spark can be ignited in Europe, 3,000 miles away, we believed it could be ignited in Canada."

Despite these patriotic sentiments, they knew it would be impossible to raise the required $3-$4 million from established sources. And they weren't going to sell the idea to some big company that could afford to market it. So they approached the investment dealers, Gardiner-Watson.

After meeting with Gardiner-Watson's corporate services division and talking to their senior people, Moore and company decided to go for the federal government's Scientific Research Tax Investment program. "We were lucky, because we qualified just before the program was folded up. Our plans for Hydrogrowers were very carefully scrutinized by a number of government experts, from Agriculture Canada, the National Research Council, and other agencies. They gave us the go ahead."

The final financing package involved a complicated formula that netted Hydrogrowers $2.7 million to work with. The rest of the money needed was raised by a small business development corporation, set up with Gardiner-Watson's help. They called it Avitas Corporation, which is *sativa* spelled backwards. *Sativa* is the Latin word for lettuce. "Investors in Avitas get 30 per cent of their money back from the provincial government, which makes it very worthwhile for them. Under the terms of the SBDC, it must have targeted investments, and in this case the investments are Hydrogrowers Corporation and Glaspod Systems Corporation." Glaspod is another new company formed to manufacture the composite pods or sections for the cultivation chambers.

In summary, Hydrogrowers got $500,000 from Moore and his partners, $2.7 million through research tax credits, and $2.5 million from the investors in the SBDC. Glaspod got another $2.5 million. The total of $8.2 million will establish a manufacturing facility for the cultivation chambers and a pilot farming project in Milton, Ontario. The Milton site was chosen because it has access to mineral-rich spring water from the Niagara escarpment.

The partners plan to have their Milton pilot project in production by November, 1985, and are already negotiating with a large restaurant chain to supply fresh lettuce daily. Once the pilot project proves itself, Hydrogrowers and Glaspod hope to provide year-round growing facilities to anybody who wants them.

"We've been approached by people from all over the world – Switzerland, Kuwait, Dubai, the U.S., Britain, and Germany. A large Canadian company, which I can't mention, is also interested," says Moore.

If Hydrogrowers' concept of year-round farming proves feasible on a commercial scale, then it will almost certainly cause major changes in the patterns of commerce and food production that have served us for so many years. The nation's fruit and vegetable terminals, necessary now to get produce to market as quickly as possible to maintain freshness, would become superfluous. Many of the truckers who now shuttle back and forth to California, Mexico, and Florida might lose their jobs, although some could probably fit into the new distribution networks that would be established to serve the year-round farms. Many American and Mexican growers would lose a large part of their Canadian business. Traditional farmers in Canada, who supply fresh produce in the late summer, might also lose market share. But the benefits of the hydrogrowing system could outweigh these concerns.

These leading-edge entrepreneurs are presenting us with the potential of a home-grown, chemical-free food supply, not subject to seasonal fluctuations in price and quality. We'd replace imports with made-in-Canada products and have a new technology to export abroad, all of which adds up to more jobs in Canada.

George Moore's vision includes handicapped people. His spinal injury many years back gave him a special appreciation for those with a disability, and Hydrogrowers Corporation actively seeks skilled individuals whose disability might impede their job prospects elsewhere. "Our only consideration when employing somebody is 'Can he do the job and is he willing to do the job?' We're all handicapped in one way or another. I know there are skilled people out there who know computers, or forestry, or farming, and those are the people we can use. We want people who want to do things, and it doesn't matter to us if other people think they're different in any way."

Moore is a money maker who believes in acting on his ideas. "I don't think concept and reality are two different things. It's always been essential to me to put theory into real practice. Think of the possibilities of this system. We're working with lettuce now. It can be used to grow tomatoes, peppers, green onions, spinach, broccoli, cucumbers, and melons. And we can do so much to help food plants grow. We believe we can grow strawberries to be the size of your fist! We think there are applications here for silviculture, and we plan to plant several thousand trees on our Milton property just to test out our theories.

"We have to do this. The southern United States has severe water supply problems, and they're getting worse. Supplying Canada with fresh food in the winter is not their priority. California is reducing tax support for farmers who export, so they'll have less incentive to grow for Canada. And I think we should be concerned about the chemicals they use to grow food, the systems they use to ripen fruit.

"I approach this task of providing fresh, pure food with glee!"

PAUL ABILDGAARD
Nanton Spring Water Company

Who said life begins at forty? Money maker Paul Abildgaard was fifty years old and had just taken early retirement from his position as a food technologist in the meat industry when he decided one day to drive around southern Alberta in a light-hearted quest for the region's legendary Lost Lemon Mine. As he entered the town of Nanton, fifty miles south of Calgary, he noticed the welcoming highway sign: "Home of Canada's finest drinking water." It struck a responsive, if painful, chord in the Danish-born Canadian. Twenty-five years before, while working with a food company in Hamilton, Ontario, he'd had the idea of patenting a process to put water in cans. It was the era when fallout shelters were something of a rage and people were building up stores of necessities; he was sure he could market such a product. But his wife vetoed the idea. Understandably, she felt the $265 patent charge was better spent buying snowsuits for their growing family. Shortly afterward, the person who did patent the process was paid $110,000 for the rights to its use.

Now in 1980, a vision quickly formed inside Paul Abildgaard's head and he did not hesitate. He stopped his car and went into a local restaurant to taste the water. It was pure, naturally sweet, and lived up to the town's billing. It was all he needed. He had chosen to part company with his last employer rather than put his family through another transfer; they had pulled up stakes so many times since coming to Canada that they had never felt really settled. But he wasn't ready to put his feet up just yet.

The same day, he purchased a rundown old honey factory in Nanton. Over the next four months he installed a bottling line with second-hand machinery he restored himself. With the help of his wife and five of his six children, he fixed up the building and gave it a fresh coat of paint. In the end it took a total of $238,000, all of it from his personal savings and assets, before the Nanton Spring Water Company was ready for business and Paul Abildgaard was ready to make his vision into reality.

Nanton's water was so pure that, at first, the company simply turned on a tap and out came its product. All it needed was a little carbonation. Abildgaard paid regular town water rates; a typical two-month bill was $42. His home bill in Calgary for the same period was a couple of dollars higher!

In the beginning he needed practically no staff. Abildgaard had been educated in food technology during a career in which he worked for more than one meat-packing operation. So he was well-acquainted with the food business. "I was able to set up the water company for a reasonable cost and, with the help of five of my kids, and one experienced mechanic, was able to bottle the water with virtually no overhead."

He still remembers his first sale vividly. "Right after start-up we sold 2,000 cases for a price of about $10,000. At the time, it left me with a net profit of $7,000." Indeed, from the March opening to July, revenues reached $400,000. The first year closed with $2.5 million in sales and the million-bottle milestone already behind. "There's been no looking back."

But the original water-supply situation was too good to last. After about a year and a half in business, the town decided to chlorinate its water. So Abildgaard simply turned around and purchased three acres of land containing a spring drawing from the same source in the Porcupine Hills that provided Nanton's liquid gold. A newly purchased stainless steel truck of the sort that usually carries milk began to roll into the plant from the spring every day, filled with 20,000 gallons of water perfect for bottling.

By keeping overhead low, Abildgaard soon was able to put Nanton water in stores and supermarkets across western Canada. Today, in Abildgaard's words, it can be found from "Minneapolis to Hawaii, from Alaska to New Mexico." He has virtually continent-wide distribution.

Along the way the company enjoyed some fortuitous publicity. One time, Abildgaard and his wife were taking some cases of Nanton water with them on a plane trip to the West Coast. But they had to leave it behind because of its potential to explode in aircraft storage. So they simply gave it to the bartender in the first-class lounge. A short time later, Joe Clark was in the same airport and ordered a Perrier for his wife, Maureen McTeer. No Perrier, just Nanton, he was told. Clark was delighted to discover that the locally famous water from his own province was now being marketed, and afterwards called the factory to order a supply for a Press Gallery reception in Ottawa. He expressed his thanks and pleasure in the quality of the bottled water in a letter that hangs framed behind Abildgaard's desk.

Nanton Spring Water was quick to branch out into flavoured waters, such as lemon-lime and orange, and it now has three production lines going full speed. The profits generated have been ploughed back into an expanded sales force (which includes six former Pepsi-Cola salesmen), and the company has diversified into the soft drink market. "Our soft drinks are better than anything you can buy in the world," Abildgaard confidently asserts. "We don't have to purify, strain, or reconstitute the water. Our soft drinks are formulated with the best spring water you can find." His root beer and a new cola now fill supermarket shelves throughout Alberta. Today, after five years in business, Abildgaard will not reveal his company's revenues. However, Nanton Spring Water has expanded steadily and now employs sixty-eight people. His 7,800-square-foot home houses several original Renoir paintings and his indoor swimming pool is so large it is classified as a public swimming pool.

Annoyed at having to pay so much in taxes, Abildgaard chose

to put money into related businesses. In 1983 he purchased another brand-name water company in Calgary, Eau Claire. He has recently built in Nanton a brand new million-dollar meat factory (specializing in making meatballs) that employs twenty-eight people and is contemplating purchasing a soft drink company to help him expand that side of his business. "I know the meat business," says Abildgaard, "and we now make 268,000 meatballs per hour at a food plant as modern as any you can find in Canada. And it's also making a profit."

Typical of Abildgaard's approach – including his love of a good bargain – he did not decide on meatballs first and then let that decision guide his entry into manufacturing. He had the available factory space and wanted to use it. Because of his industry contacts, he discovered a meatball machine was up for grabs and he bought it for a few thousand dollars. It was broken so he bought a second, put the parts he needed together, and sold the leftovers at a profit. The meat company's flash-freezing machine belonged to American country-and-western singer and sausage-maker Jimmy Dean. Nanton's acquired it for a third of its actual value.

Having built highly efficient factories for bottled water and meatballs, he then developed a delivery system that is both reliable *and* cheap. Tractor trailers traditionally carry their giant loads in only one direction; they deliver and make the return trip empty. But these days at least some of them carrying fresh produce from the U.S. are refilled with Abildgaard's mineral water, which they transport at very affordable backload rates. All in all, it's little wonder that Nanton Spring Water's price is about half that of its domestic competition and a fraction of the price of imports.

Perhaps what is most astonishing about this whole success story is the fact that the gregarious Abildgaard claims to work only about two hours a day. "I have the family to run the business now," he says, "but I have to admit that we have lots of business discussions at home, when my sons drop in for dinner." His six children, ranging in age from eighteen to thirty-two, all work in the business in important management positions. One son runs the water plant, another the meat plant; one is in charge of shipping and a daughter runs the office. Ownership of the company is also divided up democratically among the clan.

198

Nanton Spring Water's profitability has not gone unnoticed by food companies. There have been several offers to purchase. But Abildgaard thinks the potential for growth outdistances the convenience of a quick sale even if he would walk away with millions in his pocket. "I'm spending $3 million this year on expansion," he says. "But in five years the company should be worth $40 million."

Typical of entrepreneurs who have followed a hunch to profitability and independence, he doesn't hesitate to advise others to seize an opportunity when it comes along. "Don't be scared," he says. "If opportunity knocks, go ahead and open the door. I did and succeeded when everyone else was full of recession doom and gloom." He also likes to quote Henry Ford on the subject of expanding into new businesses: "You can always hire a person who has the skills that you don't have."

In retrospect it is clear that the Nanton Spring Water Company's launch was a timely one. Mineral waters were just beginning to be noticed by Canadians. But it took a man with a vision and the willingness to act on it to turn the dream into a money-making success story.

BRIAN KEENAN
International Computer Orphanage

Most in the high-tech marathon believe they must keep sprinting to stay in the race. A computer chip that cost $8 six months ago now sells for seventy cents. A circuit that took three months to design is obsolete by the time it hits the market because somebody else designed a better circuit in just two months.

Money maker Brian Keenan looks upon the victims of obsolescence as orphans. Keenan has seen many orphans in his years as a computer salesman. Bekeen Computers Incorporated (*Brian Edmond Keen*an) is the sales agency Keenan created to sell large computer systems to business. He's seen one product after another superseded by more powerful, more economical innovations that are easier to use. With every new generation of computers, older models inevitably end up in attics and forgotten warehouses.

Keenan figured that these castaways, with a bit of spit and

polish, might be attractive to students and other computer neophytes who aren't yet ready for the high-tech race and don't want to put up the money for the latest models; they just want something simpler to learn with. It was time for a computer orphanage.

Keenan comes from the small southwestern Ontario city of Chatham. "I never went to university. Eighteen years ago, after high school, I thought if I'm going to succeed without a university education, I better get into a field where I can fight my way up." He got a junior job at Sperry Computers and worked his way into marketing. He stayed eight years, learning all he could along the way and developing lots of contacts. Then, in 1976, he used his network to set himself up as a computer broker. "I did well. I sought out companies that needed computer systems and sold them systems built by most of the big companies – Sperry, IBM, Digital, Honeywell."

By 1984, Keenan had made it. He had virtually paid for his house. Bekeen Computers was doing well. But he was sure there was some unexploited potential in used computers. The idea kept nagging at him. "If I can give you an analogy. In the early 1900s, they introduced the automobile. There were hundreds of manufacturers making cars then. It wasn't until many years later that they realized they were going to have used cars. Used car lots developed. We are well into the development of new computers by hundreds of manufacturers, and it is only now that people are realizing there has to be a vehicle for used products."

Keenan approached a computer retailer in Kitchener, Ontario, A.B. Computers on Victoria Street, and suggested that they set up a counter in the store to handle used hardware. It became the first adoption centre for his newly created International Computer Orphanage Ltd. Getting stock wasn't a problem. There were plenty of people who wanted to trade up to newer computer models or who had simply lost interest in the computers they bought some time ago. Customers could either buy or rent the used computers. Like used cars, prices were set by the age, condition, and model. A used Commodore Vic-20 rented for about $30 a month.

Business was good at the counter in Kitchener. But Keenan wanted to try his idea on a larger scale. He borrowed $150,000 against his house and rented a store in the underground shopping concourse beneath the Toronto banking district. He was trying to create a market all by himself, so he knew he needed gimmicks to bring in customers. He used stuffed teddy bears and video games to dress up the store. He hired staff he called "computer paramedics" to help customers install their units, to show them how to use them and repair them if necessary.

It didn't work at the Toronto location. In the spring of 1985, Keenan gave up his lease in the underground shopping concourse and laid off his staff. He focused his energies on his other company, Bekeen Computers, to generate the cash needed to pay off his debts. He is, however, keeping the computer orphanage open in Kitchener. "You gotta know when to hold them and when to fold them," muses Keenan. "I didn't win the first round. I'm open to trying again. We really need a major corporation behind us. Perhaps we'll have to try it in the United States first. That's where you get venture capital. In Canada, venture capitalists just aren't interested in service industries.

"There's an inherent problem in the computer industry, too. It's as if General Motors said they wouldn't sanction used car lots. The IBMs and Sperrys are doing nothing to cultivate a used computer system at the public level. A used market adds value to the new products people buy. Without a market, a product has no value. If a used market develops for computers, people who buy new will know that six months later they won't have lost 60 per cent of the value of what they have bought."

Brian Keenan has retrenched. The business he dreamed of building goes on, but on a smaller scale. Yet he's still talking about ambitious goals. He's hyping a vision that could still change attitudes and create a whole new computer marketplace.

PAUL BOSC
Château des Charmes

Most people who drive through the rolling countryside near Niagara-on-the-Lake are aware that they are in the heart of southern Ontario's fruit belt. A smaller but growing number know that this is also wine country. And the fact that the reputation of Ontario wines is steadily mounting is due in no small measure to the pioneering work of Paul Bosc, founder of Château des Charmes winery.

Bosc, who is now fifty years old, was born in Algeria when it was still a colony of France. His family operated a small vineyard. They stayed in the business after Algerian winemaking became co-operative and young Paul was sent to the University of Dijon in Burgundy to study oenology. After graduation he returned to Algeria to manage one of the country's largest co-operatives. When Algeria gained independence in 1962 the Bosc family, like most Algerians of French descent, moved back to France. But he discovered the motherland was not particularly welcoming to "pieds noirs" so he emigrated to Quebec and worked decanting wines for the Régie des Alcools du Québec. But this was uninspiring work for someone with his training and expertise. Before long he landed a job with Chateau Gai Wines (owned by John Labatt Limited). Eventually he became head winemaker. In the late 1960s Chateau Gai was experimenting with higher-quality wines and Bosc oversaw the introduction of Alpenweiss, which became the firm's top-selling European-style white wine.

But Paul Bosc wasn't satisfied with making wine for somebody else. Nor was he satisfied with conventional Canadian winemaking wisdom, which held that you can't grow European vines in our harsh climate. He was convinced he could make Ontario wines that would rival the fine wines of France. So, in 1977, he quit his job at Chateau Gai and founded Château des Charmes winery. "I was determined to move beyond the usual hybrids used by Ontario growers to vinifera vines. The vineland authorities held that they would never stand up against the cold winters, but I knew that the vinifera vineyards of Dr. Konstantin Frank right next door in New York were flourishing." He also knew he was taking a big gamble in a field where success is judged by strict international standards.

Wine is not a provincial business, it's not a national business, it is an international business. And if a winemaker intends to see his product compete successfully with the best wines of France, Italy, Spain, Australia, and the United States, he has to start with the grapes. Then he has to wage war on the climate and work in relentless pursuit of quality. "I had long been adamant that this country's wineries must provide a quality dry wine free of the infamous 'foxy' flavour that characterized Canadian wines. Then we could be world class."

With two partners he purchased a sixty-acre farm near the town of St. David's and began the meticulous task of introducing chardonnay, riesling, gamay beaujolais, pinot noir, and other European grapes to Canadian soil. This was done with the help of a Small Business Development loan and a $500,000 grant from Ottawa's National Research Council to help the winery identify the hardiest and most productive "clones" of the vine.

Bosc learned to detect the strongest survivors among his vines and to use these as the base to expand his crop in successive years. "I trained the vines close to the ground to benefit from the earth's reflected heat and planted at a density of 1,300 per acre, double Niagara's conventional density." He made the furrow between each row a foot deeper than usual with the earth thrown meticulously over the vine's roots to protect it from the cold.

But even if Bosc could grow the vinifera grapes, he still had to make them into wine, an art as much as a science. But he didn't stint on technology. He purchased the best winemaking equipment. (One of his crushers can even be adjusted to crack the skins and not crush the grapes before it reaches the blending vat. "It makes," says Paul, "for a smoother wine.") Once the first crop of grapes was harvested he introduced several refinements, such as a machine that assures consistent quality from grapes with varying sugar content.

In its first year the winery produced only 6,500 cases of wine but its quality was immediately recognized by wine lovers. Bosc had already proved the unbelievers wrong. Now he had to keep refining the quality of product – and develop the market. He had based his enterprise on a key marketing decision: to produce the best wines, ones that could stand up anywhere in the world, and assume that as the Canadian palate developed there would be an appreciative audience to receive them. "Once you start drinking wine," says Paul with total conviction, "you will not be satisfied with *vin ordinaire*. Canadians will want better-quality wines, just as the Europeans do. As people become more affluent, they buy more expensive wines. It's that simple." He cites the example of a well-known Eastern European wine that at one time sold 500,000 cases in Canada, a phenomenal amount. Recently it was de-listed in Ontario, allegedly because of a persistent lack of quality.

"People are not stupid," says Bosc. "When you have a good product versus a bad product, the quality wine will always win out. Because of our quality, which extends right from the grape to every aspect of our winemaking process, we will never have a problem selling our product." He is also not hampered by the need to keep large production lines rolling, where expedience sometimes translates into mediocrity. However, unlike many cottage vintners, he has no fear of growing too large. "You don't have to be small to be good," he adds. "Just uncompromising."

Following the first successful year of production, Château des Charmes has doubled output each year and Bosc is now planning to build a new château with the capacity of producing 100,000 or even 200,000 cases. This rapid growth has meant assembling an ever larger staff, both to help grow and make the wine and to market the product. "It took me four years to get together the right team of people to work for me. Technically I had no problem because I had industry experience, but it was harder to find good salespeople or even an accountant who understood the business. My definition of a good salesperson is simple. It's someone who, when they're on the road, is not convinced that it's *your* product they're selling. It's someone who is convinced it's their own."

Château des Charmes does not have the budget to undertake a worthwhile advertising campaign, so it wisely decided to leave the publicity to the wine writers and to the publications that love to arrange wine tastings. An increasing number of people visit the winery each year for a guided tour. (One of the guides is Paul's wife.) For the moment Bosc is content to let word of mouth and a small but dedicated sales force sell his wines. However, as competition increases, as it surely will, the parameters of marketing his products will undoubtedly change.

His commitment to producing quality "international" wines has already seen his Gamay Beaujolais Nouveau recognized as one of the top Beaujolais Nouveaus by judges in Paris, France. And on February 19, 1984, at a highly publicized wine tasting at Canada House in London that was teleconferenced to a phalanx of journalists and writers in Canada, wine experts such as Hugh Johnson and Kenneth Christie selected Château des Charmes wines as the top five out of twenty-seven Canadian wines rated. Bosc's wines also tied for first and second place with two European wines thrown into the mix to keep the tasters honest.

Bosc never slackens the pace of his search for excellence, and Château des Charmes has become in recent years a centre for serious viticulture research. Scientific experimentation has been undertaken to discover vinifera mutations most resistant to winter injury; selected wines have been fermented and matured in specially imported oak barrels preferred by Burgundy vintners for Chardonnay; and, most recently, studies have been initiated on a process of reverse osmosis for concentrating grape juice to increase sugar content and intensify character.

Paul Bosc's passionate pursuit of fine wine leaves him little time for leisure – although he does enjoy a glass of Château des Charmes estate-bottled Chardonnay before dinner. He works at his business virtually seven days a week. His one relaxation is his yearly three-week visit to France, but even then he attends trade shows to check out the latest in winemaking equipment and technology. On a recent trip he discovered the French are working on a robot to prune the vines.

For Paul Bosc and Château des Charmes the future is promising. His annual sales volume has now reached $1.2 million, and despite a generally depressed market for Canadian wines, his high-quality output is snapped up each year. If a visionary is someone who sees something others don't, then Bosc qualifies. Thanks to his vision, Canadian winemaking will never again be the same.

FRANK STRONACH
Magna International

Even visionaries can be short-sighted, if only in their formative years. Today, Frank Stronach is an ambitious proselytizer of the capitalist creed, captain and creator of Magna International, which he presents as a prototype for the future. It is Canada's largest manufacturer of car parts, with over seventy factories and annual sales of well over half a billion dollars. It has made Stronach a millionaire many times over. Yet forty years earlier, sitting at a desk in an Austrian technical training school, young

Frank's vision included only improbable adventure fantasies inspired by the North America he found in picture books. Somehow, a teacher penetrated his wandering fourteen-year-old mind with dry lessons about blueprints and mechanical drafting. For four years he learned the trade of a tool and die maker, the skill that would become the ticket to an extraordinary entrepreneurial adventure.

In spite of his parents' pragmatism – they wanted him to work in the factories to help rebuild post-war Austria – the young man's whimsical dreaming drew him away from a hometown machine shop to seek passage to Canada. "All I wanted to do, at the time, was see the world. I didn't have money, so I thought I'd find jobs in different places to pay for my travelling and keep. It was difficult to get into most countries. You needed working visas and permits, but Canada wanted immigrants and was easy to get into then."

In 1954, Stronach landed in Montreal, where he searched vainly for a job and burned up most of his savings. He used his last few dollars for bus fare to Kitchener, where he had a friend. "I had a lot of pride. I really didn't want to ask anybody for help. But when you're down, you have to do something, so I landed on this guy's door, told him I had no money, and I needed help. He put me up."

That year, Canada was suffering from a recession and jobs were hard to find. Stronach finally found work in the kitchen of the Kitchener-Waterloo hospital. "It paid $120 a month, plus room and board, for working six days a week."

It was the kind of difficult working experience that breeds bitterness and hopelessness in some people, but it helped Stronach to develop the entrepreneurial business philosophies for which he is known today. "It's up to business to be sure we go in the right direction. We've got to show people that there is an alternative to socialism. If we can show the working class that we can create a class of owners, show them that they can accumulate capital, then the thinking process will change. Part of the problem is that politicians are always trying to cater to the masses. They know that nobody likes to swallow bitter medicine. But in the long term, they're only creating more poor people. Instead, they have got to provide people with a formula for accumulating their own wealth."

For a man who tells people, "If you want to be economically free, you can't do it working for someone," the job market remained his only alternative for many years. He found his first tool and die making job in Canada building jet aircraft parts for the Avro Arrow. He was also one of the thousands thrown out of work when Prime Minister John Diefenbaker, alarmed by the plane's cost, cancelled the Arrow project and forfeited Canada's leadership in aerospace technology. Many of the country's leading technologists and engineers headed south, ultimately to help put the Americans on the moon. But others, including Stronach, found new work in Canada. In his case, it was with the Don Tool and Die Company on King Street in Toronto. There he began to discover what he now calls "corporate culture": "You've got to create a working environment where people will have their hearts in their work. You do that by being totally honest with workers. You can't hide anything from them. You've got to say 'This is what I make. This is what we make. This is what I take. This is what you take. When we do better, I'll make more, and you'll make more.' "

Stronach sensed some of this openness at Don Tool and Die. "The owner of this small company let me run the place for him. He told me he wanted to make me a partner in the business. At first, I was very enthusiastic. It meant a lot to me. But the boss was very vague about it, and the partnership never amounted to much. I left the company and moved to Peerless Engineering in Toronto. There, I began to realize that there is no great magic to running your own shop."

If great magic wasn't required, firm convictions and the brashness of mid-twenties youth did help. Frank Stronach rented a small garage at Dufferin and Dupont in east-end Toronto. He put his small savings into a workbench and a kit of tools. "I'd walk into these places and ask to speak to the tooling engineer. I'd work my way into the engineering department, and say, 'If you've got a problem, I'd like to give you free advice. I'll build something for you. I'll correct your problem. If it doesn't work, then you don't have to pay me.' I did that just to get my foot in the door. I created a bit of curiosity, you know, this young guy walking in off the street. I'd go back to my shop, do up some sketches, and build whatever was needed by myself."

There was enough business in a month to hire an assistant. In a year, he'd hired ten people. In two years, thirty people were employed in Frank Stronach's tool and die works. The evolution of the business seemed obvious. But he observed another type of evolution occurring among his employees. "I noticed my foreman acted a little different. I asked what was the matter. He said he had wanted to talk to me for the longest time. He told me that he really wanted to go into business for himself. I figured, this foreman is going to leave me now, and that's a bad deal for Stronach. If I hire a new foreman, a good foreman, he'll leave me eventually, too, to go out on his own. That's when I realized the only way to succeed was to offer people a piece of the business. You've got to make them partners."

The foreman established Stronach's second tool and die shop. The two businesses were working together to achieve the same corporate goal, but they worked independently to capitalize on the creative energies of individual entrepreneurs. It was the genesis of Stronach's philosophy of corporate growth. He says the growth is due to the fact that "I want every good person I meet to be my partner. The only way my business is going to succeed is to be in business together with good people. I've always felt the reason so many businesses fail is because too many people try to keep it all for themselves.

"If I lose a good person, I'm losing somebody who could become a competitor. I want those people in my camp. That's what business is all about – people management."

By 1969, Stronach had eight parts plants, each under autonomous management, humming with orders from the big car assemblers. But he wanted to go public to implement a plan for employee share ownership. So he merged with a publicly traded company that was then known as Magna Electronics Corporation. He kept the name but substituted "International" for "Electronics" to reflect both the expanding product mix and his bold ambitions.

Since then, Magna's performance has been dazzling. The company has grown by 30 per cent or more during almost every one of the past fifteen years. In 1970, Magna sales were $10 million. At the close of the 1984 fiscal year, they had zoomed to $500 million. In 1985, they were heading for $700 million. By 1988, Magna projects annual sales of a staggering $1 billion! The company intends to supply an average of $100 in parts for every single automobile built in North America by 1988. In 1985, it is estimated that Magna is opening one new factory every six to eight weeks to deal with its burgeoning order book.

That order book looks like a car parts catalogue from Canadian Tire. Magna is now manufacturing nearly 4,000 components and assemblies for General Motors, Ford, Chrysler, Volkswagen, American Motors, and Japanese and European car makers. The company makes parts for every section of the automobile: bumpers, body panels, sections for the car frame, fan and wiper motors, pumps, pulleys, door, hood, and trunk latches, instrument clusters, alarms, fans, motor mounts, heat shields, seat parts, head rests, foot pedal assemblies, catalytic converters, hinges, windshield and body mouldings, and taillight bezels. Many of them are made to specifications set by the car makers. Many others were designed by Magna's engineers and purchased by the car makers as original equipment because of their innovative designs. Magna sales and technical staff now stream through car makers' offices in the quest for even more component contracts.

Stronach may have stumbled upon his management philosophy by accident. But he has honed it over the years. "Most large companies are like an ocean liner. In order to make a right turn, or a U-turn, it takes a long time. In many cases, guys running large corporations don't want to make drastic changes, so nothing can go drastically wrong. That leaves them feeling secure in their position. But it often doesn't do the company a lot of good. It might be sinking slowly, and nobody is noticing it.

"We provide every employee with a blueprint to create a Magna. It's a cloning process. We have profit-sharing, and employee ownership, and small units of 100 people in a factory for close communication. We show our people how to open up another factory. People move up in each factory to assistant manager, then manager, then they can open their own factory and even move on to create a whole new group of factories. They're like cells splitting in an organic structure. As long as the soil is right, and the climatic conditions are right, the seeds will sprout like an oak tree. More seeds will fall and create more oak trees and more oak trees. If you have an environment which doesn't nurture the individual, then everything is stifled.

"People gotta have hope. In our plants, they can see the foreman there. The reason he's a foreman is because he worked hard. He was interested. They see all of a sudden that the foreman has got his own factory!"

Magna facilities do not multiply indiscriminately. The company is run by tool and die makers like Frank Stronach, people trained to work within exact tolerances and precise plans. At the nucleus is corporate headquarters, where Stronach and a handful of senior executives set broad corporate policy and provide a link for all of Magna's diverse operations. Headquarters is a lean, efficient group of less than a hundred staff housed in a two-storey office building in the suburban Toronto Apple Creek business park.

Radiating from this nucleus are a number of smaller nuclei, or group management units. They are located in various Toronto suburbs, and in the state of Iowa. At the moment, there are five of these groups, but they are destined to divide and form more groups as Magna expands. Each group is responsible for specific technologies and product lines. Each has its own marketing, research and development, and planning responsibilities. Each maintains its own sales office in Detroit and in Toronto and launches its own marketing program in Europe and Japan. Magna's executive vice-president responsible for marketing, Michael Hottinger, says this allows closer contact with the engineers and buyers in each of the large automobile companies.

Each of these group management nuclei has an average of ten factories orbiting around it like electrons on the corporate diagram. Magna has tried to keep them together geographically, but until recently it was limited by whatever factory space could be found in various industrial parks. Now, the company has grown sufficiently to develop its own parks. Stronach calls them campuses. The first was purchased in Newmarket, Ontario, in 1983. Another campus began construction in Guelph, Ontario, in 1985. The most ambitious industrial campus plan involves an abandoned piece of the Toronto waterfront, near the foot of Leslie Street, where Stronach envisages a mixed development of housing, recreation facilities, and car parts factories, if he can get government approval.

The campus system allows Magna to build ten to fifteen factories together around one group management nucleus. Such a system provides group management with the financial resources to construct daycare, recreational, educational, and health facilities to be shared by the employees of all the factories. Stronach estimates that every fifty cents spent on such facilities results in $1.50 of improvement in productivity. A working parent knows his or her offspring are well cared for and close at hand. A lower-level worker has easy access to a company classroom where new skills for better jobs can be learned. A health problem can be quickly tended to without much time lost from work. Weekend recreation is available at no cost to employees. They are the kinds of services people often demand from governments. Stronach believes they can be provided more efficiently with his industrial campus concept.

The factory concept also means that a group's research facility is close to the production lines where new developments and products go into production. And group management has much closer contact with the plants in its jurisdiction.

There are now five distinct manufacturing groups within Magna. The Downsview Group, in the northwest part of Metropolitan Toronto, operates eleven factories. They are engaged principally in metal stampings, such as floor sections, hinges, and car door parts. The Iowa Group specializes in motor and transmission parts and units for air conditioners and catalytic converters. The MACI Group, least defined by geographic location, concentrates on electrical components for instrument panels and car accessories. The Concord Group, in the Regional Municipality of York, north of Toronto, is engaged in making various trim components. And the Maple Group, also in the Region of York, makes bumpers and other car body parts with glass-reinforced urethane plastic, as well as a line of pulleys for car engines and air conditioners.

Developments at one of the Maple Group factories, Polyrim, best illustrates Stronach's blueprint for growth. Polyrim won several large contracts to supply urethane plastic bumpers for some of the Ford Motor Company's best lines – the Tempo/Topaz and the Thunderbird/Cougar. Polyrim's general manager, Wilfried Woelfe, an Austrian tool and die maker like Stronach, put the plant on a twenty-four-hour schedule, with three shifts of about 100 people each. They still couldn't produce enough bumpers. But Woelfe's independence under Magna's operating system allowed him to build a second factory to fill the orders. As a result both Woelfe and his supervisory staff moved up the corporate ladder. As they win more contracts, more new factories might be needed. Eventually Woelfe could find himself head of his own Management Group within Magna, with its own group of factories, its own marketing and sales team, and its own business objectives. If we take the scenario even further, one of Woelfe's people might develop an entirely new product line, open new factories, and create another Management Group of factories.

Stronach sticks with the small, one-hundred-workers-to-a-factory concept because of his insistence that management and employees maintain close working relationships. He believes the smaller units spark individual initiative and entrepreneurialism. Smallness also permits direct communication between the plant manager and his employees. "Communication is very important," he says. "If you have a few thousand people under one roof, you need a hundred thousand rules. You lose the human touch. You create a faceless kind of management."

Therefore, each of Magna's factories has an individual character: its own product mandate, its own research and development department, separate marketing responsibilities, and production and profit goals set by each factory's management team. Management textbooks would describe this as classic decentralization. At Magna, they see it as just part of their corporate culture. It allows the entrepreneurial spirit to thrive because it gives every worker access to management and a voice in how things are done. An assembly-line suggestion to make a product better can lead to promotion, more profit-sharing, and increased equity participation, since all Magna employees earn shares in the company. The smallness of the operations makes it evident to everyone that they must be nimble and creative to meet the demands of the marketplace. The emphasis on factory-floor technical skills means staff know how to rebuild and restructure manufacturing equipment to make it turn out new products when old product lines face obsolescence. Magna factories even make their own machine moulds rather than buying them from somebody else. That capability means the company can make almost any size component and leads the company's most ambitious thinkers to talk of building entire cars soon.

Growth as rapid as Magna's cannot usually be sustained

without broader stimuli. The firm has entered into a number of international joint ventures to gain offshore technology and open up new markets for its products. An agreement with Switzerland's Brown Boveri gives Magna exclusive North American rights to a sulphur battery, which Stronach thinks could be used to power small electric vehicles. Magna is using its expertise in urethane plastic body moulding, electric motors, and the Swiss battery technology to plan an electric delivery van, which Stronach thinks could be useful for mail delivery and other light-duty work.

Frank Stronach subscribes to the theory that advances in technology always create more jobs in the long run than they eliminate. "Robots and automation are unavoidable. It should help us, and help labour. There is lots of room for robotics, and also lots of room for people. It means that the size of a factory doesn't matter anymore. With robots and a hundred people you can supply the world with a product." Tool and die makers and computer experts in one Magna factory have designed their own production-line robot. They hope to manufacture and market their own robots to other companies.

Surprisingly, for someone who has no unions in his plants and whose wages are below North American auto industry standards, he is a supporter of unions. Not that the unions haven't tried to organize Magna. One attempt in a company factory fizzled when the workers in the plant voted against the United Auto-workers trying to represent them. "Unions fulfil a good role. They act as a watch dog. They perform a great role in creating a better society, but they have to modify the way they operate. Business also has to come up with better solutions, because if you run a lousy shop, you deserve a union."

Paying lower wages has helped Magna remain competitive. But, as Stronach points out, increases in productivity mean wages are going up. "They're not high enough yet. We feel that over the next few years, we should be catching up to what bigger corporations pay. We can do that as we improve our product lines, our technology. But we have to stay competitive. If we can't compete there just won't be any jobs. So we have to be concerned about more than just wages – like job security, safety, and the work environment."

And employees deserve a share of the profits. "Employees have a moral right to some of the profits they help generate. Even if they have a reasonable wage, they might buy a better television or a better car, but at the end of the year, they won't have much saved up. If they get profit, and they can put it into company equity, there's a sort of discipline which helps the employee. We've got some people on machines who've got $30,000 sitting there. That's a lot of money for an average person.

"Here's how we divide the corporate pie," Stronach says. "Ten per cent of the profit is for the employees. Twenty per cent is for the investors. We've got to make our company attractive for investors. Seven per cent goes for research. Unless you do research, you've got no future. Two per cent is for the community – arts, theatre, universities, youth programs. Six per cent is for management. The rest is re-invested in building the company."

Frank Stronach's sees his version of benign capitalism with an emphasis on worker participation and initiative as having wider applications. "We have to create a society where people start to own things. If you live in a rented apartment, you're not as careful as you would be if you owned your own house. When you own something, you have something at stake. Your capital is invested. If you provide a worker with an environment in which he can accumulate equity in the company that employs him, the worker's thinking process changes, he sees things differently. That's because the company is partly his."

On October 16, 1984, deans and professors and leading academics gathered in the dining room of the University of Toronto's Massey College. The banquet was to honour Frank Stronach, who had granted $400,000 to the university's Faculty of Management Studies. Other universities and colleges have also benefited from his largesse. It is Magna's way of encouraging schools to provide the skills the company – and the economy – needs. Education allows society to embrace change and fend off obsolescence. It protects and produces more durable jobs. The $7-an-hour stamping-machine operator can become tomorrow's $20-an-hour computer auto parts designer if Stronach's corporate blueprint is as well drawn as he describes it.

Stronach has become a regular on the business-college speaking circuit where Canadian management students seem as keen to hear his views as their American counterparts are to listen to Chrysler's Lee Iacocca. The Stronach speeches are laced with memorable one-liners: "You can't tell people to work less" – a swipe at union mentality. "Attitude is difficult to teach. Use candy instead of a whip" – a warning to those who advocate management by desk-pounding. "The only way to get a customer is with a better product at a better price" – his rallying cry for all industry. "Too many people are sucking at a creature called government" – a blunt criticism of state intervention. "Learning a trade can be a ticket to independence" – a suggestion that colleges turn out fewer social scientists and more product-oriented professionals, such as the tool and die makers who dominate the executive and management ranks at Magna International.

Stronach's brand of entrepreneurialism is most effectively understood in a Magna factory and it is epitomized by Klaus Niemeyer. Niemeyer is manager of Magna's Normark Manufacturing plant, which makes, among other things, the structural struts for the Ford Tempo and Topaz. Like Frank Stronach, Niemeyer is an Austrian and a tool and die maker by trade.

On a typical day Niemeyer can be found on the shop floor huddled in conversation with a group of his colleagues. Around them is all the activity of the shop: starburts of sparks from the spot welders and the air-shaking racket of two dozen metal-stamping machines. But the group is oblivious to all the hubbub. It is pondering a peculiar array of hammered steel that no one else is paying attention to at the moment. It is a prototype frame for a new model of sports car, a hand mock-up assembly made by Niemeyer's workers on his own initiative. By 1987 he hopes his plant will be producing the frame for one of the big three Detroit automakers. But first his marketing staff must talk one of them into the plan.

There are over 7,000 employees at Magna, but Niemeyer manages just one hundred of them. He knows, however, that he has the freedom to expand the factory, or build a new factory and add new staff, if he wins the contract for the sports car frame. The blueprint he follows was drawn by Frank Stronach nearly twenty-five years earlier, when Stronach landed his first auto industry contract, a mere $20,000 deal with General Motors. Stronach convinced GM that his small tool and die shop could produce brackets to hold sun visors to car roofs at a lower price and with higher quality than his competitors. Only the scale of the operation has changed at Magna. Klaus Niemeyer and dozens of other Magna people are all Frank Stronachs knocking on opportunity's door.

Whether Magna's operating methods can be applied to other companies and enterprises will only be known as others try them. They seem unlikely to be effective everywhere. Uranium mines and aircraft factories must be large by definition; they can't be divided into small, one-hundred-worker units like Magna. But Stronach's personal experiences at the workbench and on the production line, his talent for spotting talent, and his glowing corporate record at Magna all lend credence to his insights into the entrepreneurial mind. He wants all those who work for him to feel that they're also working for themselves. He believes in economic independence for everyone as the way to achieve individual happiness. It's a vision others will undoubtedly follow.

Conclusion:
We Can Do It! (Goya)

Walter Light reportedly earned a million dollars a year while he was chairman and chief executive officer of Northern Telecom, Canada's world-class high-tech giant. He is widely recognized as the man who led a modest manufacturer of cables and telephones for the Canadian market to become a world leader in computer-driven communications. When Light retired from Northern in 1984 (he was recently appointed to the position of chancellor at Queen's University in Kingston, Ontario) the company employed more than 47,000 people and sales were approaching $5 billion. And the Americans, Japanese, and Europeans were scrambling to catch up to Canadian technology in the communications business. Under Light, Northern proved that innovation, risk-taking, and world leadership can thrive north of the 49th parallel.

In addition to his glittering achievements at Northern Telecom, Walter Light has always been a generous patron of Canada's artistic community. His office in Northern's world headquarters in Mississauga, Ontario, became a gallery for the works of contemporary Canadian artists and sculptors.

There was, however, one exception. On a corner table of the office, he kept a book of prints by the eighteenth-century Spanish artist, Francisco Goya. Goya was stubbornly independent, and subjectively passionate. Ernest Hemingway wrote that "you don't look at Goya if you want neutrality." Walter Light enjoyed the beauty and sensitivity of Goya's works, but those were not the only reasons a book of Goya's paintings sat in the corner of his office. It was there as a constant reminder of one of Light's lifelong philosophies, encapsulated in one of those nifty phrases people often carve in their minds to drive them onward against all odds. The artist's name – *Goya* – served as an acronym for Light's reminder to himself to "Get off your ass!"

The slogan is a reflection of one successful man's strong bias for action. This bias is common to every winner, every achiever, every money maker profiled in these pages. It is such a crucial element because it turns dreamers into doers, spectators into participants, and followers into leaders. Whatever motivates people to act, to "get off their asses" as we might crudely put it, is difficult to define or measure. However, throughout our journey over the Canadian entrepreneurial landscape, we have come across factors, conditions, and forces that either starve or nourish the economic growth process, that determine whether people will take risks, invest their time and capital, test their ideas, and seek new opportunities. The following summary is grouped under two categories – You the Person and We the People – because there are things you must have as an individual that will determine whether you might make it as a money maker, and there are things we as a nation of people must provide to support our money makers.

You the Person
We wish we could tell you exactly how to become a successful money maker. But there just isn't a single golden rule that will guarantee success. Every one of the money makers profiled in this book did it his or her own way. The process is unpredictable, unrestrained, and usually unlike anything anybody has ever tried before.

Many people have driven the same route as Paul Abildgaard, when he set out on his quest for Alberta's legendary Lost Lemon Mine. Many have, like him, stopped at a restaurant in Nanton and asked for a glass of water. But nobody except Abildgaard ever tried to bottle Nanton's water and sell it across the country. Nobody but Abildgaard invested his life's savings in a used bottling machine and installed it in an abandoned Nanton honey factory to build his fortune.

Many people have lost their jobs, just as Robert Isserstedt did when his employer went broke. But nobody reacted quite like Isserstedt did, when he invested only his knowledge to build GEAC, Canada's largest mainframe computer manufacturer. Ken and Heather Dafoe mortgaged their home, as many others have done, but only they defied industry wisdom to carve out a

$100-million-a-year niche in the personal hygiene products business. Any number of people are weekend balloonists, yet only Wayne Metler turned his hobby into Fantasy Sky Productions. Thousands of people have trained in the tellers' cages of Canada's banks, but Ron McLelland's bank training led him to build a large mobile home business, which gave him the capital to become a McDonald's restaurant owner.

Are they geniuses? Were they extraordinarily lucky? Were they wealthy? Neither genius, luck, nor wealth was a determining factor in any of the money-making success stories we have chronicled here or have heard of. It takes no unusual gift of knowledge or intelligence to match the achievements we have described. In many cases, our money makers had bad luck, but they used it to fill their quiver with the experiences they needed to take aim at the future. If they had money to start their ventures, they had earned it and saved it themselves. The lack of money, in many instances, spurred them to take on great challenges.

Money makers mix dreaming with pragmatism. They tune their minds to the future and its opportunities and promises, and they accept the required struggles and sacrifices. They have faith in their abilities and they trust their instincts, even if these run counter to the wisdom and expertise of professionals who warn them that their efforts might be merely exercises in folly.

We have read how the individuals, partners, and families profiled in these pages have followed the money makers' maxims: everybody did it his or her way; they challenged the status quo; they escaped the comfort of the crowd; they embraced risk and defied the odds; they exploited their most valuable assets – their time, energy, experience, and ideas; they made the market and created opportunities; they attracted people better than themselves; they seldom feared failure; and they proved that anybody can do it.

What personal qualities help money makers succeed? A survey published by D.C. McClelland in the book *Entrepreneurship and Venture Capital* (edited by Joseph R. Mancuso and Clifford M. Baumback), and quoted in the recent Canadian Foundation for Economic Education booklet "Entrepreneurship: A Primer for Canadians," finds that entrepreneurs themselves list these qualities, in descending order of importance, as most necessary for success:

1. Most important for success – perseverance, desire and willingness to take the initiative, competitiveness, self-reliance, a strong need to achieve, self-confidence, and good physical health.
2. Important for success – a willingness to take risks, a high level of energy, an ability to get along with employees, versatility, a desire to create, and innovativeness.
3. Least important for success – ability to lead effectively, a willingness to tolerate uncertainty, a strong desire for money, patience, being well organized, a need for power, and a need to associate closely with others.

That is how money makers see themselves as a group; however, the qualities each individual brought to his or her enterprise vary widely, as we have discovered in our stories. With Ian Innes self-reliance was primary when he brought together a group of partners to start Feathers pub. He never again wanted to be in a position where somebody could fire him. Ken and Heather Dafoe had already reached a comfortable position in life with Ken's executive income, but they wanted new challenges and an outlet for their creative impulses. A willingness to take the initiative was common to the groups of partners at Linear Technology and SPAR Aerospace, who both took orphans from major corporations and built successful independent enterprises from them. Perseverance is an outstanding quality in Clem Gerwing, whose Alberta Boot Company fought off major foreign competition to carve out a unique market niche. Innovativeness is a shining quality in George Moore, who plans to change the face of farming in North America and elsewhere.

A strong desire for money is a quality we can find in every money maker, of course, but in none of our examples is it the supreme factor. Some have become extremely wealthy as a result of their enterprise. When they started, however, none expected extraordinary wealth. In adding value to the productive capacity of the economy, they made money for themselves. But much of that is paper wealth, because it is still invested in their companies to allow them to grow and thrive.

For those launching a new enterprise, the forethought and preparation required for success can be broadly grouped in the following categories.

The Idea

Most ideas are – to use an old phrase – a dime a dozen, and that's exactly what they're worth in most cases. You won't come across a valuable idea, however, without commitment and effort. Be tuned into the world about you and question everything. Is there a better way of doing something? Can a service be provided that would meet the needs of others? Can a product be changed or developed to better serve the needs of prospective customers? What are the things nobody has thought of, or nobody has done anything about?

Read voraciously and investigate thoroughly. The more you learn and experience, the more likely you are to discover good ideas. A formal education might be a good beginning, but relatively few successful money makers are highly educated in the formal sense. They have excelled, however, in educating themselves by being inquisitive and interested. The workplace is usually rife with new ideas for those who choose to see them. Any employer who has encouraged suggestions from employees can attest to the wealth of shopfloor ideas that have helped improve his business. Work experience helps you to spot market opportunities other companies have missed while giving you some of the skills you might use in launching your own enterprise. Travel, movies, books, and even a walk through a shopping centre can provide the stimuli that might lead to market opportunities.

The Business Plan

Typically, you'll start small. You won't have the resources to launch a major company right away. Consider how you can bring your idea to market in the most efficient, least expensive way. Your time will likely be your major investment, so plan to use it wisely. Decide who your customers will be; how you will convince them to buy; how much they'll be prepared to pay you; how much they'll buy in the first year, the second year, and so on; who the competition is and how it might respond to your invasion of their marketplace; whether the market can accommodate both you and your competitors; how you are going to produce your product or service; how you will keep your costs under control and below the price you'll be able to charge your customers; how you will promote and sell your product; how you'll recruit good people as employees or partners and how you'll be able to keep them.

You would be wise to seek professional advice in developing your business plan. A professional knows what questions you should ask and how best to answer them so that you'll be on the right track, and you'll be able to satisfy bankers, investors, and customers that you know what you're doing and where you're going. An accountant can be very helpful in development of a business plan, and these services need not be expensive if you use the accountant's time wisely. Some accountants will spend an hour or two with you at no charge, because they hope you'll bring them your business once your enterprise is off the ground. A local banker can also offer good advice.

Governments all operate departments dedicated to helping small business people. They operate under various names in Ottawa and the provincial capitals, but generally you'll find they are known by names such as the Ministry of Industry and Trade, or the Ministry of Small Business, or the Ministry of Industrial Development. Be persistent in seeking information and advice from your government. Because they are large organizations, a number of phone calls, letters, or visits might be required before you find the right person to help you. The Federal Business Development Bank maintains a list of consultants (Barbara Caldwell found them useful when she established Cleanwear from the basement office in her home). Governments are beginning to recognize that new businesses are the major force in the creation of jobs, and they have established hundreds of programs on the municipal, provincial, and federal levels to support small businesses.

Your local chamber of commerce, the provincial chambers of commerce, and the Canadian Chamber of Commerce in Ottawa are other extremely useful sources of business advice and support. The chambers are organizations of business people who've all been through what you face, and they are committed to helping prospective businesses succeed. They know how to tap into government assistance programs, and they know where you can get help.

The Canadian Federation of Independent Business, the Canadian Manufacturers' Association, and dozens of industry organizations can offer research and expert advice. Approach the universities and colleges for help. Graduate students can often be hired at reasonable fees to give planning and technical advice, and professors are sometimes interested in helping with research or the development and marketing of new products. Eugen Hutka used professors at the University of Toronto to develop products for Exceltronix. The Canadian Foundation for Economic Education in Toronto has published a number of booklets that will help you plan your business.

While it is only prudent to arm yourself with as much advice as possible, and to plan carefully, only you can assess your own abilities and commitment, because you will be the major determining factor in the success of your enterprise.

The Money
So many of our money makers started with nothing, or almost nothing. There comes a time, however, when most businesses need financing and capital. Sadly, too many businesses in Canada borrow too much money. The problem with borrowing is that it must be paid back, and it must be paid back at a price: the cost of the interest on the loan. That means money that should go into the development of the business goes instead to the people or banks that have loaned you the money. Debt is a major cause of business problems, and it should be avoided if possible. Ideally, the money for a business should come from investors. They take an ownership position in the company by buying shares, and their payoff will come when the company gains value. It is riskier for them because, unlike lenders, they have no claim on the company's assets if things go wrong, but their potential for gain is many times greater if the company does well.

Usually, investors in a start-up business are members of the entrepreneur's family or are friends. It is becoming easier in Canada, however, to attract other investors because of new initiatives announced in the May, 1985, federal budget. It is now possible to create Small Business Investment Corporations and Small Business Investment Limited Partnerships (contact the federal Ministry of Finance for information) that allow people to invest part of their retirement funds and savings in exchange for income tax credits. Various provincial governments also give tax credits to those who invest in small businesses. Contact your local member of the provincial legislature, who can put you in touch with the proper government officials. Investment experts on the staffs of investment dealers can also be helpful, as they were for George Moore when he put together the financing for Hydrogrowers. Accounting firms also are aware of potential sources of investment funding, as are various business organizations such as the Canadian Federation for Independent Business (offices in most Canadian cities) and the chambers of commerce.

The type of investment funding small businesses seek is usually called venture capital. Since governments now recognize the pressing need for venture capital and have provided tax incentives to encourage more of this type of investment, a number of companies specializing in this kind of funding have been started. Contact the Association of Canadian Venture Capital Companies at 908 Oxford Tower, Edmonton Centre, Edmonton, Alberta, for information on venture capital companies in your area. The ACVCC was created in 1974 and conducts seminars and conventions that might provide useful contacts for those seeking business funding.

Venture capital clubs, common in the United States and Britain, are also being established in various Canadian cities. They usually require a membership fee, but they give aspiring entrepreneurs an opportunity to appear before an audience of potential investors. Once you've made your business presentation at a club meeting, those you have impressed might seek you out to arrange an investment package. Such clubs are beneficial because they bring together people who need money with those who have money.

The best source of investment funding comes from your business itself. Put as much of your company's profit as you can afford back into the business to fund expansion and growth. That way you maintain control and it forces you to take a disciplined approach to the way you manage your enterprise.

Just Like Money
Some things available to help build your business don't require cash. A phenomenon called incubators is becoming common in many communities. Universities, municipalities, provincial gov-

ernments, and even private corporations are establishing office and factory complexes that offer space at no cost or at low cost to businesses going through the incubation stage. Statistics show that companies given this kind of incubation assistance in the first one to three years have as much as a seven times greater chance of surviving. Survivors are then able to take their place with other successful businesses and pay normal taxes or rents to the governments or organizations that helped them through incubation. In some communities, office and industrial park space is offered to qualifying business people at no cost. Sometimes, secretarial and other support services are thrown in for nothing as well. After the first half year or so, the businesses are expected to be earning enough cash to pay nominally for these services, and after eighteen months or two years, they must pay full costs. The March, 1985, issue of *The Magazine That's all About Small Business* lists the following contacts for those interested in incubator space: Winnipeg Business Development Centre, Winnipeg; Innovation Place, Waterloo, Ont.; Multi-Tenant Research Facility, Burnaby, B.C.; The Discovery Foundation of the B.C. government, Victoria, B.C.; Regional Small Business Complex, Dieppe, N.B.; Calgary Research and Development Authority, Calgary; General Realty Ltd., Halifax; Ontario Ministry of Industry and Trade, Toronto; and TIEM Canada Inc., Toronto.

Many new businesses don't need a special business location to start at all. Maureen and Jim Baufeldt began Granny Taught Us How in a Toronto apartment; Anton Dissanayake began out of his Thornhill home; Barbara Caldwell and Dennis Covill from basement offices; and George Spark and Nigel Hill from a Saskatoon garage. David Archibald and Ian Cumming initially worked out of hotel lobbies. Product, quality, price, and service win sales, not an impressive business address. Dallas Howe of BDM served his first American customers with an 800 telephone line to Canada, which saved him the cost of opening a U.S. office.

If you can stand the red tape and bureaucracy, the federal and provincial governments often operate job placement and training programs that subsidize the cost of employees hired under the programs. Your local Manpower office is usually aware of any government programs available in your community.

Of course, the best investment you can make, which won't put pressure on meagre financial resources, is the time you invest in your enterprise. Eighty-hour weeks might be frustrating, tiring, and demoralizing at times, but the business will benefit and chances are that you'll reap the dividends later. And you'll always have the satisfaction of knowing that you're working for nobody but yourself.

We the People
Most of us will never own businesses. But all of us depend on them. There are over 700,000 small businesses in Canada. They were started by a million entrepreneurs, if we count all the partnerships. Those million employ another four million people. Once we subtract the million or so who are directly employed by governments, we find that roughly half the Canadian work force is directly dependent on the small business sector. Many more are indirectly dependent on small business because the taxes it generates fund a large part of the government payroll, and the services small businesses supply and purchase help support the 28,000 medium- and large-sized companies in Canada.

Small businesses create nearly 90 per cent of all the new jobs in the country simply because that's where the action is; that's where most economic growth takes place. If that growth is to continue – so that Canadians can have the things we want; so that we can help those who are disadvantaged, such as the elderly, single parents, women seeking equal pay and equal opportunities, native peoples, and the poor – then we have a responsibility as a society to support measures that create new wealth.

So many of the arguments over our economic problems focus on the division and distribution of wealth rather than on the creation of wealth. Currently, our federal government is $210 billion in debt. Our provincial and municipal governments owe additional tens of billions of dollars. Government debt is so large that, on a per capita basis, every man, woman, and child in Canada owes roughly $10,000. Within five years, payments on the government debt are expected to be such that they will consume every penny of all the personal income taxes paid by all Canadians. Various economists argue over the seriousness of the debt, but none can deny that payments on the debt are consuming too much of our governments' revenues. Governments might spend less and tax more, but we submit that the most painless solution to our national financial woes lies in the entrepreneurial process, the process that creates new wealth.

We believe the good life is possible in Canada, if we the people take up the cause. This means support for entrepreneurial effort and an understanding of how it functions and how it makes all of our lives better. Through our attitudes as a society we can foster a climate for innovation; we can encourage people to take risks and explore new opportunities; we can remove roadblocks to progress; we can protect the rewards for toil and achievement. Ideological arguments about the right or the left are pointless. The plain, simple truth of arithmetic supports our thesis that jobs and improved lifestyles for all come only from an effervescent and unfettered marketplace. Arithmetic tells us that taxing and legislating against the "rich," however they might be defined, will never lead to an economic revival. (Even if we were to confiscate everything all the so-called rich have in Canada, it wouldn't add up to enough to finance the nation for more than a month.)

The power and the potential for new wealth resides in the population at large. We are a broad, fathomless river of opportunities and resources. Whether we allow the ebb and flow to follow a natural, progressive course or choke it off with a dam of regulations and restrictions is up to us, collectively. Here are some of the ways we can support this money-making process.

Tax Policy
Less can be more. You might have noticed that the higher tax rates get, the more governments get into debt. That's only one reason taxes should be reduced in Canada. Lower tax rates can result in higher government revenues, strange as that might sound. But lower tax rates have an even more beneficial effect: they tend to lead to the creation of new businesses and enterprises and a surge of new economic activity.

Taxes affect the entrepreneurial process in two extremely significant ways: first, money taxed away cannot be saved for investment in entrepreneurial ventures, nor can it be spent to purchase the products brought to market by entrepreneurs; second, high taxes remove the incentive to invest time and money in new ventures, wipe out the rewards for achievement, and discriminate against extraordinary effort and risk-taking. What sane person would submit to the toil and turmoil of starting a new business venture when she or he must share more than half of the rewards with the state? It is a wonder that so many do so in Canada.

The way people react to taxes through the financial decisions we make as consumers, investors, and entrepreneurs is seldom given consideration by economic experts and tax authorities. The several hundred pages of the recent federal budget documents contain not a word about the impact of taxes on our work habits, savings, and entrepreneurial decisions, although the budget did provide for investment incentives to help create new businesses.

Consider for a moment a situation faced by millions of wage earners when their employers offer them the chance to earn overtime income. Often, the response is: "Why bother putting in the extra hours, when I'll lose a third or a half of it in taxes?" Our tax rates are progressive, which means the higher your income goes, the greater the percentage of the tax bite. The rationale for this system is based on "ability to pay." The more you earn, the more you can afford to pay a higher rate of tax. The unfairness of this system, however, is the way it ignores the time spent earning income. It is entirely possible that those who choose to work twice as many hours as the average worker will end up paying three times as much tax! Even those commonly described as "ordinary workers," such as steelworkers and autoworkers, can quickly work their way into tax brackets that categorize them as "rich." The top marginal tax brackets in Canada are among the highest in the world. With the new surtaxes imposed in the May, 1985, federal budget, the accounting firm of Clarkson-Gordon calculated that taxpayers in the various regions of Canada will now pay the following percentages of their top income dollars in tax:

Quebec	61.82%
Manitoba	57.73%
Newfoundland	56.10%
New Brunswick	55.42%
Nova Scotia	54.91%
P.E.I.	53.55%
B.C.	53.47%

Sask.	53.37%
Ontario	52.02%
Yukon	51.00%
Alberta	50.49%
N.W.T.	50.32%

Still, these figures do not tell the full tale of taxes in Canada. In addition to income taxes, we all pay municipal taxes, either as home owners or as part of monthly home rental fees; we pay fuel taxes, federal and provincial sales taxes, import duties, cigarette and liquor, wine, and beer taxes; we pay taxes on our car licence plates and taxes for our dog tags. The Fraser Institute, an economic think tank based in Vancouver, estimates that the average Canadian works half the year for the governments that serve him or her and the other half of the year for himself. Since an average person surrenders fifty cents of every dollar earned, those who hit the highest marginal tax rates could easily pay seventy or seventy-five cents on every dollar earned. Why there has not been a tax revolt in Canada can only be ascribed to the genial nature of our people!

What is needed in Canada is radical surgery on the tax system. It is becoming evident that nations adopting low tax rates benefit from an enormous surge of new business activity and job creation, which in turn replenishes and even surpasses the revenue loss caused by tax cuts. This is not just New Right rhetoric or Reaganomics. It's backed up by historical evidence.

George Gilder, author of *The Spirit of Enterprise*, points out that "The American tax cuts of the 1920s – reducing the top rate from 73 per cent to 25 per cent in four years – increased the actual tax payments of the rich by nearly 200 per cent and raised the share of total taxes paid at the top from 27 per cent to 63 per cent. The less dramatic Kennedy-Johnson tax cuts of 1964 and 1965 had similar, though smaller effects, and the cut in the top rate from 70 per cent to 50 per cent in 1981 led to an increase of 11 per cent in payments by the rich in fiscal 1982." According to Louis Rukeyser, in his book *What's Ahead for the Economy*, "The Kennedy cuts lowered these [tax] levels [from as high as 91 per cent] to 50 to 70 per cent.... The cuts produced more revenue from those whose rates were lowered. Even adjusted for inflation, tax receipts from those with incomes over $50,000 increased by 34 per cent in 1965 over 1963."

Milton and Rose Friedman, in their book *Tyranny of the Status Quo*, agree that "The income tax does indeed 'soak the rich' – but that soaking does not yield much revenue to the government. It rather takes the form of inducing the rich to acquire costly tax shelters and rearrange their affairs in other ways that will minimize actual tax payments. There is a very large wedge between the cost to the taxpayer and the revenue to the government. The magnitude of that wedge was illustrated by the reduction [by Ronald Reagan] in 1981 of the top rate on so-called unearned income from 70 to 50 per cent. Despite ensuing recession, the taxes actually paid at rates of 50 per cent went up, not down, as a result."

Economist Arthur Laffer, designer of the Laffer Curve, observed in a recent appearance on the PBS television program, *The Nightly Business Report*, that the Western industrial nations with the highest unemployment rates also had the highest taxes. According to Laffer, the connection between the launching of new enterprises and tax rates is undeniable.

The Laffer Curve plots the course of economies under various tax regimes. At zero per cent tax, government won't collect any revenue, of course. And at the opposite end of the graph, with 100 per cent tax, government won't collect any tax either, because people refuse to work or engage in entrepreneurial risks when all of their rewards are confiscated. Between the two points, economic activity and government revenue collection vary with the tax rates. His graph shows the optimum level of economic activity and government revenue at the 11.5 per cent tax rate.

We certainly don't expect Canadians will wake up one day soon to discover a flat 12 per cent tax rate. But significant tax cuts in Canada would reverse a long-time trend continued by the Mulroney government and give some much needed stimulus to entrepreneurial activity.

Doug Wills, an economist with the Fraser Institute, told us that "We should have a flat tax of around 20 per cent in Canada, because then people would put their money where they prefer to put it, which is usually more productive than government spending. Our current progressive tax rates haven't worked well. People don't work harder, they do less, when you keep so much of their money. A flat tax is a very common sense position."

Labour Force
While participation in the work force provides a rich tapestry of experiences to help foster entrepreneurialism, a motivated and skilled work force is also essential to help entrepreneurs do their job. Behind every successful entrepreneur, it could be said, is a phalanx of dedicated employees.

So many of our money makers have spoken of the difficulties they have had finding and keeping good employees, even in industries where unemployment is high and salaries are attractive. They complain that many workers don't have adequate skills, some aren't motivated, and some are unwilling to move to other cities to take work. Those who inveigh against employers for offering low wages that attract few workers ignore the realities of the marketplace. The setting of wage rates is purely a democratic process, and we're not talking about membership votes in union halls or votes of approval at corporate board meetings.

The marketplace casts a vote on wage rates each time a consumer decides to buy or not buy a product or service. Employee wages are usually a major component in the cost of anything a business sells. If the wages force up selling prices, consumers either buy less or buy elsewhere. A company that must force up selling prices because of high wages risks losing sales and can go broke, putting everybody out of work – so unions have a duty to be responsible in their wage demands. Companies can reduce wage costs by increasing productivity, through automation or incentives to make employees work harder and produce more.

In the 1960s and 1970s, government employees were granted all the privileges of private-sector workers, in addition to the not insignificant benefits of public employment. The results have been damaging to the economy and the marketplace. The postal service, a government monopoly, is vital to all businesses, and particularly new businesses, which use the post office to market and distribute goods and collect income from sales. Small businesses can not afford to have expensive courier services take over when the post office is shut down. Others who count on government pensions and income supplements have suffered when civil servants picketed. Strikes and slowdowns by municipal employees, from police to garbage collectors, have also been damaging and needless. Surely, in a modern society, compulsory arbitration or some other mutually satisfactory negotiating arrangement is preferable.

Unemployment insurance – a touchy subject – has had an impact on the labour force that many entrepreneurs find damaging to their efforts. Marie-Josée Drouin and B. Bruce-Biggs made these observations in their 1980 Hudson Institute study, *Canada Has a Future*: "In effect, Canada is now paying people to be unemployed. We are not implying that unemployment is not serious, nor maintaining that nothing should be done about it, nor are we advocating that unemployment benefits be curtailed. Rather we are making the simple economic point that the more you pay people to be unemployed, the more people will be unemployed. Unemployment is not particularly rewarding, but its duties are extremely light: it requires no investment in education, clothing, tools, or transportation, and offers a large amount of leisure time. Therefore, we should not be surprised that a small percentage of the population at any given time has taken up this economic 'activity'." According to the study the number of unemployed in Canada grew dramatically when unemployment benefits were increased, even as the number of job vacancies grew.

John Bulloch, president of the Canadian Federation of Independent Business, told us that "unemployment benefits in Canada are the most generous in the world. They are four-and-a-half times more generous than in Sweden, and four-and-a-half times more generous than in the United States! Our benefits are a tremendous disincentive to work. In the U.S., when there are labour surpluses, the cost of labour falls. In Canada, labour costs always go up, and more people go on welfare. In the period between 1975 and 1985, labour costs in Canada rose by 125 per cent. In the U.S., they only went up 75 per cent.

"Our benefit system allows people here to be choosier. In the U.S., they'll take wage cuts and move somewhere else if they have to take work. With our compensation system in Canada, people tend to stay out of the work force longer."

Bulloch's organization has identified a staggering $2 billion that could be cut from unemployment payments annually in Canada. "Even with such a cut, we would still have the most generous system in the world. We need to increase the period needed for eligibility for unemployment insurance. How much people receive should be dependent upon how much they contributed. There's a tremendous political dimension to this, but right now we're pouring money down the drain, and that's very costly to the economy."

Political attempts to make life comfortable for as many voters as possible have had deleterious effects on the work-force mobility required in progressive societies. The Hudson Institute concludes: "In effect, we have said that people have the right to remain in their home communities, even if there are no jobs." As well, employers who do have jobs available must draw from a smaller labour pool and have difficulty attracting people with the necessary skills and experience.

James Fallows, Washington editor of *The Atlantic Monthly*, offers these comments in the magazine's March, 1985, issue: "Societies find ways of deflecting the things that frighten them. When they see change as a threat, they manage to retard it." Fallows quotes Canadian-born economist John Kenneth Galbraith, who himself sought richer opportunities away from his home on the shores of Lake Erie: "Migration, we have seen, is the oldest action against poverty. It selects those who most want help. It is good for the country (or region) to which they go.... What is the perversity in the human soul that causes people to resist so obvious a good?"

Attitudes toward Money
Attitudes and perceptions shaped by national policies and conditions determine what people will do with their money. Canadians are among the greatest savers in the world. We happily plunk 13 per cent of our disposable incomes in savings accounts and government savings bonds. Superficially, this seems a wise habit. Unfortunately, it can be self-defeating. Our savings get burned up by a sluggish economy in the same way a car driver would waste his fuel towing around a trailer-load of gasoline to be sure he would never run out of gas. The rate at which we save and the rate of unemployment and the lower value of the Canadian dollar are all related. We save for rainy days, but the saving only makes the rainy days come sooner. Why do we do this to ourselves?

First, because savings appear to earn a handsome return on our money. Investment certificates at banks and government savings bonds have been paying savers at least 10 per cent annual interest, and as high as 20 per cent interest, over the past five years. Those high interest rates have been determined by the Bank of Canada's benchmark rate, set in Ottawa every Thursday afternoon. The Bank of Canada uses interest rates to control the supply of cash in the economy, thereby keeping inflation under control. It also uses interest rates to shore up the value of our dollar in the world marketplace. In a way, that is self-defeating, because the marketplace judges our dollar's value on our economic performance, which in turn is affected by domestic interest rates. When they are high, they act like a powerful magnet, attracting our disposable cash when it should go into the investments that build our economy.

Second, Canadians prefer to lend their money to big institutions – the banks and governments – because they are almost guaranteed a return. It seems safer, even though a declining dollar and inflation can erode those savings. Putting money into the stock market and other business investments is seen as a gamble, and Canadians don't like to gamble – with the exception of lotteries. Fewer than one in ten Canadians has ever had a dollar directly invested in the stock market. Yet we unknowingly expect others to do the stock market gambling for us, through our union and company pension plans and insurance policies. The handsome returns of stock market investment are evident in the growth of our institutionalized savings. Those professionals who manage those savings for us know that the best way to make money grow is to invest it in business. Sadly, government policies and faulty perceptions prevent millions of individuals from following their example.

Therefore, the pool of cash available for business investment in Canada is limited and restricted. Money tied up in savings isn't available to start and expand many businesses because professional money managers tend to invest our cash only in proven stock market performers. Small, new businesses suffering from a lack of investment capital then borrow their cash and become hostages to interest rates.

The role of interest rates is seldom discussed on the national scene, other than how they affect home owners' mortgages and car loans. The current double-digit interest rates that our generation pays are an unprecedented economic aberration. Just because prices of homes, cars, and other goods have trebled over the past twenty years, it does not mean that trebled interest rates should follow. Twenty years ago a business might have borrowed $100,000 at 5 per cent to finance operations. As a result of inflation, today a business might borrow $300,000 to finance the same kind of business operations. But the interest rate might be 15 per cent! Once all the effects of inflation are factored out of this example, a business must be three times more successful than it had to be twenty years earlier to cover both the trebling of business financial needs and the trebling of interest rates. High interest rates force business to be lean and mean. It has to be inordinately competitive to survive. The pressure of high interest rate payments discourages entrepreneurs, business expansion, and riskier ventures.

The challenge, then, is not only lower interest rates. We must encourage people to invest in business rather than lending business what has been put away in savings. If public policies make saving less attractive, then business should benefit from a larger investment pool. Governments that spend no more than they earn don't have to issue savings bonds at high interest rates and therefore don't set an interest rate pattern throughout the economy. Tax policies favouring investors rather than savers strengthen the economy because many millions of Canadians become active participants in the entrepreneurial decision-making process. Such decisions are not left up to a handful of professional money managers in the employ of government agencies, such as the Federal Business Development Bank, and the chartered banks and pension and life insurance funds.

A strong business sector helps take the risk out of business investment and makes the apparent security of savings less palatable.

Rules of Law
Peace, order, and good government are the tenets of the Canadian way. We have put the American-style "life, liberty, and the pursuit of happiness" second in the management of our national affairs. Many would affirm that we do live better than Americans with cleaner and safer cities and better schools. But we're

not happy about it. We complain about the prices we pay for homes, cars, and other goods and services. A Gallup poll completed in the winter of 1984 found that more than two-thirds of Canadians, 69 per cent, believe our taxes are too high. Other polls show that unemployment and the fear of unemployment are still Canadians' number-one concern. Seldom, however, do we consider how the rule of law can interfere with the entrepreneurial process and the dynamics of the marketplace, which lead to the creation of money makers.

Many of us must live within the bounds of rules and regulations put in place by four levels of government. The federal, provincial, regional or county, and municipal governments have passed tens of thousands of laws and regulations governing almost every aspect of our lives. It often seems that we don't trust our fellow citizens to do anything right without ordering them how to conduct their affairs exactly as prescribed in law books. Consider what money maker Ian Innes faced when he opened Feathers pub in Toronto's Beaches neighbourhood. He couldn't do what he thought was best for his business. He had to do what the rules forced him to do, whether they made good business sense or not. Liquor-licensing rules told him how much liquor he could sell, or rather, how much food he *had* to sell. Other regulations governed the design and fixtures he put in the pub and the food he served. He must spend countless hours keeping records and filling in forms to satisfy government regulators. Any number of municipal, provincial, and federal officials could shut down the pub at any moment. It is all done to protect the public at large, because in the past some business people have been dishonest or careless. Too often, it seems, the regulatory system that governs entrepreneurial money-making efforts presumes guilt rather than innocence.

Governments originally passed rent control laws to protect voters from a short-term aberration in the rental marketplace. New York has had rent controls for forty-five years, and Harlem is a shambles. Most Canadian provinces have had rent controls for a decade, and vacancy rates are at an all-time low. Meanwhile, the unregulated office, factory, and house sectors of the real estate industry are booming, with lease and sale prices lower than they've been in years. The marketplace enforces a competitive pricing system that's far more effective. When prices go

236

up, more entrepreneurs want a piece of the action, increase the supply and the competition, and drive prices lower. Government regulation tends to freeze high prices in place and discourages entrepreneurs who could increase the supply.

In *Tyranny of the Status Quo* Milton and Rose Friedman observe that most government regulations and programs have an effect opposite to the one intended. Statistics show that minimum wage laws tend to push more people out of work than push up their wages, when the free marketplace could have created labour shortages and bid up wage rates. Generic drug laws intended to guarantee low drug costs in Canada so angered drug companies that they shut down research labs, put Canadian scientists out of work, and impeded the introduction of new drug products in the Canadian marketplace. Oil industry regulations – now rescinded – sent hundreds of independent Canadian drill rig operators to the U.S. oil patch and set Canadian energy development back nearly a decade.

Lamentably, our elected representatives believe they are judged by the number of new laws and spending programs they implement. Vocal self-interest groups are largely responsible for this. A national political environment that encouraged fewer laws and simpler regulatory systems might be more fruitful. The number of people who abandon money-making endeavours because of frustration with the regulatory environment is difficult to measure. Surely, however, the statistics on joblessness and business failures underline the need for a freer marketplace.

Canada's money makers are not a peculiar and entertaining appendage to the mainstream of national economic life. They are not exploiters and profit-takers who should be taxed and derided for their self-serving ventures. They cannot be dismissed for their roles in job creation and economic development, although they don't make as much noise as big business, big labour, and big government.

The people in this book, and the hundreds of thousands like them across this land, comprise an independent, free-thinking, risk-taking, bubbling brew of innovation and enterprise that makes most everything possible, in spite of the considerable difficulties they face with financing, the labour force, and regulations. Our money makers discover what society needs before society discovers it. They experiment and test and push and pull the marketplace until they've created and produced the goods and services we all want and will pay for. They leave behind the redundant, dying products and processes of yesterday and concentrate on the products of tomorrow. They feed our economy and give it nourishment. That is why, if we want to build a nation that offers everyone rich, rewarding lives, we will need many more money makers.

We hope that the examples of all the innovative, risk-taking men and women profiled in this book will help to cultivate in others a sense of adventure!

Acknowledgements

The process which resulted in this book started many years ago, and it has involved many people. It began with the pioneering efforts of the Global Television Network, which nearly twelve years ago became the first television broadcaster in Canada to offer daily reports of business and financial news. Six years ago, a trio of network executives – Paul Morton, David Mintz, and Raymond Heard – saw a need for a weekly, nationally syndicated television program about business and responded to a proposal from Ken Barnes to create *Everybody's Business*. They won the support of a number of independent television stations to make the series available to as many Canadians as possible. CKVU Vancouver, CFAC Calgary, CKTV Regina, CITL Lloydminster, CKND Winnipeg, and TV Ontario joined the Global grid of transmitters to broadcast *Everybody's Business* in major centres across the country. Additional support came in the form of production grants from over forty major corporations to help underwrite the costs of the program. *Everybody's Business* has been a resounding success, with a following of some half million viewers.

The producer of *Everybody's Business*, Mark Jacot, has worked tirelessly and brilliantly to uncover and present the many entrepreneurial success stories that have been featured on the program. Reporter Avis Favaro was instrumental in developing a key element in the program, the Money Maker segment, which became the title of this book. Mark, Avis, senior cameraman Dan Laffey, and sound recordist Sandy Pimenoff, in bringing the initial stories of many of the money makers in this book to television, also brought them to our production offices. And with Global Television's support, we were able to use their contacts and research for *Everybody's Business* as the genesis for our text.

Production assistant John McKenna contributed further research and spent many hours transcribing interviews.

The *Financial Post* provided research material from its extensive business library.

Rick Archbold lent his wisdom, organizational skill, and sharp editor's pencil to the manuscript, which always seemed to face impossible deadlines, because publishing, as we have discovered, is a business as demanding as any profiled here. Thanks are extended to Betty Ewing and Nancy Gilmore for their assistance to Ken Barnes in checking and finishing parts of the manuscript.

Finally, we are particularly indebted to all the money makers who happily gave up many hours from their enterprises to tell us of their experiences and knowledge so that others might benefit by having their stories told here.

E.B.
K.B.